DAVID WHITWELL

ESSAYS ON MUSIC OF THE FRENCH BAROQUE: PHILOSOPHY AND PERFORMANCE PRACTICE

WHITWELL BOOKS

Essays on Music of the French Baroque: Philosophy and Performance Practice
Dr. David Whitwell

Copyright © 2015 David Whitwell
All rights reserved.
Published in the United States of America.
These essays were first published between 2000 and 2010.

Cover image: *A detail of the roof at Palace of Versailles* by Jopparn. CC BY-SA 3.0

ISBN-13 9781936512843

Whitwell Publishing
Austin, TX 78701
WWW.WHITWELLPUBLISHING.COM

Contents

1	On Some Views of French Baroque Musicians	9
2	Mersenne on the Nature of Music	27
3	Voltaire on Music	53
4	Mersenne on Performance	67
5	French Philosophers on Music	85
6	French Philosophers on the Character of French Musicians	115
7	Descartes on Music	129
8	On Court Music in the French Baroque	143
9	Music in the French Dramatic Theater	159
10	French Philosophers on Opera	175
11	Voltaire on Opera	189
12	Music in French Fiction	203
13	Music in French Non-Fiction	217
14	On French Military Music of the Baroque	231
	Bibliography	241
	About the Author	251

I want to express my appreciation for my colleague, Craig Dabelstein of Brisbane, Australia, for his contribution to this volume. His own musicianship, broad education and skill in editing is responsible for thus preserving my essays. Any reader who places value in having these essays in his library is in his debt.

1 *On Some Views of French Baroque Musicians*

NOTHING SETS IN BETTER PERSPECTIVE the significance of the contributions of Rameau than the writings of Marc-Antoine Charpentier (1634–1704), who was actually a gifted composer. What he writes under the title, "The Definition of Music," reads like some medieval Scholastic pronouncement at the University of Paris.

> Music is a harmonious combination of high, medium, and low sounds. The third either against the bass or among the parts creates all the harmony.
>
> Diversity alone causes all perfection, just as uniformity creates all staleness and disagreement. Changes of motion and of mode aptly done contribute marvelously to the diversity which music demands.[1]

In Jean-Philippe Rameau (1683–1764) we have one of the most brilliant men among all early musicians. Born not only a prodigy, but with profound instinctive feelings about music, he also had such an inquisitive and penetrating intellect that he found correct answers in the area of harmony which had eluded the best minds for one thousand years. With this balance, as we might say of left and right hemispheres of the brain, and living in the stimulating first years of the Enlightenment, we believe he might well be thought of as the first *modern* thinker in music.

One can see this sense of balance in his definition of a musician. In the following, written in 1727, he first refers to the long medieval Scholastic tradition which esteemed music only from the perspective of rules and mathematics. Such a

[1] Quoted in Jon Kuyper, "Marc-Antoine Charpentier's *Règles de Composition*" (Iowa City, Unpublished dissertation, 1971), 53.

musician he clearly rejects. Then, in the second paragraph, he refers to the opposite kind of musician, one who operates purely from instinct, responding to his own emotions. He points as well to the limitations of this kind of musician. Finally, perhaps reflecting his view of himself, he reserves his praise for the balanced musician, one who engages both the rational and experiential sides of himself.

> A learned musician is generally understood to be a man who understands everything about the various combinations of sounds. At the same time, however, he is so engrossed in these combinations that he sacrifices everything: good sense, feeling, imagination, and reason. Such a musician is an academician, of a school that is concerned with notes alone and nothing further. We are right to prefer to him a musician who prides himself less on learning than taste.
>
> The latter, however, whose taste is limited by the range of his sensations alone, can excel only in certain types of music that are natural to his character. If he is naturally tender, he will express tenderness. If his temperament is witty, lively, playful, his music will correspond accordingly. Moreover, since he draws on his imagination for everything, without the assistance of art, by this means of expression he soon burns himself out. In his first fire he was all brilliance, but this fire consumes itself as he tries to rekindle it, and nothing remains but banality and repetitions.
>
> Therefore we should like to find for the theater a musician who would study nature before painting it; not only his taste, then, but his learning and judgment would enable him to select the coloring and shading appropriate to the desired expression.[2]

Rameau, with his balance of the intellect and native instincts, and perhaps following the fashion of wide-ranging investigation which characterized the Enlightenment, was by nature a keen observer. A few passages in his writing reveal that he had given considerable thought to the physiology of the perception of music. In the following he touches on a very significant topic and yet one which still has not received more than preliminary research. We know that the overtone series is a natural law of physics.[3] It follows that our species has heard, no matter how unconsciously, the overtone series

[2] Letter to Houdart de la Motte, October 25, 1727, quoted in Gertrude Norman and Miriam Shrifte, *Letters of Composers* (New York: Knopf, 1946), 18ff.

[3] After the initial observations, it took two thousand years for theorists to understand it correctly!

in all sounds since its very beginning. Is it possible, through adaptation, that our species has an internal genetic tonal system? In 1734, Rameau was clearly pondering observations which he had made along these lines.

> In music the ear obeys only nature. It takes account of neither measure nor range. Instinct alone leads it.
> Whether a novice or the most experienced person in music, the moment one sings an improvisation, one ordinarily places the first tone in the middle register of the voice and then continues up, even though the voice range above or below this first tone is about equal; this is completely consistent with the resonance of any sounding body from which all emanating overtones are above its fundamental tone which one thinks one is hearing alone.
> On the other hand, inexperienced as one may be, one hardly ever fails, when improvising on an instrument, immediately to play, ever ascending, the perfect chord made up of the overtones of the sounding body, the major form of which is always preferred to the minor, unless the latter is suggested by some reminiscence.[4]

Twenty-five years later he was still struggling with this idea. He begins by discounting the ancient explanations based on faith and wonders why these early philosophers did not pursue natural rules, that is understanding based on Nature.

> [The ancient writers] found the relationships between sounds in divinely inspired order; they discoursed a great deal on that subject, and every reason they were able to advance evaporated like a wisp of smoke. Finally the geometricians and the philosophers became disheartened. Can it be true that up to the present time man has always been so enthralled by this single inspiration that it never occurred to anyone to seek the reason why, despite ourselves, we should be compelled to prefer certain intervals to others after certain sounds, especially after the first sound? Allow your natural feelings to operate in yourself with no preconceived expectation and then try to see if you can ever ascend a semitone after a given semitone, and whether you can do the same thing after two successive tones. Why was this suggested to me in this way? Whence this sensation? What could have given rise to this sensation in me, if it was not in the moment itself?

[4] Jean Philippe Rameau, *Observations sur notre instinct pour la musique, et sur son principe* (1734), quoted in Sam Morgenstern, *Composers on Music* (New York: Pantheon, 1956), 44.

It was necessary to test the effect of the sound, and from it three sounds would have been distinguished which form that enchanting harmony, and from there one would have proceeded with certainty, as I believe I have done.[5]

[5] Letter to A. M. Beguillet, October 6, 1762, quoted in Norman and Shrifte, *Letters of Composers*, 20.

We presume that it was from this observation of the natural aspects of music, the overtone series, that Rameau concluded that it was harmony, and not melody, which was the fundamental element of music. From the perspective of the listener, this is a conclusion which is not substantiated by modern clinical research in psychology.

Music is generally divided into harmony and melody, but we shall show in the following that melody is merely a part of harmony and that a knowledge of harmony is sufficient for a complete understanding of all the properties of music.[6]

[6] Jean-Philippe Rameau, *Treatise on Harmony*, trans. Philip Gossett (New York: Dover, 1971), 3.

Later Rameau elaborates on this contention, beginning with the admission, "it would seem at first that harmony arises from melody."[7] However, he suggests, whatever logic one might discern in a melody, it all becomes unintelligible as soon as other voices are added, for they will have their own, and therefore conflicting logic. All this is avoided, he proposes, if one builds melodies solely from the harmony.

[7] Ibid., 152.

It is harmony then that guides us, and not melody. Certainly a knowledgeable musician can compose a beautiful melodic line suitable to the harmony, but from where does this happy ability come? May nature be responsible? Doubtless. But if, on the contrary, he has refused her gift, how can he succeed? Only by means of the rules.

Since it was the reflections on ancient Greek music by earlier humanists which initiated the whole Baroque movement in music, and since interest in Greek philosophy remained strong, Rameau realized he was in need of further explanation. Because the humanists understood ancient Greek music to be unaccompanied, and therefore consisting of melody only, Rameau's harmony-based philosophy denied, in effect, everything admired in ancient Greek testimony on music. He deals with this by simply saying the ancient Greeks did not know what they were doing.

The Ancients defined the properties of the modes perfectly well, in terms of the different effects they produce and the way in which they control harmony and melody. But the Ancients were always ignorant of their true nature, for they attributed all the power of these modes to melody. They assumed that melody had to be derived from the seven diatonic notes of the perfect system, without distinguishing among them further. As they thought that by using each note of the system as the principal one they would be able to create as many different effects as there are notes in the system, they simultaneously lost sight of what should have been their model.[8]

[8] Ibid., 159. We must point out that Rameau was quite mistaken in his interpretation of Greek modes here.

On Taste in Music

THE MOST IMPORTANT accomplishment of the Baroque in music was the freeing of music from the old Scholastic understanding that music was a branch of mathematics. It was this fact which made the question of taste immediately important, for in the past "good taste" was tied to "following the rules." Therefore, when Jean Rousseau (not to be confused with Jean-Jacques Rousseau) considered this question in 1687, it was the proper role of the rules which had to be addressed.

> But genius and fine taste are gifts of nature, which cannot be learnt by rules, and it is with the help of these that the rules should be applied, and that liberties may be taken so fittingly as always to give pleasure, for to give pleasure means to have genius and fine taste.[9]

Similarly, when François Couperin, in 1717, mentions the "old" style, it was the rules-dominated polyphonic style he was thinking of.

> Let the style of playing be directed by the good taste [*bon-gout*] of today, which is incomparably purer than the old.[10]

Rameau, writing in 1726, makes the same point.

> It is often by seeing and hearing musical works (operas and other good musical compositions), rather than by rules, that taste is formed.[11]

[9] Jean Rousseau, *Traité de la viole* (Paris, 1687), quoted in Robert Donnington, *The Interpretation of Early Music* (New York, 1964), 425.

[10] François Couperin, *L'Art de toucher* (Paris, 1717, reprinted Wiesbaden: Breitkopf & Härtel, 1933), 33.

[11] Rameau, *Le Nouveau Système de musique théorique* (1726), quoted in Morgenstern, *Composers on Music*, 43.

The following year Rameau views the question from a more practical perspective. Perhaps more significant is the fact that he does not include the theorists, the "learned," among those with "good taste."

> You will then see that I am not a novice in the art and that it is not obvious that I make a great display of learning in my compositions, where I seek to hide art by very art; for I consider only people of taste and not at all the learned, since there are many of the former and hardly any of the latter.[12]

It follows that during the Baroque it was therefore "taste" and not rules alone which governed the elements of performance. As Michel de Saint-Lambert, writing in 1702, states, in the questions of inequality[13] in rhythm and of tempo, "taste judges."[14]

The interest among French philosophers in *Gout*, or taste, led to much discussion regarding taste, or style, including the music of the various national peoples. The French composer, Sebastien de Brossard, in his *Dictionaire de musique* (1703), defined style as follows:

> Style is understood in music as the form and method that each person has especially for himself to compose, perform and to communicate. And all of these [forms and methods] are quite different, according to the measure of the genius of the composer, the country, and the people according to which the material, the place, the time, the subject, the expression etc. are rendered. Thus one says: the style of Carissimi, Lully, Lambert etc ... The style of joyful and merry music is very different from that of the serious; the church style is very different from the theatrical or chamber styles; the Italian style is sharp, colorful, expressive; the French in contrast, natural, flowing, tender. From these facts result various descriptive phrases in order to stress all of these different characteristics: the old and new style; the Italian, French, German styles; the Church, Opera, Chamber styles; the joyful, merry, colorful, sharp, moderate, expressive, tender, excited styles; the grand, sublime, galant styles; the normal, common, vulgar, fawning styles.[15]

François Couperin, in thinking of the difference between French and Italian style, observed in 1717,

---

[12] Letter of Rameau to La Motte (1727), quoted in Julie Anne Sadie, "Paris and Versailles," in *The Late Baroque Era* (Englewood Cliffs: Prentice Hall, 1994), 182.

[13] De Bacilly, in *L'Art de bien chanter* (Paris, 1668), 232ff, suggests that the practice of performing with inequality came about because composers were reluctant to write dotted rhythms for fear they would become in performance jerky.

[14] Michel de Saint-Lambert, *Principes du clavecin* (Paris, 1702), quoted in Donnington, *The Interpretation of Early Music*, 452.

[15] Quoted in George J. Buelow, "Music and Society in the Late Baroque Era," in *The Late Baroque Era* (Englewood Cliffs: Prentice Hall, 1994), 15ff.

The French gladly swallow what is novel, at the expense of losing what is fit and proper, which they believe they understand better than other nations.[16]

[16] François Couperin, *L'Art de toucher*, 22.

On the Purpose of Music

THE HALLMARK OF THE BAROQUE STYLE is a new appreciation of the communication of feelings through music. Marc-Antoine Charpentier (1643–1704) wrote at length at this time on the subject of expressing the feelings in music. He first mentions this subject in a brief discussion of modulation. The first virtue of modulation, for Charpentier, was a rather practical one, to facilitate the range of singers. However,

> The second and principal reason is for the expression of the different emotions for which the differing power of the modes is most appropriate.[17]

[17] Quoted in Kuyper, "Marc-Antoine Charpentier's *Règles de Composition*," 54ff.

We see how literally he meant this, in his list of keys and associated emotions. It is an interesting list, although the reader may be surprised to find the key of Eb major, home to so much pleasing music of the Classical Period, described here as "Cruel and harsh."

C major	Gay and martial
C minor	Somber and sad
D minor	Serious and devout
D major	Joyous and very martial
E minor	Effeminate, amorous, and plaintive
E major	Quarrelsome and crude
Eb major	Cruel and harsh
Eb minor	Horrible, hideous
F major	Furious and fiery
F minor	Gloomy and plaintive
G major	Sweetly joyous
G minor	Austere and magnificent
A minor	Tender and plaintive
A major	Joyous and rustic
Bb major	Magnificent and joyous

Bb minor	Gloomy and terrible
B minor	Lonely and melancholy
B major	Harsh and plaintive

Charpentier does not elaborate on this list, but he evidently took the subject seriously. He does not forget to include "good choice of meters and of modes which suitably make the passion which one wants to represent," when he later sums up the elements which "cannot fail to make music as beautiful as it is good."[18]

[18] Ibid., 62.

For Couperin, the first obstacles to the communication of feelings lay in notation and tradition.

> In my opinion, there are faults in our way of writing music, which correspond to the way in which we write our language. The fact is we write a thing differently from the way in which we execute it; and it is this which causes foreigners to play our music less well than we do theirs. The Italians, on the contrary, write their music in the true time-values in which they have intended them to be played. For instance, we dot several consecutive eighth-notes in diatonic succession, and yet we write them as equal; our custom has enslaved us, and we hold fast to it.[19]

[19] Couperin, *L'Art de toucher*, 23.

For Rameau, as he points out in 1726, a greater concern for the composer was to find a deeper meaning of feeling in the musical materials.

> We may note that the semi-skilled generally use a chord because it is familiar to them or pleases them, but the expert uses it only to the extent that he feels its power.[20]

[20] Rameau, *Le Nouveau système de musique théorique*, 42.

For Rameau, the "rules" now take second place.

> While composing music is not the time to recall the rules which might hold our genius in bondage. We must have recourse to the rules only when our genius and our ear seem to deny what we are seeking.[21]

[21] Ibid., 41.

The following year he observed that it is Nature which, for him, precedes rules.

Nature has not completely deprived me of her gifts and I have not surrendered myself to mere combinations of notes so far as to forget their intimate relationship with that beautiful Nature which by itself suffices to give pleasure.[22]

[22] Letter to Houdart de la Motte, October 25, 1727, quoted in Norman and Shrifte, *Letters of Composers*, 19.

Regarding the role of the performer, we have two points of perspective. There is the discussion of this question in the literature, but then there are also descriptions of performers themselves.

The first strong focus on communicating feeling came with the beginning of opera and its use of the voice. It is no surprise the instrumental comments tended to follow the inspiration of the voice. For example, Pierre Trichet discussing string technique in 1631 observed,

After the human voices, there is nothing so captivating as the affecting vibrato [*les mignards tremblements*] which can be produced on the fingerboard, and nothing so ravishing as the sobbing bow strokes [*les coups mourants de l'archet*].[23]

[23] Quoted in Peter Walls, "Strings," in *Performance Practice: Music after 1600* (New York: Norton, 1989), 71.

Among French commentators, the reader must guard against confusing "movement" with form or time. "Movement," to these writers had to do with expressing feeling. Charles Masson writing in 1699 finds,

Measure is the soul of music, since it excites with such truthfulness of emotion [*fait agir avec tant de justesse*] a great many people, and by the variety of its *mouvmens* can again stimulate so many different feelings, being able to calm these and arise those, as has always been observed.[24]

[24] Charles Masson, *Nouveau Traité* (Paris, 1699), quoted in Donnington, *The Interpretation of Early Music*, 412.

Couperin was one who gave great significance to the role of time in relationship with the expression of feelings. In the following he makes several important points. First, in addition to his distinction between "Measure" and "Time," he reminds us that the Italian terms familiar to us as "tempo" designations had earlier a strong mood or character connotation as well. It is also a significant point, which Couperin mentions here, that the notation system has no symbols whatsoever for feeling.

I find we confuse Measure or Time [the number of beats in a bar] with what is called Cadence or Movement [tempo, together with accent phrasing, or expression or feeling]. Measure defines the number and quality of the beats; and Cadence is literally the intelligence and the soul which must be added to it. The sonatas of the Italians hardly admit of this Cadence, this expression or feeling. But all our melodies for the violin, our pieces for the harpsichord, for the viols, etc., describe and seem to be trying to express some feeling. Thus, not having devised signs or characters for communicating our specific ideas, we try to remedy this by indicating at the beginning of our pieces, by some such word as Tenderly, Quickly, etc., as far as possible the idea we want to convey. I hope that someone will take the trouble to translate us for the benefit of foreigners; and may it procure for them the possibility of judging of the excellence of our instrumental music.[25]

[25] François Couperin, *L'Art de toucher*, 24.

This seems also to be what was intended in Jean Rousseau's viole treatise of 1687.

> There are people who imagine that imparting the movement is to follow and keep time; but these are very different matters, for it is possible to keep time without entering into the movement, since time depends on the music, but the movement depends on genius and fine taste.[26]

[26] Quoted in Donnington, *The Interpretation of Early Music*, 425.

In another place, Couperin considers the relationship of time and expression on a much lower, although no less important, level.

> As the sounds of the harpsichord are determined, each one specifically, and consequently incapable of increase or diminution, it has hitherto appeared almost impossible to maintain that one could give any "soul" to this instrument. However, by investigations which have lent assistance to what little native talent Heaven has granted to me, I shall endeavor to show by what means I have managed to gain the happiness of touching the hearts of people of good taste, who have done me the honor of listening to me ...
> The feeling or soul, the expressive effect, which I mean, is due to the cessation and suspension of the notes, made at the right moment, and in accordance with the character required by the melodies of the preludes and pieces. These two *agremens*, by their contrast, leave the ear in suspense, so that in such cases where string instruments would increase

their volume of sound, the suspension [slight retardation] of the sounds on the harpsichord seems (by a contrary effect) to produce on the ear the result expected and desired ...

With regard to the expressive affect of the aspiration, the note over which it is placed must be detached less abruptly in passages which are tender and slow than in those which are light and quick. As for the suspension, it is hardly employed at all except in slow and tender pieces. The duration of the rest which precedes the note over which it is marked must be left to the taste of the performer.[27]

[27] François Couperin, *L'Art de toucher*, 14ff.

Sebastien de Brossard, in an early dictionary of music (1703), considered time from a different perspective with regard to the recitative. Writing of rubato in Largo tempo, he observes,

> In Italian recitatives we often do not make the beats very equal, because this is a kind of declamation where the Actor ought to follow the movement of the passion which inspires him or which he wants to express, rather than that of an equal and regulated measure.[28]

[28] Sebastien de Brossard, *Dictionaire de Musique* (Paris, 1703), "Largo."

Similarly, under "Recitativo," Brossard comments on the importance of adjusting tempo to the emotions of the words.

> This is a manner of singing which holds as much of declamation as of song, as if one declaimed in singing, or as if one sang in declaiming, hence where one has more attention to expressing the passion than to following exactly a timed measure ...[29]

[29] Ibid., "Recitativo."

It seems clear that all of Couperin's contemporaries would have at least agreed with him when he observed,

> Just as there is a difference between grammar and declamation, so there is an infinitely greater one between musical theory and the art of fine playing.[30]

[30] François Couperin, *L'Art de toucher*, Preface.

These have been theoretical comments, written observations on the role of the performer with respect to the communication of emotions. They seem almost disinterested in comparison with descriptions of actual performance. A manuscript by Diderot, purporting to describe the nephew of Rameau, seems, among other things, to have been inspired by performers whom Diderot had actually observed. The nephew is in a cafe and is singing tunes from opera.

> While singing fragments of Jomelli's *Lamentations*, he reproduced with incredible precision, fidelity, and warmth the most beautiful passages of each scene. In that magnificent recitative in which Jeremiah describes the desolation of Jerusalem he was drenched in tears, which drew their like from every onlooker. His art was complete—delicacy of voice, expressive strength, true sorrow . . .
>
> Worn out, exhausted, like a man emerging from a deep sleep or a prolonged reverie, he stood motionless, dumb, petrified. He kept looking around him like a man who has lost his way and wants to know where he is. He waited for returning strength and wits, wiping his face with an absent-minded gesture. Just as a man who on waking should see a large number of people around his bed and not remember or be able to conceive what he had done, he began by asking: "What is it, gentlemen? Why do you laugh? You look surprised—what is it?" Then he added: "This, this merits the name of music. There is your true musician."[31]

[31] Quoted in *Rameau's Nephew and Other Works*, trans. Jacques Barzun (Garden City: Doubleday, 1956), 69.

The possibility that there were French singers so lost in their feelings seems evident in the reaction of a French critic in 1702, when he similarly described a violinist as,

> an ecstatic who was so carried away with the piece that he was playing that he not only martyred his instrument but also himself. No longer master of his own being, he became so transported that he gyrated and hopped around like someone overcome by a demon.[32]

[32] Quoted in Hans-Peter Schmitz, *Die Kunst der Verzierung im 18. Jahrhundert* (Kassel: Bärenreiter, 1955), 12.

An account of a singer finds her to be not a demon, but an Italian!

> She caused a great sensation, but it was short-lived: several people concluded that she could not even sing properly, for this *is quite in the Italian tradition*, and she pulled the most horrible faces. She seemed to be suffering from convulsions.[33]

[33] Quoted in David Maland, *Culture and Society in Seventeenth-Century France* (New York: Scribner's, 1970), 80ff.

One can find many earlier references by French composers and theorists to the role of the listener, with respect to music's ability to soothe, or to affect character, etc. In the eighteenth century, however, there is something new added:

the reference to listening to music as music. This is what Couperin had in mind when he observed,

> There is no doubt that a certain song or melody, a certain passage, if executed in a certain way produces a different effect on the ear of a person of taste.[34]

[34] François Couperin, *L'Art de toucher*, 13.

It is in this sense, the modern concept of a completely non-utilitarian art music, that Rameau writes in 1726: don't think, don't put academic rules first, just let yourself be carried away.

> To enjoy the effects of music fully, we must completely lose ourselves in it; to judge it, we must relate it to the source through which we are affected by it. This source is nature. Nature endows us with the feeling that moves us in all our musical experiences; we might call her gift *instinct*. Let us allow instinct to inform our judgments, let us see what mysteries it unfolds to us before we pronounce our verdicts, and if there are still men sufficiently self-assured to dare make judgments on their own authority, there is reason to hope that none will be found weak enough to listen to them.[35]

[35] Jean Philippe Rameau, *Le Nouveau Système de musique théorique*, 43.

In a remarkable passage eight years later, which represents a dramatic departure from the contentions of the sixteenth century French philosophers who placed all meaning in the words, Rameau says find your meaning in the music, don't force your impressions of the music to fit the accepted meaning of the words. He might as well say, listen with the right brain, not the left.

> Often we think we hear in music only what exists in the words, or in the interpretation we wish to give them. We try to subject music to forced inflections, but that is not the way to be able to judge it. On the contrary, we must not think but let ourselves be carried away by the feeling which the music inspires; without our thinking at all, this feeling will become the basis of our judgment. As for reason, everybody possesses it nowadays; we have just discovered it in the bosom of nature itself. We have even proved that instinct constantly recalls it to us, both in our actions and in our speech. When reason and instinct are reconciled, there will be no higher appeal.[36]

[36] Jean Philippe Rameau, *Observations sur notre instinct pour la musique et sur son principe*, 44.

In a more extended passage from this same treatise, Rameau's reasoning is only flawed by his error that "harmony alone can stir the emotions." We know today, from clinical research in the perception of music, that it is primarily melody which carries emotional meaning for the listener, and furthermore it is genetic, as is demonstrated in part by the fact that it also holds true for lower species.

> A mind preoccupied, while listening to music, is never free enough to judge it. For instance, if we think to attribute the essential beauty of this art to changes from high to low, from fast to slow, soft to loud—means which do give variety to sounds—we will judge everything according to this prejudice, without considering how weak these means are, or what scant merit there is in making use of them; we will fail to perceive that they are foreign to harmony, which is the sole basis of music and the true source of its glorious effects.
>
> A truly sensitive spirit must judge quite differently! If the spirit is not moved by the power of the expression, by the vivid colors of which the harmonist alone is capable, then it is not absolutely satisfied. The spirit may, of course, lend itself to whatever may entertain it, but it must evaluate things in proportion to the impact the given experience exerts.
>
> Harmony alone can stir the emotions. It is the one source from which melody directly emanates, and draws its power. Contrasts between high and low, etc., make only superficial modifications in a melody; they add almost nothing ...
>
> If the imitation of noise and motion is not used as frequently in our music as in Italian music, it is because with us the main object is feeling. Feeling has no predetermined rhythms, and consequently cannot be everywhere reduced to a regular measure without losing that verity which is its charm. The musical expression of the physical lies in beat and rhythm; that which touches the emotions comes, on the contrary, from harmony and its inflections, a fact which we must carefully weigh before deciding what should carry the balance.
>
> The comic genre almost never aims to express emotion and consequently is the one genre that lends itself to those cadenced rhythms by which we do honor to Italian music. We do not always notice, however, how our own musicians have made felicitous use of them. Our enjoyment of the few attempts which the delicacy of French taste has permitted our

composers to risk, has proved how easily we can excel in this genre.³⁷

[37] Ibid.

On Performance Practice

AT THE END OF THE SEVENTEENTH CENTURY, we are attracted to two observations by Charpentier on the subject of "practical music." First, he concludes his book on the rules of composition by admitting,

> Practice teaches more about this than all the rules.

Charpentier also addresses a word to the accompanist:

> Those who make too much of a disturbance, who raise their hands in order to overpower their clavier, are incapable of accompanying well.
>   What can be said about one instrument can be said and has to be true about all the others.
>   When the voice rests, the brilliance of the hands may appear without destroying good taste.³⁸

[38] Quoted in Kuyper, "Marc-Antoine Charpentier's *Règles de Composition*," 65ff.

Couperin, in 1717, offers some interesting and self-explanatory advice to players. It is also worthy of note that this is one of the earliest documentations of performers playing (written music) from memory.

> With regard to making grimaces, it is possible to break oneself of this habit by placing a mirror on the reading-desk of the Spinet or Harpsichord ...
>   It is better and more seemly not to beat time with the head, the body, nor with the feet. One should have an air of ease at one's harpsichord; not gazing too fixedly at one object, nor yet looking too vague; in short, look at the assembled company, if there be one, as if not occupied with anything else. This advice is only for those who play without the help of their books.³⁹

[39] François Couperin, *L'Art de toucher*, 11.

The most interesting topic discussed by these musicians is improvisation, by which we mean both true improvisation [ornamentation] and the simple addition of ornaments. As with other countries, it is quite clear that improvisation was assumed, as we can see in Michel de Saint-Lambert's *Les Principes du clavecin* of 1702.

> If the choice of the fingering is arbitrary in playing the clavecin, that of adornment is no less so. Good taste is the only rule to be followed. There are ornaments that are essential in the music and that it would be hard to do without. The most important of these is the trill; the others are the mordant, the arpeggio, and the falling tone. But though those we shall talk about later are not so necessary nor so much used, they lend much grace to compositions and one would be wrong to neglect them.[40]

This same writer also gives two general rules for ornamentation. First, he advises against taking too many liberties for fear that "you will spoil that which you are trying to embellish." Second,

> The ornaments should never alter the melody nor the pace of the piece. Thus in the pieces with gay movements the runs and arpeggios should go faster than in slow movements. You must never hurry in making an ornament, however fast it should be played. You must take your time, prepare your fingers, then execute it boldly and freely.[41]

François Couperin also clearly implies an expectation of improvisation.

> Although these preludes are written in measured time, there is nevertheless, a style, dictated by custom, which must be observed. I will explain what I mean. A prelude is a free composition, in which the imagination gives rein to any fancy that may present itself. But as it is rather rare to find geniuses capable of production on the spur of the moment, those who have recourse to these non-improvised preludes should play them in a free, easy style, not sticking too closely to the exact time, unless I have expressly indicated this by the word *Measure*. Thus one may venture to say that in many things, Music (as compared with Poetry) has its prose, and its verse.
>
> One of the reasons why I have written these preludes in measured time was to make them easier, as will be found to be the case, whether in teaching them, or in learning them.[42]

A rather extraordinary comment by de Bacilly, urges singers to slow down the beat in order to have more time to improvise, especially in dance forms such as the gavotte.

[40] Michel de Saint-Lambert, *Les Principes du Clavecin* (1702), quoted in Carol MacClintock, *Readings in the History of Music in Performance* (Bloomington: Indiana University Press, 1979), 218.

[41] Ibid., 224.

[42] Ibid., 33.

It is completely unfair to criticize this style of performing by saying that the melodies [are then no longer] danceable, as thousands of ignoramuses have done. If this were to be the intention of the performing singer, then his function would be no more than that of a viol.[43]

We are also given several aesthetic goals for improvisation. One is that the end must still be to please the listener, as Benigne de Bacily writes in 1668:

A piece of music can be beautiful and please not, for want of being performed with the necessary embellishments, of which embellishments the most part are not marked at all on paper, whether because in fact they cannot be marked for lack of signs for that purpose, or whether it has been considered that too many marks encumber and take away the clearness of a melody, and would bring a kind of confusion; besides, it is useless to mark things, if you do not know how to fashion them with the appropriate refinements [*avec les circonstances necessaires*], which makes all the difficulty.[44]

Another goal was that the end must be natural to the performer. But, Louis Bollioud de Mermet, in 1746, complained that now all sonatas sounded the same as performers had begun to standardize types of ornaments and their use.

One could easily persuade oneself that he who plays music in such a complicated and unnatural manner is an evil-doer on whom this labor was imposed for punishment.[45]

Because this aspect of performance was so much a part of the very understanding of music itself, from the perspective of the player, even in those cases where composers were beginning to "write out" or to realize the ornamentation, their wishes were ignored. Couperin complains in 1722 that the information in his prefaces is being ignored and pleas that his music,

will make a certain impression on people of good taste only if everything which I have marked is observed to the letter, without addition or subtraction.[46]

[43] Quoted in Ellen Harris, "Voices," in *Performance Practice: Music after 1600* (New York: Norton, 1989), 108.

[44] Bénigne de Bacilly, *L'Art de bien chanter* (Paris, 1668), quoted in Donnington, *The Interpretation of Early Music*, 155.

[45] Louis Bollioud de Mermet, *De la corruption* (Lyon, 1746), quoted in Ibid., 156.

[46] François Couperin, *Pieces*, Liv. III (Paris, 1722), Preface.

2 Mersenne on the Nature of Music

MARIN MERSENNE (1588–1648) studied mathematics, physics, the classics and metaphysics at the Jesuit College of Le Mans and later at the college at La Fleche, where one of his classmates, and life-long friend, was René Descartes After becoming a Jesuit priest, and a member of the Minorite friars, Mersenne began teaching Hebrew, philosophy and theology at the Sorbonne in Paris in 1619. His residence became a required stopping place for every intellectual visiting Paris, which, together with his correspondence with persons throughout Europe, including Galilei, Huygens and Descartes, made him a virtual one-man academy.

His studies and experimentation in music resulted in his *Harmonie universelle* (1636), a work of encyclopedic proportion organized in five treatises. They are,

I *Traitez de la nature des sons, et des mouvements de toutes sortes de corps.*

II *Traité de mechanique.*

III *Traitez de la voix, et des chants.*

IV *Traitez des consonances, des dissonances, des genres, des modes, et de la composition.*

V *Traité des instruments.*

The first two treatises deal with mathematics-based music theory and acoustics. The final three deal with vocal production, composition and instruments.

Reflecting his background, the perspective of Mersenne is as thoroughly mathematics-based and theologically oriented as any late medieval Scholastic university theorist. Nowhere is this more evident than in the second treatise, *Traité de mechanique*, which, in addition to subjects such as the soul and relationship of the senses to man, deals with pure science, which he attempts to correlate with music. His discussion in this treatise reflects clearly his twin centers of gravity, mathematics and theology, as well as his very impressive breadth of knowledge of earlier treatises. His purpose was an attempt to prove mathematically the ancient Greek thought that music must be related to a great harmony of nature created by God. While the treatise's value as science is weakened by errors in mathematics and by his acceptance of contemporary deductions, especially in astronomy, which are now understood to be incorrect, it is nevertheless an interesting and very valuable reflection of seventeenth century French intellectual thought.

The entire thrust of philosophical thought in music beginning with the sixteenth century was centered on the understanding that the central purpose of music is to express feelings, the vital concept which was to carry musical development into the future. Since these ideas were synonymous with the specific rejection of the old Scholastic mathematics-based explanations of music, it is curious to read Mersenne's extensive attempts to base explanations of music on mathematics in his *Traité de mechanique*. In great mathematical detail, he attempts to relate consonance and dissonance to solid geometry, physics and mechanics. For Mersenne, this mathematical knowledge was central to the "theory" of music and like a medieval academic this, in turn, was central to the definition of "musician."

> Those who know only singing and the manner of composing, as well as singers and those who play instruments, do not merit the name of musician, just as bricklayers do not deserve to be called architects, since the former do not know the ratio of the harmonics which they make or in which they assist, as the latter do not know why palaces and other edifices have

one figure rather than another. Thus the practice of music is like a body without a soul if one does not know the theory, which surpasses practice as much as the spirit surpasses the body and the heavens surpass the Earth.[1]

In his fourth treatise, Mersenne seems to suggest that goodness in a composition is a matter of mathematics. Those who teach analysis in universities today, those who teach the analysis of the "grammar" of music, but not the "music" of music, will find comfort in this definition.

> Since the goodness of composition consists in the natural order of the consonances, in their succession, and in the harmony which they make, we can say that the examination of this order is the idea of all the examinations which can be made of all the other kinds of compositions.[2]

In this same treatise Mersenne presents a detailed theory on voice leading and intervals, as the basis for composition.[3] It is entirely mathematics-based, resulting in musical examples expressed in a kind of tablature-notation consisting entirely of numbers.

> This manner of composing can be used by learned theoreticians, who wish to compare and send their compositions to each other, or who wish to have their compositions printed without using the [normal musical] notes of practice, which not every printer has.[4]

For the modern reader, perhaps the most interesting pages within the maze of mathematics in the *Traité de mechanique* are those which discuss the ancient theory of the "music of the spheres." To understand this subject, observes Mersenne, is a natural thing for musicians who wish to "contemplate celestial things while playing" or for the admiration of God, "who has preserved such beautiful proportion in the order which he has placed in all parts of the universe."[5]

Mersenne begins his discussion with the statement that he will not attempt to prove the existence of the music of the spheres and then devotes many pages to doing precisely that.

> Of course, we shall not be able to show whether the planets and stars make any sound. If the air extends as far as the

[1] Marin Mersenne, *Harmonie universelle*, II, ii. The English translation is taken from John Egan (Bloomington: Indiana University, unpublished dissertation, 1962). [All translations from the Second Treatise are taken from this source]

[2] Marin Mersenne: *Fourth Treatise of the Harmonie universelle*, ed. Robert Williams (Rochester: Eastman School of Music, unpublished dissertation, 1972), IV, iv, 24. As hereafter, these numbers represent: Treatise, Book, and Proposition. [All translations from the Fourth Treatise are taken from this source.]
[3] IV, iv, 5ff.

[4] IV, iv, 17.

[5] II, viii.

firmament or infinity, as some people believe, having no doubt
that God created it infinite, since it is an opinion fairly well
received in the [ancient] schools that God was able and is
still able to create an infinite air, and since we have neither
known nor revealed principles which oblige us to believe that
God did not create it infinite, then it is probable that the stars
and planets make some sound, inasmuch as they do move in
the air. We do not hear the sound, for we are accustomed to
it from the wombs of our mothers. Sometimes the sound is
too far from us, too low, too high, or too great to be heard, as
happens with certain other phenomena. We are, for example,
unable to hear the sound or noise which ants and other little
animals make when they walk, run, crawl, or fly, inasmuch as
the sound is too little and too feeble.

It may be concluded that sound has two imperceptible
extremities. It may be too strong or too violent. It may be too
feeble or too small. It may be made by too slow movement or
too small movement. It may be made by a too swift, too large,
or too precipitous movement. Both extremities exceed the
sphere which the ear has for its activity and understanding.

Now, if the celestial bodies do make sounds, one may
ascertain what their qualities are by considering the size and
movement of the celestial bodies.[6]

[6] II, v.

Mersenne next paraphrases the conclusions of the ancient
Greek Pythagorean school of philosophy, not a single word
of which, by the way, is extant in the writings of Pythagoras
himself.

The seven planets contain not only the consonances, but also
the dissonances. Orpheus invented his heptachord or lyre of
seven strings, each of which represented one of the planets,
but the Pythagoreans added the *Proslambanomenos* from
the Earth up to the Moon in order to create their lyre with
eight strings. There was a whole-tone from the first acquired
string up to the principal, which they called *Hypate*; there
was a semitone from *Hypate* to *Parhypate*, which represented
the distance from the Moon to Mercury. From *Hypate* up
to *Lichanos* there was a whole-tone, which represented the
distance from Mercury to Venus. From *Lichanos* to *Mese*, or
from Venus to the Sun, there was another whole-tone. From
there to Mars, or from *Mese* to *Paramese*, there was a semitone.
Finally, from the *Paranete* or from Jupiter there was a whole-
tone, and from Jupiter to *Nete* or Saturn there was another

whole-tone. Consequently they placed the octave from the Earth to Saturn, the perfect fifth from the Earth to the Sun, the perfect fourth from the Moon to the Sun, the perfect fifth from Venus to Saturn, and the perfect fourth from the Sun to Saturn. Thus they based their music on planetary movement from east to west, for the movement of the lowest planets is the slowest, and that of the highest planets is the quickest, since the latter make a greater journey in the same time.

If, however, we tune a lute according to planetary movement from west to east, it is necessary to change the order of the names and give the *Proslambanomenos* to Saturn, the *Hypate* to Mars, etc.[7]

Mersenne quotes at length another contemporary who believed in the music of the spheres, the German astronomer Johann Kepler (1571–1630). Kepler, who concentrated on planetary motion, speculated on combinations of sounds, chords, which might be created by the passing of the planets.[8] Mersenne suggested that if the planets produce harmony, "it would be necessary to make Saturn and Jupiter the bass, Mars the tenor, the Earth and Venus the alto, and Mercury the soprano, because Mercury has a greater range and is livelier than the others."[9] If there really is music of the spheres, Mersenne recommends that musical instruments should be tuned to these pitches. Unfortunately, he adds, there will always be something missing in this celestial harmony because of the great time intervals involved—Saturn and Jupiter, for example, only coinciding every 800 years.

In another treatise, Mersenne cites Gosselin and Guy Aretin relative to their theories that the musical intervals and the voice can be related to the planets, concluding that Jupiter is the root, Saturn is the second, the Moon is the third, Mercury is the fourth, Venus is the fifth, the Sun is the sixth, Mars is the seventh and Jupiter again the octave. Mersenne, however, finds this knowledge not necessary for practical musicianship.

But it is not necessary that the musician know the properties of the planets in order to compose good songs. For all kinds of music can be composed without knowing the planets, which have no particular influence on the voice.[10]

[7] II, v.

[8] Kepler, in view of the recent discovery that the planets revolve around the Sun, and not the Earth, concluded that a listener could only hear these chords if he resided on the Sun!

[9] II, viii.

[10] Marin Mersenne, Treatise Three, Book One, *Traitez de la voix, et des chants,* trans. Edmund LeRoy (New York: Julliard School, unpublished dissertation, 1978), III, i, 7. [All translations from Treatise Three, Book One, are from this source.]

Turning to the senses, Mersenne suggests that colors correspond with music in a similar manner. He cites a few examples taken from the sixteenth century Italian philosopher, Girolamo Cardano (1501–1576), beginning with white and black corresponding to the major and minor sixth. Cardano's theories of colors in their harmonic ratios, says Mersenne,

> will enable one to judge how the splendor and light of colors may be compared with the splendor of music or with that which heightens harmonies and consonances. Music is like perspective. Harmonies are like paintings which artists enhance with shading just as musicians set off consonances with a silence and dissonances. Silence can be compared with darkness, and vocal or instrumental sounds with diverse lines or the traces of the brush, colors, light, and shadows which ameliorate painting. Some sounds and intervals wound the ear, just as some colors offend the eye. Perhaps bulls and elephants really are terrified when they see red, and there are also certain sounds and intervals by which bulls and other animals can be enraged.
>
> As green refreshes the spirit primarily, and blue the eye, even so the perfect octave and the perfect fifth delight the ear more than do the other intervals.
>
> Everyone will be able to judge the consonances and sounds most agreeable to himself and compare them with colors, tastes, smells, paintings, qualities of touch, and all other things which give him pleasure.[11]

[11] Ibid., II, ii.

In his third book, Mersenne attempts to make similar correspondence between music and "Isorropics, weights, machines of war and peace, the beating of the pulse, and the health of body and soul." Regarding the soul, he paraphrases Ptolemy in saying,

> The octave is similar to the reasonable or intellectual spirit because of its uniformity and equality ... He compares the perfect fifth with the sensitive spirit and the perfect fourth with the vegetal, inasmuch as the perfect fifth approaches the octave more closely than does the perfect fourth, just as the sensitive spirit is closer to the intellectual than is the vegetal. The vegetal spirit contains three parts, namely, growth, strength, and decline of life, just as the perfect fourth contains three intervals. The sensitive has four faculties

[although he lists five], namely, sight, hearing, smell, taste and touch, just as the perfect fifth has four divisions. The intellectual spirit has seven faculties, namely, imagination, thought, memory, ratiocination, opinion, reason, and science, just as there are seven divisions of the octave.[12]

[12] II, iii.

The position of the Church had long designated the eye as the most important of the five senses, for its obvious relationship to the intellect. Mersenne presents an interesting, and more balanced, comparison of the importance of eye and ear.

If the eye discovers a greater array of things present, the ear discovers a greater array of things absent ... If the eye enjoys light and colors, the ear enjoys harmony of sounds and discourse that surpasses all that is comprehended by the eye ... If the eye is more prompt in its actions, the ear hears in recompense all that is said in front, behind, and to the sides, [while] the eye sees only what is in front.[13]

[13] III, i, 53.

On the Definition of Music

IN THE FIRST PROPOSITION of the second book of his third treatise, Mersenne provides his most concise definition of music, in the context of a discussion of song.

The song, or air, is a derivation of the voice, or of other sounds, by certain intervals either natural or artificial, which are agreeable to the ear and to the spirit, and which signify joy, or sadness, or some other passion by their movements.[14]

[14] Marin Mersenne, *Treatise Three, Book Two* ("Second Book of Songs") of the *Traitez de la voix et des chants ...*, trans. Wilbur F. Russell (Princeton: Westminster Choir College, unpublished dissertation, 1952), III, ii, 1. [All translations from Treatise Three, Book Two, are from this source.]

Having written this, it is interesting that he seems compelled to clarify the distinction between song and the vocal qualities of speakers and actors. Here he observes that the regular tessitura of preachers encompassed a fifth.

An objection can be made here, saying that the definition of this first theorem pertains to harangues, or discourse, and to the recitation of tragedies and comedies, for an orator, or someone representing a personage of the theater can observe all the intervals; diatonic, chromatic, or enharmonic within the octave. Experience has shown us how preachers use the half tone, the tone, the major third, the minor third, the fourth and the fifth, according to their accents or movements which they employ. From this it can be seen that several excellent musicians state that the discourse made by such men form a *Faux-Bordon*. This is verified by the preachers who speak as if they sang. That is why their discourse is less agreeable, and less profitable.

Later in this book he adds a few comments on the aesthetic qualities of song.

I say that the song which is best proportioned will be best of all. It will have all parts which correspond exactly to the letter and subject chosen, and this will never be better than when it describes the grandeur and praise of God, and the love and ardor which we must eternally consider.

It is easy to conclude that all the chansons of the court which have only profane subjects, and contain the praises of men, or flattery, and vanity and lies, cannot be perfect since truth is lacking in them ...

As for the note and song that must be given the chanson, I say first that it must have the range of a 19th, in order that it is not without the number which is employed to celebrate the grandeur of Him who has used the six days of creation to make the Universe ... Secondly, the chanson must contain all the beautiful and ravishing passages which can be imagined, and all the sweet consonances, for if it lacks these things it will not be the most perfect possible. In the third place, it must be sung by an excellent voice.[15]

[15] III, ii, 22.

Mersenne makes only a few references to the actual elements of music with respect to their aesthetic qualities. In one passage where he is arguing for the importance of the triad, it is interesting that he knows no explanation for its absence in medieval and early Renaissance music.

Composers maintain as a certain rule that thirds or their replicas should never be lacking in compositions in three or more parts, since they do not have charm without them ... Thus we have reason to be astonished that the ancient Greeks and Latins rejected the third from the category of the consonances, since without them music in several parts has almost no charm at all.[16]

[16] IV, iv, 28.

He seems to revert to his perspective as a priest with respect to dissonance, finding that it has the same effect among chords as "the vices do among the virtues."[17] A dissonance resolved, he says, is like a pardon.

[17] IV, v, 2.

The remainder of Mersenne's attention to the definition of music is focused on the problem of the classification of the many kinds of music. Almost as if he were not quite sure which type of classification would be most functional, he proposes several means by which one can organize and discuss types of song.[18] One can organize them according to "Diatonic, Chromatic and Enharmonic," by the twelve modes or by their emotional character.

[18] III, ii, 4.

> In the third place, the songs divide into as many types as there are passions, for there are sad and languishing; there are joyful ones; ones fit for war, and others for peace.

They can be further divided into "Dactylic, Anapestic, Iambic, etc."

Mersenne then proposes the division of songs into one of three genres: the Vaudeville or Chanson, the Motet or Fantasie and the third being all kinds of dances. Or,

> If one wishes even a more definite division, he can consider twelve types of compositions of music practiced in France; Motets, Chansons, Airs, Passamezzi, Pavanes, Allemandes, Gaillards, Voltes, Courantes, Sarabandes, Canaris, Branles, and Ballets.

Before continuing his discussion on classification, in particular before his discussion of dance forms, Mersenne makes the interesting observation that he understood that "the chanson and dances accompany each other ordinarily."[19] Following are some of the more revealing comments he makes relative to the nature of the basic musical forms.[20]

[19] III, ii, 22.

[20] III, ii, 23.

> The *Vaudeville* is the most simple of all the Airs, and can be applied to any kind of poetry sung note against note, without being [notated], according to the longs and breves found in the verse ... The Vaudevilles are simple indeed, because the least artisans are capable of singing them, since the author is content with presenting something which is agreeable to the

ear, rather than making counterpoint, fugues, syncopes, or other formal arrangements.

The *Motet* is so called because it is used in a short period of time, as if one had only a few words to say, and is used to present some brief idea in music ...

When the musician takes the liberty of using everything which comes into his spirit without expressing passion in words, the resultant composition is called *Fantasie*, or *Recherche* ...

The *Passemezze* is an Italian song for dancing. It was used in former times as an entree to the basse danses. It is danced by making several turns around the room with certain posed steps, and then crossing the middle, as the word bears ...

The *Pavane* comes from Spain, and is called thus because those who dance it make wheels in front of each other as the Pagans do, and with such seriousness that the cap and sword are not awkward at all, but necessary to better perform the step ...

The *Allemande* is a dance of Germany, which is measured like the Pavane, but it is not used in France as much as the others ... Today it is usually played without being danced ...

The *Sarabande* was invented by the Saracens, or Moors, and took its name from them ... It is danced to the sound of guitar, or castanets ... Its steps are composed of stretches or slides.

The *Volte* shows by its name (meaning to turn) that it comes from Italy, and is a turning dance ...

The *Courante* is the most practiced of any dance in France, and is performed by two people at a time, who run in time to the Iambic foot ...

The *Galliard* is a dance which took its name from the liveliness, or *Gaillardise* used in dancing, and the liberty which allows the dancers to go on the bias, across, or the length of the hall. Some say that it comes from Rome ...

On the Perception of Music

MERSENNE IS ONE OF VERY FEW early writers who ventured beyond the mathematics-based discussion of the theory of music to speculate about the psychological perception of music. He begins by observing that the brain is capable of processing sounds beyond those used in music, indeed capable of hearing musical sounds in the forces of Nature.

> The brain, which is more universal than the will, can contemplate the natural noises, and examine whether the different thunderings, roarings, and rumblings of the sea form consonances and dissonances.[21]

He wonders if the pitches used in music, specifically in singing, are somehow innate, provided by Nature, or if they are entirely taught by man. It is a question of Art versus Nature in terms of pitch. While Mersenne concludes on the basis of his experience that pitch is artificial, taught by man, some studies today suggest man may carry a genetic, natural pitch template.

> Now there is no doubt that the degrees and intervals of voices take after Art ... for if they do not depend on Art, those who teach singing to children would have no trouble at all in making them intone and sing exactly; and all men would make the exact intervals without having to learn them. This is against experience.[22]

Mersenne now turns to the perception of pitch in terms of high and low. From his experience he concludes that it is the highest voice which is most prominently perceived, something which has also been confirmed by modern clinical research to be a specific function of the brain. Mersenne finds a "natural" example in the peasant.

> Experience shows us that nature without artistry does not ordinarily use a bass at all, for peasants and shepherds sing only the treble or the tenor whenever they sing.[23]

He has also found this principle demonstrated by the performances of trained musicians in the concert hall.[24]

> We experience that the trebles in concerts, as much vocal as instrumental, awaken the attention best and are very much more agreeable, as if approaching more nearly to heaven and life, than the basses. Now we take more pleasure in drawing to us those who are more perfect and more full of life than those who are more imperfect and nearer to death. Thus it

[21] Marin Mersenne, Treatise Five, *Traité des instruments*, trans., Roger Chapman (The Hague: Nijhoff, 1957), V, i, 5. [All translations from Treatise Five, are from this source.]

[22] V, i, 3.

[23] IV, iv, 3.

[24] In III, i, 23, Mersenne discusses the construction of concert halls relative to acoustics, concluding that an ellipse shape produces the best results.

happens that we love and caress infants more than old people who are like great and weighty sounds and like winter, just as children are like spring and summer and heat or fire. Bass voices are like gloom, sought after only by owls and goblins; but high voices are like light and day, serving as ornaments to nature as high sounds do to music which loses all her charm when she does not have good trebles. Bass voices serve almost as nothing more than to make the high sounds perceptible, and to make them enter the ear and the mind with more diversity and pleasure.[25]

He does, however, offer one aesthetic objection.

Although the high may be more agreeable, nevertheless the intensity and the work necessary to produce this voice withdraws and diminishes the pleasures of the ear, for when the pleasure does not surpass the pain, it cannot be great.

Mersenne contends that in everything we experience, "we receive more pleasure in knowing one thing distinctly and perfectly, than in knowing several things indistinctly and imperfectly." After giving several illustrations of "simpler is better,"[26] Mersenne advances the contention that a simple unaccompanied melody is "more agreeable" to the listener than multi-part music.[27] He finds this idea opposed not only by composers, who are afraid their works will be discredited, but by Nature, where nothing is simple, but rather composed of elements. Nevertheless, for Mersenne, experience still taught that simple solos brought more delight than music in several parts. He curiously fails to distinguish the separateness of the senses in his discussion here, as he advances the argument that *smelling* a single flower produces a more distinct pleasure than *seeing* a bouquet of mixed flowers. Musically, he focuses on the observation that hearing *fa, me* sequentially, as in a melody, is pleasurable, but hearing them together is not.

For the sake of discussion, however, Mersenne considers the perception of multi-part music with respect to aesthetics. If pleasure comes from hearing distinctly, he asks, does it not follow that duos should be more pleasing than trios? Can this not be considered, Mersenne wonders, as an analogy to

[25] III, i, 17. The final line refers to what we call today the "pyramid principle," by which lower tones must be played louder, and higher ones softer, to counterbalance the action of the brain which makes us imagine we hear higher pitches louder than we do.

[26] For example,

> Even the sweat and the other excrements, of men as well as of animals, who subsist more simply, for example, of those who eat only bread or plants, and who drink only water, do not have as bad an odor as those who subsist on meat and who drink wine.

[27] Behind his pronouncements, however, is his personal preference for the performance of chant in the church.

the difficulty in following a single soldier in battle [a single line in multi-part music] as opposed to watching a duel [two-part music]? Here, he interrupts himself to tell a rather extraordinary anecdote about the great composer Claude Le Jeune.

> It is believed that when Claude Le Jeune showed his musical pieces in five, six, and seven voices to the masters of Flanders and Italy, they did not even want to look at them, and he had no audience at all, and that after having composed in two parts, in which he succeeded so poorly, he acknowledged to himself that he did not understand the true composition of music.[28]

[28] IV, iv, 2.

Mersenne continues with arguments pro and con, in judging the virtues of two- versus three-part music, including analogies from Nature and theology. His consideration of why three or more parts are more agreeable than two, includes analogies with geometry and another detailed attempt to correlate color and musical tones.[29]

[29] IV, iv, 4.

In the end, he concludes that the greater number of voices the better, so long as each sings in perfection.[30] Indeed, in another place he mentions in passing,

[30] IV, iv, 2.

> The third part increases the pleasure of duos so perceptibly that it is almost not possible to express it.[31]

[31] IV, iv, 24.

If he finds himself admitting that "songs in several voices have a great number of beauties of which the simple solos are deprived," he acknowledges as well his realization that others will disagree with him. Thus, he says, "this distinction will remain problematical."[32]

[32] IV, iv, 3.

On the Purposes of Music

IT IS EVIDENT that Mersenne considered that the essential purpose of music was closely tied to the expression of emotions. This, in turn, was inseparable from the natural "passions" in man, a subject to which he devoted considerable attention and which we have discussed in a previous essay. Here we present his observations on the role of the composer, performer and listener regarding the general question of the communication of emotions in music.

With regard to the role of the composer, Mersenne seems, as he often is, torn between opposing values. First, he had a certain loyalty to the ideas put forward by Baïf during the attempts of his famous Academy to reproduce Greek song. In spite of the strong support for Baïf's ideas here, we must point out that Baïf's concept was not carried forward. Baïf's conclusion that ancient Greek melodies proceeded on a basis of one note for each syllable was probably based on the Greek poetry rhythms. Attempts by Baïf's Academy to create music in this way only resulted in songs which were staid, lifeless and without feeling.

> We must place each note with each syllable in such a way that we never make a barbarism, which consists in lengthening a short syllable, or in making short that which is long. This makes the composer ridiculous, and makes him pass as a dunce or a dunderhead.[33]

Mersenne now turns his focus to those elements which make an effective song. It is an interesting discussion, including the influence of intervals and the objections frequently found in seventeenth century literature that French music did not communicate deep emotions.

> The art of writing good songs on all kinds of subjects does not depend solely upon the genius, the caprice, and the inclination of those who write them, but also upon the judgment, which should serve as guide for composers, as for other craftsmen …
>
> With regard to melody, there is no need to explain its degrees and intervals [having done this in an earlier book, thus] nothing more can be desired except a good judgment to use them suitably, according to the different subjects which are presented. For example, sorrowful and amorous things are quite well represented by major, mean, and minor semitones, and still better by enharmonic dieses, if we wished to accustom the voice to them, and similarly, by the minor third, which follows the nature of the semitone, and by the minor sixth, which is suitable for representing the greatest

[33] IV, v, 10. In IV, vi, 29, Mersenne seems to approve of this, on the basis of his belief that this was the principle of the practice of song by the ancient Greeks.

moans and pains. Things which possess something great and arduous, or rustic, such as martial and vigorous actions, are better represented by the tones and by the major thirds and sixths, or by the perfect or augmented fourth . . .

We must consider the entire text, and the purpose or intent of that which it contains, and where it inclines the mind, so that we might accommodate to it an inflection and movements so suitable, that when sung, they have at least as much force on the listeners as if it were recited by an excellent orator. Thus the composer, or rather the singer, bends and inclines his mind to all that he wishes. For this purpose, the composer should indicate all the places of the song in which the voice must be strengthened or weakened, and where the accents of the passions . . . should be made, so that the singer might follow the intent of the composer punctually.

He must also indicate the tone on which the voice should begin, for experience shows that songs recited on certain tones are much more agreeable and have more effect upon listeners than when they are sung a tone higher or lower . . . [34]

There is still something else in melody, however, which is more difficult to indicate and execute when singing than all that of which we have spoken up until here, namely, a certain grandeur, which accompanies the agreeableness of singing in the harmoniousness of the voice, and gives a single song something great and beautiful. This occurs with almost all other things which can be executed by the skill of man, which consists in action, as happens with dances, with the manner of bearing oneself on horseback, which has given the name of *fine and handsome man on horseback* in the academy of Pluvinel. This is noted also in perspectives, in scenes, in buildings, and everywhere else where there are things which partake of greatness and beauty. Hence the simplest clothes appear better on a well-formed body than the most handsome in the world on a badly formed body . . .

We must acknowledge that the accents of the passions are lacking most often in French melodies, since our singers are content with tickling the ear and with pleasing by their affectations, without concerning themselves with exciting the passions of their listeners, according to the subject and the intention of the text. They also do not have this grandeur, which arises from beauty and greatness of which I have spoken, and the song does not always express the significance of the words, for which we should have quite a particular care.[35]

[34] Mersenne may be referring to a performance practice discussed at more length by Praetorius, regarding the singer's freedom to begin a melody on a pitch other than that written by the composer.

[35] IV, vi, 8.

Aside from this discussion of the elements which influence the emotions communicated in music, Mersenne also recognized that there was something else—the composer himself must be inspired.

> We should consider well, understand, and express the meaning and intent of the words and the subject, in order to accentuate and animate it in such a way that each part makes all the effect of which it is capable. This happens particularly when the composer himself is struck by the feeling which he desires to impress upon the minds of his listeners when writing and singing his airs, just as it happens that the orator has more power upon his audience when he is moved and completely convinced of his reasons.[36]

[36] IV, vi, 9.

And beyond this, there was something which had to be supplied by Nature. Composers, he concluded, are born and not made through "Art."

> Whatever rules we could give for composing fine and beautiful melodies on all kinds of subjects and texts, it appears that they cannot bring this to pass until we are induced by the favorable genius and natural inclination of those who write excellent ones without having learned or established any other rules than those which their imagination furnishes ...
>
> I shall be of the opinion of those who say that the genius of music is like that of the poet, the painter, the orator, and of several other craftsmen, to whom nature, or rather the Master of Nature, has dispensed certain gifts to which art cannot attain.[37]

[37] Ibid.

In another place, Mersenne calls upon several analogies, including color, in attempting to explain how music expresses emotion.

> If we can find and establish infallible rules for making songs, we shall have accomplished one of the most difficult things in music ... And if one demands why it is [more] difficult to make a good song, [than] it is to add parts to a song already composed, and to compose in two, or several parts, I reply that one must be more learned to recognize good songs, than to compose in several parts.

......

I say now first that the infallible rule for songs is that they follow and imitate the movement of passion which they wish to excite in their hearers. For example, if one wishes to arouse war passion, or color, the Iambic or Anapestic movement should be used ... He who knows the real movements, knows the best part of music, and the rules which are most necessary in singing.

The second part pertains to intervals, and the degrees used in chansons, for here also the same degrees must be used according to the passions which are to be aroused. For example, if anger rises or falls by degrees, it is necessary that the song does the same, [for] it is certain that songs were invented to arouse the passions. For example rejoicing pertains to the passions, and it is their beginning, foundation, and the end, for pleasure is nothing other than perfect love. I do not believe that other rules are necessary for making good songs on all types of subjects ...

......

It should be noticed here that songs are similar to the nuances of colors, which follows the idea of not being able to pass from one extremity to another without passing through a central shade. That is why one can be instructed in making good songs by the consideration of the nuances, for as one has seven intervals, or eight sounds in the octave, so one takes seven or eight colors for each shade, as is seen in the shade of purple, blue, and chartreuse, or lemon yellow. In this way one can compare each song to each color ...

One can add that if songs are made of the twelve tones in the octave, one has also twelve colors, and that a shade may have as many colors as the octaves do sounds, or intervals, for each may be divided into an infinity of degrees.

One can be instructed by an analogy to other things. Simple tones compare to simple colors. Intervals of sounds compare to mixtures of the colors, and the songs to paintings.[38]

[38] III, ii, 6.

Regarding color, it is interesting that Mersenne thought it might be helpful if the composer arranged to have his music actually printed in color to help identify the emotions he had in mind. Therefore, the diatonic, a joyful set of intervals, might be printed in black; the chromatic, whose half-steps arouse sad, amorous, and ravishing feelings, could be printed in red; and the enharmonic, since it is particularly fitting "for ravishing the mind in the contemplation of heavenly things," could be reproduced in blue.[39]

Turning his attention to the listener, Mersenne makes an error which is frequently made even today. Mersenne assumed that music produced its impact on man in a process similar to painting. But here he is mistaken, painting is a representation, but music is not—it is a *direct* communication between its source and the listener.

> Music is an imitation or representation, as is Poetry, Tragedy, or Painting ... for it does with sounds or with the articulated voice what the Poet does with verses, the Comedian with gestures, and the Painter with light, shade, and colors.[40]

Mersenne did recognize that to some degree taste is an individual matter. This has more than ordinary significance, for in a series of treatises so highly dependent on mathematics, it is an admission that mathematics and science cannot account for everything in music. We would say today that math and geometry are left-hemisphere grammar—something someone told us.

> Since the rules have been formulated only upon the different observations of the mixture of sounds, some of which have been more agreeable to those who formulated the rules than others were, it is free to those who are as capable, or more so, than they, to observe that which pleases them, since their ear is as good and as well trained, and since that which is offensive to some can be pleasing to others. For the rules of harmony are not like those of geometry, which force the mind of all those who have common sense to adopt them. They depend upon the ear and upon custom.[41]

But Mersenne also recognizes that the listener's preference can be influenced by experience.

> If perchance someone finds it a little harsh in certain places, he will judge it quite good when his ear is accustomed to it. The same thing will happen to him as to the disciples of Pythagoras who did not wish to approve of thirds and sixths until time and their use, based upon Reason, made them understand the excellence of these consonances, so that he will judge that the fourth is an excellent chord.[42]

---

[39] "Embellissement des chants," according to David Duncan, "Persuading the Affections: Rhetorical Theory and Mersenne's Advice to Harmonic Orators," in *French Musical Thought, 1600-1800* (Ann Arbor: UMI Research Press, 1989), 156.

[40] II, 97.

[41] IV, iv, 21.

[42] IV, v, 5.

Next, Mersenne makes one very important point: one can only judge music by hearing it. He reminds us that before the advent of recordings, persons heard much less music than we hear today. Perhaps more than anything else this helps explain the emphasis on theory over practice in earlier periods, for they had to work from imagination rather than from direct, live experience.

> If we wished to have all the pleasure which can result from music, it would be necessary to have all the ways of singing and make them appear one after the other, in order to judge how one surpassed the other. For example, it would be necessary to have one or two madrigals or other Italian melodies sung by a dozen fine Italian voices, as well as sarabandes by the Spanish, and courantes and melodies by French; and then to have the best pieces of music written for instruments played by each of them ... Since, however, no book can furnish the practice of this music, and since it is not easy to encounter it, it is sufficient to show what our France has invented, or what it has added to music, or at least its attempts, which can only be praiseworthy, even though they have not attained perfection.[43]

[43] IV, vi, 24.

Mersenne assumed that "happy" songs should be more agreeable to the listener than sad ones. But to his astonishment, he found the opposite was sometimes the case! This led him to formulate the proposition, "To determine if chansons which are sad and languishing are more agreeable and pleasant than those which are gay."

> This proposition is not useless, for being well explained it will give us insight into the nature of man, and of music. It seems that one cannot doubt that gay chansons are not more agreeable than sad ones, since all men desire to rejoice and disperse sadness which ruins health and state of the body.
>
> One sees that the Ballet melodies, and the violins arouse men of their gaiety, derived from the quick movements, and high-pitched sounds, rather than those melodies played on the lute, or bass viols, which are ordinarily more serious and languishing.
>
> The trumpets are another proof of this when they use the first mode, which is the gayest of all, and arouses all sorts of emotion in men. We know from experiences that the

movements of heart and imagination follow the sounds and movements of the trumpet.

    To which one can add that sounds, and rhythms of gay songs approach life, rather than the sad melodies, since life consists of perpetual movement. The vibrations of air which make the high sounds, and rhythmic movements which are quicker approach nearer this continuity than those which are serious, or weighty and slow sad songs. They represent broken and dying life. One experiences that gay songs are proper for dancing, and even those who have never learned to dance derive some pleasure from these chansons. This does not happen in the case of sad or lugubrious melodies, which are only proper for making their auditors weep and die, rather than for laughing or life. These melodies are composed of rhythms suitable for engendering sadness, and consequently for making the inactivity fall upon the limbs which cause them to become paralytic and incapable of movement.

Mersenne now offers the proposition: "The accent of which we speak here is an inflection or modification of the voice or the word with which we express the passions and the affections naturally or artificially." He finds this a natural expression in speech, but he is suspect of singing for through the study of the art of singing, singers may learn, like actors, to only imitate an emotion.

> The difference of this definition is explained in the words *with which we express*, etc. For nature itself teaches us which accents we must use to show and designate our passions and affections, which are expressed solely artificially with the simple word or with singing. For the song and discourse depend upon art and instruction. We cry, shout, and give certain accents to the voice and the words, without having learned to make them. These accents of passion are common to men and animals, who cry differently to show their joy than to show their sorrow.[44]

Mersenne now turns to the role of rhythm in the communication of emotions in music. In the following proposition, the word "movement" is used to refer to emotional character, not as a term to distinguish part of a larger form as we use the term today.

---

[44] IV, vi, 12. Mersenne adds,
> If we had observed the different accents which the animals make use of to express their passions, we could perhaps have some knowledge of their temperaments and their humors, but it would be necessary to make a great number of observations on this subject.

> Rhythmics is an art which considers movements and which regulates their succession and their mixture to excite the passions and to maintain them, and to increase, decrease, or calm them.[45]

[45] IV, vi, 18.

He begins here a discussion of the application of the Greek rhythmic modes to composition. His aim in his discussion under this proposition was apparently to justify and encourage the continuation of the ideas of Baïf, which he discusses in another place.[46]

[46] IV, vi, 24.

> This description contains the principal effects and the highest intent of rhythmics, whether we consider it speculatively, or insofar as practice is concerned. For those who use it on drums and trumpets, in dances and ballets, in songs and in lines, etc., have no other intent than to please the listeners and the spectators, or to excite them to some passion or affection, either of joy or of sorrow, and of love or hatred, etc. Thus fine poets, such as Virgil, use quick movements, represented by short syllables, by dactyls, anapests, and other similar feet, to give a similar impulse or a similar imagination to the reader or the listener ... It is certain that when these movements are well-regulated and arranged they have a great power over the mind or over the blood and the other humors, since some feel inclined to sing and dance in rhythm when they see this practice, even though they had no intention, and that just as we often yawn when seeing others yawn, we also find ourselves singing, leaping, or dancing without any preceding deliberation, which the imitative nature anticipates in several of its movements. From this it is easy to conclude that he who gives beautiful movements to his melodies and who expresses better for listeners the passion of the text, should be preferred to all the others.[47]

[47] IV, vi, 18.

Mersenne admits it is difficult to persuade composers to observe these, not only because they find the application of these modes result in tedious rhythms, but because they would prefer to write what comes to them solely from their imagination.

No doubt following the ideas of Baïf and his sixteenth century Academy, Mersenne now discusses the Greek term, "rhythmopoeia," which he defines as "the art of making beautiful movements on all kinds of subjects."

We have explained all these species of feet and of lines, so that it is only necessary to add to their properties, so that composers might use them and so that before beginning a fantasy or any other musical piece which can be imagined, they might know the movements which must be used, if they desire that their music make some impression upon the minds of the listeners ...

For example, he should choose the genus and the mode of music so that if it is more appropriate to use the degrees of the diatonic [*genus*] and the Phrygian mode, he avoids the chromatic degrees and the pitches of the Lydian, and if the song should be made in the first or lowest pitches of the system, which are called by the Greeks *hypatoides*, he does not touch at all those in the middle, nor above, which they call *mesoids* and *netoids*, according to the passions which he wishes to excite ...

After having chosen the melody, it is necessary to join to it the proper movement ...

Secondly, we should choose the species of movement and times necessary to execute the required effect. Since equal movement is suitable for minds which love tranquility and peace and which are favorable to repose and solitude, if we wish to induce this affection, or if we wish to maintain it, it is necessary to use the Dorian mode of the ancients and their hesychastic with spondaic movement, which admits all feet whose lowering is equal to the lifting ...

When, however, we wish to change this affection to enter into more turbulent passion, it is necessary to use the Phrygian mode and the double movement and feet whose lowering or *thesis* is double the lifting or *arsis*.[48]

[48] IV, vi, 27.

In relating these ideas to instrumental music, Mersenne adds,

Those who are not tied down to words, however, and who are content to write branles and other species of fantasies and dances for ballets, can apparently use more kinds of movements, since they subject themselves neither to prose nor to verse. If it is permitted to philosophize in this matter, we can say that the iamb is suitable for expressing choler, since it imitates the quickness and lightness of fire at its beginning, and it doubles its force in the second part of its movement, which is double the first which the Greeks make in lifting, as is that of the *pyrrhic*. Practitioners call this iambic and trochaic movement *ternary beat*, although it is actually *double*. Those who desire to pass beyond this to find the reason for the effects of each movement, foot, or line, can endeavor to know the movements of the passions, the blood, and the other humors, which ordinarily follow and accompany. For it appears that there is no more powerful means for exciting the passions of listeners than to use the same times and movements which the same passions make use of in those who are touched by them.

Thirdly, we can pass from one genus of movement to another as well as from one mode to another … It is good, however, to return to the first kind of movement before ending, just as we return to the mode …

Fourthly, we must choose good words to make good effects, and must use the vowels *a* and *o* several times when we wish to represent great and magnificent things, and the feminine *e* and the short *i* and *u* several times to express sorrowful, abject, and small things. This is portrayed quite well by the word *petite*.

We should also choose words full of harsh consonances, such as *r*, to express troublesome things, and those which have more pleasant consonants, such as *d*, *l*, and *z*, to represent that which is pleasant and agreeable.

Beyond this focus on the communication of emotions, Mersenne found other important purposes in music. First, of course, as a priest, an important purpose in music was to bring man to God. In particular, Mersenne found in the strings, which never fail to sound when played, a metaphor for how man should respond always to the will of God.

> For since there is no movement that does not lead the way to the first Motive Power, it is reasonable that the movements from which one receives so great contentment and whence one draws so great a harmony, lead us to that, of which Providence incessantly beats the measure of the harmony of the universe and governs the grand concert of everything, lest it be said in Eternity that the musicians were more stupid and irrational than the inanimate creatures.[49]

[49] V, iii, 17 (Collary 8).

Another purpose of music, which he mentions in a letter to the great Dutch mathematician and physicist, Huygens, is to offer delight.

Similarly melodies are not made to excite anger, and some of the other passions, but to delight the minds of listeners, and sometimes carry them to devotion ... I do not want to deny that certain songs carefully joined to the text, cannot move one to pity, to compassion, to regret, and to other passions, but only that this is not their principal goal, but rather to delight, or even to fill knowledgeable listeners with admiration, which will make them investigate the causes of so signal an effect.[50]

[50] Letter to Constantin Huygens [November 14, 1640], quoted in Duncan, "Persuading the Affections," 165.

Mersenne only briefly mentions the important topic of dance and music, making clear he lacked the personal experience to judge the validity of the medical claims in this regard.

Some believe that the ancients practiced certain well regulated dances, which cured men of certain maladies, when they were sick. If one could put this art into practice, one would save great sums of money now used in medicine. But we have no knowledge of the movements necessary to cure or to prevent sickness, and when we shall have, there would be few people who would be willing to undergo such a test.

......

As for the perfection of these dances, it consists in perfecting the spirit and body, and putting them in the best possible condition. The best perfection of nature consists in knowing and contemplating the works of nature; the movements of the stars, the elements, their greatness, light, and perfection, and to elevate one's self, by means of them to the Author of the Universe, who is the great master of the Ballet which all creatures dance by well-regulated movements, and which ravish the sages and savants, and bring pleasure to the angels, and to all the blessed.[51]

[51] III, ii, 22.

Finally, Mersenne also mentions as a purpose of music the concept of ethos of which the ancient Greeks were so enthusiastic. In only one place does he suggest that he may have believed music can affect the manners of men. This comes at the end of an interesting discussion in which he contends that since all voices are unique, it might be possible to create a *phtongonomie* or *phoniscopie* to identify individual voices. While he does not further describe these terms he has invented, he adds that "the face and the voice are mirrors of the soul."

Mersenne also wonders why man was made with the ability to make only one sound at a time.[52] He doubts that man would be able to accomplish anything he cannot do with one voice and concludes that God made it necessary for man to need another man to make harmony, "so that the harmony of voices might invite men to the harmony of manners."[53]

However, in a letter to Huygens, he privately confessed great doubt whether music can in fact have significant influence on the actions of man.

> Now to begin this examination, it is first necessary to assume that music, and consequently melodies, are made particularly and principally to charm the mind and ear and to make us pass our lives with a little sweetness among the bitter things encountered in it. For to think that music serves to persuade us of the intention of the musician as perfectly as could a good orator, and that it has as much power to conduct us to virtue and to make us hate vice as much as the voice of a good preacher, even though the same things are sung as he recites in the pulpit, and to believe that singing can be used as easily for instruction as can speaking and lecturing, it is this that it is difficult for us to accept.[54]

[52] III, i, 21. In III, i, 22, Mersenne mentions that the "son of Pierre d'Avignon" astonished everyone by singing one part and whistling another simultaneously.

[53] III, i, 6.

[54] Letter to Constantin Huygens [November 14, 1640], quoted in Duncan, "Persuading the Affections."

3 Voltaire on Music

FRANÇOIS MARIE AROUET (1694–1778), known as Voltaire,[1] was the son of a successful attorney and a lively and intelligent woman who hosted a minor salon in Paris. His father advised him, "Literature is the profession of the man who wishes to be useless to society and a burden to his relatives, and to die of hunger." The son responded by becoming one of the most prolific writers of the Baroque Period, supporting his family and dying wealthy. His works include drama, poetry, history, fiction and above all philosophy.

Voltaire arrived in Paris in 1715 as France was in transition from the era of Louis XIV to the regency for the young Louis XV. His brilliant wit, and sharp tongue, soon brought him to the attention of high society and earned him several visits to the Bastille. One comment remembered from this time followed an announcement that the regent, for reasons of the economy, had sold half the horses of the royal stables. Voltaire suggested it might have been better if he dismissed half the asses at court!

Regarding the purpose of music, in Voltaire's poetry there are several instances of the familiar reference to music's ability to soothe. In Voltaire's poem, "The Maid of Orleans," we find for example,

> Paris felt sorrow at their fate so tragic,
> And was consoled with comic Opera's magic.[2]

Similarly, in the poem, "The Nature of Pleasure,"

> That man is born to a propitious fate,

[1] He took the name Voltaire, a name which had been in his mother's family, while in the Bastille.

[2] "The Maid of Orleans," in *The Works of Voltaire* (New York: St. Hubert Guild, 1901), XL, Canto III.

Who to the muse his time can dedicate;
He from the tuneful art derives repose,
The Muse his anguish soothes, dispels his woes:
He laughs at all the follies of mankind,
And from his lyre a sure relief can find.[3]

And again in Voltaire's epic poem, "The Henriade,"

Thy accents too, sweet music, strike mine ear,
Music, descended from the heavenly sphere.
'Tis thine to soothe, to soften, and control
Each wayward passion of the ruffled soul.[4]

In Voltaire's poem, "The Answer," there is a reference to the purpose of music to communicate emotions which is especially interesting. He uses a very ancient expression for music, "harmonious numbers," as well as an often used metaphor in which the ear, and not the eye, is the passage to the heart.

Ye boys called Cupids by mankind,
Who whilst our meadows bloom in spring,
Inspire men love's soft joys to sing,
Assist a poet with your skill,
The charms 'twixt sense and rhyme to fill.
The enchanting pleasures well I know
Which from harmonious numbers flow;
The ear's a passage to the heart,
Sound can to thought new charms impart.[5]

In a letter to a connoisseur of art, Voltaire also reveals that he understood quite correctly the fundamental nature of music, that it communicates 'passions' and not the intellect. It is not, he says, an *idea*.

It seems to me that sculpture and painting are like music: they do not express ideas. An ingenious song cannot be performed by a musician; and a clever allegory, intended only for the intellect, cannot be expressed either by the sculptor or the painter. I believe that a subtle idea, in order to be represented, must be animated by passion, be characterized in a non-equivocal manner, and above all that the representation of this idea must be as pleasing to the eye as it is to the mind.[6]

---

[3] "The Nature of Pleasure," in Ibid., XXXVI, 246.

[4] "The Henriade," VII, in Ibid., XXXVIII, 109.

[5] "The Answer," in Ibid., XXXVI, 98. "Numbers" was a frequent Scholastic synonym, reflecting the association of music with mathematics, during the latter Middle Ages and Renaissance.

[6] Letter to Anne Claude Philippe de Tubières Grimoard de Pestels de Levis, Comte de Caylus (c. January 1739), in *Select Letters of Voltaire*, trans., Theodore Besterman (London: Nelson, 1963), 59.

That music was an "idea," or consisted of concepts, was propagated by the Scholastic tradition of the University of Paris. This long professed dogma of "speculative music" demanded that music be judged by knowledge of theoretical concepts and not by the ear. Voltaire makes fun of this idea in the course of a fictional debate among the inmates of the hospital *Quinze Vingt*.

> A deaf man reading this short history, acknowledged that these blind people were quite wrong in pretending to judge of colors; but he continued firmly of the opinion that deaf people were the only proper judges of music.[7]

[7] "The Ignorant Philosopher," in *The Works of Voltaire* (New York: St. Hubert Guild, 1901), XXXV, 293.

Voltaire also makes a few observations about the development of musical style and traditions. Two of these comments contain interesting references to Rameau.

> The rude beginnings of every art acquire a greater celebrity than the art in perfection; he who first played the fiddle was looked upon as a demigod, while Rameau had only enemies. In fine, men, generally going with the stream, seldom judge for themselves, and purity of taste is almost as rare as talent.[8]

[8] *Philosophical Dictionary*, "Amplification," in Ibid., V, 153.

......

> "Easy" applies not only to a thing easily done, but also to a thing which appears to be so. The pencil of Correggio is easy, the style of Quinault is much more easy than that of Despréaux, and the style of Ovid surpasses in facility that of Persius.
>
> This facility in painting, music, eloquence, and poetry, consists in a natural and spontaneous felicity, which admits of nothing that implies research, strength, or profundity. Thus the pictures of Paul Veronese have a much more easy and less finished air than those of Michelangelo. The symphonies of Rameau are superior to those of Lully, but appear less easy.[9]

[9] *Philosophical Dictionary*, "Ease," in Ibid., VIII, 174.

Finally, twice Voltaire mentions music with regard to language. The first is the case of a word whose musical roots are quite forgotten today.

> Enchantment (*incantatio*) comes, say some, from a Chaldee word, which the Greeks translate "productive song."[10]

[10] *Philosophical Dictionary*, "Enchantment," in Ibid., VIII, 222.

The second instance contrasts the performer and composer.

> The word *able* is applicable to those arts which exercise at once the mind and the hand, as painting and sculpture. We say of a painter or sculptor, *he is an able artist,* because these arts require a long novitiate; whereas a man becomes a poet nearly all at once ...
>
> A mere player of an instrument is *able*; a composer must be more than able; he must have genius.[11]

[11] *Philosophical Dictionary*, "Able," in Ibid., V, 28. He adds, that to say "an *able* courtier," implies blame rather than praise, since it too often means an able flatterer.

In his discussion of the various kinds of love, Voltaire points to the love of art, including music, as a kind of love which is without any reference to self. In view of the fact that today we regard music as a fundamental means of expressing feeling, it is certainly incorrect to suggest that the listener receives nothing from his experience.

> If we must pass from the thorns of theology to those of philosophy, which are not so long and are less piercing, it seems clear that an object may be loved by anyone without any reference to self, without any mixture of interested self-love ... We view some masterpiece of art, in painting, sculpture, architecture, poetry, or eloquence; we hear a piece of music that absolutely enchants our ears and souls; we admire it, we love it, without any return of the slightest advantage to ourselves from this attachment; it is a pure and refined feeling; we proceed sometimes so far as to entertain veneration or friendship for the author; and were he present should cordially embrace him.[12]

[12] *Philosophical Dictionary*, "Love of God," in Ibid., XI, 144.

In a very interesting comment on acoustics, Voltaire seems to have been unusually interested in the relativity of the perception of music as sound.

> The harmony of a concert, to which you listen with delight, must have on certain classes of minute animals the effect of terrible thunder; and perhaps it kills them.[13]

[13] *Philosophical Dictionary*, "Appearance," in Ibid., VI, 7.

......

> He who, for the first time in his life, hears the noise of a cannon or the sound of a concert, cannot judge whether the cannon be fired or the concert be performed at the distance

of a league or of twenty paces. He has only the experience which accustoms him to judge of the distance between himself and the place whence the noise proceeds. The vibrations, the undulations of the air carry a sound to his ears, or rather to his sensorium, but this noise no more carries to his sensorium the place whence it proceeds than it teaches him the form of the cannon or of the musical instruments.[14]

[14] *Philosophical Dictionary*, "Distance," in Ibid., VIII, 136.

Voltaire was clearly a participant in the discussion at this time of the relative merits of ancient and modern aesthetics in the arts. In his essay, "Revolutions in the Tragic Art," he writes of the functional role of music in religion in ancient times.

These public diversions were, among the Greeks, connected with their religious ceremonies. It is well known that among the Egyptians, songs, dances and representations made an essential part of the ceremonies reputed sacred. The Jews borrowed these customs from the Egyptians, as every ignorant and barbarous nation endeavors to imitate its learned and polite neighbors; hence those Jewish festivals, those dances of priests before the ark, those trumpets, those hymns, and so many other ceremonies entirely Egyptian.[15]

[15] "Revolutions in the Tragic Art," in Ibid., XXXIX, 152.

In another place he speaks of functional music in both ancient Greece and modern Paris, in the latter case the songs of the street peddlers.

Law was promulgated in Athens nearly as in Paris we sing an air on the Pont-Neuf. The public crier sang an edict, accompanying himself on the lyre.
   It is thus that in Paris the rose in bud is cried in one tone; old silver lace to sell in another; only in the streets of Paris the lyre is dispensed with.[16]

[16] *Philosophical Dictionary*, "Singing," in Ibid., XIII, 208.

The philosophical debate over the artistic rules of the ancient Greeks and the "moderns" had continued since the sixteenth century. Voltaire was struck by those who were so enamored by the past that they seemed oblivious to the accomplishments of their own era. He singled out the Englishman philosopher, William Temple, as one who "closed his eyes to the wonders of his contemporaries, and opened them only to admire ancient ignorance."[17]

[17] *Philosophical Dictionary*, "Ancients and Moderns," in Ibid., V, 159ff.

"What," he says, "has become of the charms of that music which so often enchanted men and beasts, fishes, birds, and serpents, and even changed their nature?" This enemy to his own times believed implicitly in the fable of "Orpheus," and, it should seem, had never heard of the fine music of Italy, nor even of that of France, which *do not* charm serpents, it is true, but *do* charm the ears of the connoisseur.

In an interesting review of Renaissance music in France, Voltaire seems curiously uninformed of the scope of musical activity during the period of François I, in particular the important art music played by *Les Grands Hautbois*. He also appears to have no knowledge of Machaut and his period.

The arts that do not depend absolutely upon the mind, such as music, painting, sculpture, architecture, etc., made but small progress in France before that period which we distinguish by the name of the age of Louis XIV. Music was as yet in its infancy; all that we knew were some songs, and a few melodies for the violin, the guitar, and the oboe, most of which were composed in Spain. The taste, the skill of a Lully, amazed the world; he was the first who in France introduced bases, stops, and fugues. However easy and simple his compositions may now appear, the execution of them must have cost him some trouble. There are at this time a thousand people who understand music for one who was proficient in the days of Louis XIII, and the art has, by degrees, arrived at perfection.

What music may have gained in composition it seems to have lost in expression, for the modern refinements of this art are calculated to tickle the ear rather than wake or assuage the passions of the heart.

Few great towns are now without a public concert; whereas then there was not one, even in Paris. The king's orchestra, of twenty-four violins, was all the music of France. The different species of science belonging to music, and its dependent arts, made such progress that, about the end of Louis XIV's reign, the art of notating dances was invented; so that it may now be truly said we dance by book.[18]

[18] "Ancient and Modern History," in Ibid., XXX, 112ff.

He makes several other interesting references to the period of Louis XIV, beginning with a reference to the participation of the nobles. By way of background, beginning at the end of the sixteenth century the fashionable thinking began to be that the noble could listen to music, but not actually be a performer. Not only did being a performer require too much effort, which a gentleman does not expend, but there was also an inappropriate association with the professional musicians (who were considered of a lower class).

> The word Academy became so celebrated that when Lully, who was a sort of favorite, obtained the establishment of his Opera, in 1692, he had interest enough to get inserted in the patent, *that it was a Royal Academy of Music, in which Ladies and Gentlemen might sing without demeaning themselves.* He did not confer the same honor on the dancers; the public, however, has always continued to go to the Opera, but never to the Academy of Music.[19]

To one of his correspondents, Voltaire writes of the musical awareness of Louis XIV.

> Do not regard Louis XIV merely as a happy man who had no part in the glory of his reign. He alone reformed the taste of his Court in more than one field. He chose Lully as his musician, depriving Lambert of his license because Lambert was mediocre and Lully was excellent. He knew how to distinguish wit from genius. He gave Quinault the subjects of his operas, directed the paintings of Le Brun, sustained Corneille and Racine against their enemies.[20]

In one of his essays he suggests that one may judge the importance of past artists by observing the nature of their burial.

> There is an immense difference between consecrated ground and profane ... the value of the ground is increased in proportion to that of the man. That in which Molière was interred has acquired reputation. Now as this man was buried in a chapel, he cannot be damned, like Mademoiselle Le Couvreur and Romagnesi, who were buried upon the highway ... I have no doubt of the salvation of Jean Baptiste Lully, fiddler to the king's sister, king's musician, superintendent of the king's music, who played in *Cariselli* and *Pourceaugnac* and was, moreover, a Florentine; he is gone to heaven as surely as I shall go thither myself; that is evident, for he has a fine marble monument at St. Eustache's church: he was not thrown upon a dung-hill: fortune rules the globe.[21]

[19] *Philosophical Dictionary*, "Academy," in Ibid., V, 58ff. Later in this volume, under "Anecdotes," Voltaire quotes a book by Durand, *Anecdotes Littéraires* (1752), III, 183, as follows:

> Louis XIV was so much pleased with the opera *Isis* that he ordered a decree to be passed in council by which men of rank were permitted to sing at the opera, and receive a salary for so doing, without demeaning themselves. This decree was registered in the Parliament of Paris.

[20] Letter to John Hervey (c. June 1740), in *Select Letters of Voltaire*, 66ff.

[21] "Dialogue between the Intendant des Menus and the abbé Brizel," in *The Works of Voltaire*, XXXVII, 244.

Voltaire's reading seems to have been so extensive that he noticed even some interesting trivia regarding music. Of particular interest to us is the subject of the relationship between music and light, or color. This was a topic discussed at length by Mersenne, but was also a subject taken very seriously by the great Isaac Newton. Voltaire mentions Newton, but seems unaware of his interest in the association of light and music.

> Thus, after Newton discovered the nature of light, Castel, to outdo him, suggests an ocular harpsichord.[22]

This is a reference to the French mathematician, Castel, and his treatise *Optique des Couleurs* (1740), which discussed the correspondence between melody and color. To demonstrate his theories, he apparently constructed an *clavecin oculaire*.

Another passage which caught our eye leaves us disappointed that Voltaire failed to provide more details.

> I know that men have disorders in their brain. We have seen a musician die mad, because his music did not appear good enough.[23]

Voltaire rarely discusses specific performances or even circumstances of performance. We find interesting one reference to the long tradition of sung poetry, which now in England had evolved into larger choral forms.

> It is surely of all the employments in a great house, that which is the most useless. The kings of England, who have preserved in their island many of the ancient usages which are lost on the continent, have their official poet. He is obliged once a year to make an ode in praise of St. Cecilia, who played so marvelously on the organ or psalterium that an angel descended from the ninth heaven to listen to her more conveniently—the harmony of the psaltery, in ascending from this place to the land of the angels, necessarily losing a small portion of its volume...
>
> It is asked, why poetry, being so unnecessary to the world, occupies so high a rank among the fine arts? The same question may be put with regard to music. Poetry is the music of the soul, and above all of great and of feeling souls.[24]

[22] Letter to Mdlle Quinault (May 1776) in *Voltaire in His Letters*, trans. S. G. Tallentyre (New York: Putnam, 1919), 257.

[23] "The Ignorant Philosopher," in *The Works of Voltaire*, XXXV, 284.

[24] *Philosophical Dictionary*, "Poets," in *The Works of Voltaire*, XII, 216.

In an article on "Somnambulists," Voltaire makes a passing comment worthy of mention. While the French humanists were the most avid advocates for music being written to the poetry, with the words being the most important, here Voltaire suggests that by the early years of the eighteenth century he was familiar with a practice which was quite the reverse, with the music coming first. Voltaire claims there was a young priest who not only wrote sermons in his sleep, but also music "notating it with precision, and after preparing his paper with his ruler, placed the words under the notes without the least mistake."[25]

In Voltaire's poem, "The Maid of Orleans," we find a description of the type of brief concert performed after banquets, after the tables had been cleared. The music in this case included epic poetry.

> The banquet finished, music played awhile,
> The song Italian, in chromatic style;
> Flutes, hautboys, viols, softly breathed around,
> While three melodious voices swelled the sound;
> They sang in allegory, and the strain
> Told of those heroes mighty love had slain,
> Who fled of sounding glory the career,
> To please the tender fair they loved most dear.
> The concert echoed from concealed alcove,
> Close to the chamber, then the scene of love.
> Thus beauteous Agnes, the discreet and wise,
> Heard all, but was not seen by human eyes.[26]

The most interesting reference to art song in the poems of Voltaire is found in Canto XVI of Voltaire's poem, "The Maid of Orleans." Here the poet creates a scene based on the rural singing contest, which was a staple in the works of the ancient lyric poets of Greece. In this case, St. Peter invites St. George (represented by "Austin") and St. Denis to compete in composing "A Hymn in verse, but not an Ode in prose . . . [and then] To music set the whole immediately."

Austin begins with an ode about ancient Egypt and the Hebrews, together with various characters of ancient literature.

[25] *Philosophical Dictionary*, "Somnambulists," in Ibid., XIII, 249ff.

[26] "The Maid of Orleans," in Ibid., XL, Canto I.

> Dull was the litany and somewhat long,
> While interspersed these brilliant traits among,
> Were mighty deeds detailed in sounding [songs],
> Those acts so cherished in remotest days . . .

His song was not well received.

> Austin was silent, his Pindaric strain
> Called forth amid the bright empyreal train
> A doubtful murmur—sounds made to infuse
> Ill-favored thoughts on his odaic muse.

Now Denis rose, "low bent his eyes serene, which straightaway reared, displayed his modest mien." He sings of the heroes of the Catholic Church, pauses and is encouraged to continue.

> With prudence Denis once more struck the lyre:
> "Mine adversary may have charmed the choir,
> The arm of vengeance hath he loudly praised;
> Whereas my sounding plaudits shall be raised,
> To honor clemency's bright power with skill,
> Hating is good; but loving's better still."
>
> Denis more confident in voice and mind,
> Then sang in pleasing verse, the shepherd kind . . .

At length, Denis is declared the winner, that is, France over England.

> Hailed was of Denis the odaic treasure,
> The prize it gained, and praises without measure,
> Of England's saint was foiled the boldness dread;
> Austin blushed deep, and skulking, forthwith fled.

In Voltaire's epic poem, "The Henriade," there is a reference to a civic victory song.

> Now was all Paris filled with joyful cries,
> And odious songs of triumph rent the skies.[27]

[27] "The Henriade," Canto V, in Ibid., XXXVIII, 81.

Voltaire's poem, "The Maid of Orleans," which describes French society at the time of Joan of Arc, contains a number of interesting references to functional music. First, we read of the use of the serpent in the French cathedrals, a practice which would continue into the nineteenth century.

To Heaven's high King, preferred a solemn prayer;
Te Deum sung by Drone from Serpent Bass ... [28]

Otherwise, Voltaire rarely wrote of Catholic church music, although an extraordinary exception is this sarcastic discussion of the relationship of the traditional Latin *Te Deum* with the slaughter of war.

> The most wonderful part of this infernal enterprise is that each chief of the murderers causes his flags to be blessed, and solemnly invokes God before he goes to exterminate his neighbors. If a chief has only the fortune to kill two or three thousand men, he does not thank God for it; but when he has exterminated about ten thousand by fire and sword, and, to complete the work, some town has been leveled with the ground, they then sing a long song in four parts, composed in a language unknown to all who have fought, and moreover replete with barbarism. The same song serves for marriages and births, as well as for murders; which is unpardonable, particularly in a nation the most famous for new songs.[29]

Curiously, a letter to a friend speaks of this form in quite a different light.

> Far be it from me to ask you to reply to me: but while I chant a *De Profundis* with my failing health, I sing aloud *Te Deum laudamus* for you.[30]

We might also mention here that in one place, in his, "The Maid of Orleans," Voltaire offers a description of Hell which includes, "songs in praise of drinking loudly roar."[31] A resident of Hell observes,

> Cursed and tormented here, why care a jot
> For psalms and praises sung where we are not?

The most interesting discussion of entertainment music by Voltaire is relative to a Comédie-ballet, "Princesse de Navarre" (1745), which he was writing for the Dauphin's wedding, with music by Jean Philippe Rameau. Voltaire had worked with Rameau in some attempts at opera libretto, but here he seems very nervous to have Rameau participate.

[28] "The Maid of Orleans," in Ibid., XL, Canto XV.

[29] *Philosophical Dictionary*, "War," in Ibid., XIV, 195ff. When Gossec was commissioned to write a large-scale work for the anniversary of the fall of the Bastille, and elected to write a Te Deum, he was much criticized in the press for this same association of this form with past military exploits.

[30] Letter to M. Turgot (July 1774) in *Voltaire in His Letters*, 240.

[31] "The Maid of Orleans," in Ibid., XL, Canto V.

Why did you give this entertainment to Rameau? I quite understand that Monsieur de Richelieu would like to have it rehearsed before he leaves for Spain, but if he tries to hurry everything he will spoil everything. He has already done it much harm in compelling me to invent the plot in one day at his house at Versailles . . .

There is one more thing I want you to decide: the proportion of [musical] interludes my play ought to have. It must not be stifled by double quavers; the entertainment must be short so that the play does not appear to be long. I don't know whether Rameau will put up with so small a share. Anyway, what a man! He has gone mad. Judge of it by the criticism he has made. And what is worse is that he will be encouraged in his madness by people who take pleasure in sowing discord in the path of pleasure. You ought first of all, my dear angel, to withdraw from Rameau the entertainment I am going to correct, but you should also have someone tell Monsieur de Richelieu that Rameau is not at all fitted for this kind of entertainment, the music of which intermingles all the time with the spoken declamations, that this genre requires as great harmony and union between the author and the composer as there exists between Francoeur and Rebelle. Monsieur de Richelieu ought to have chosen both of them for my interludes, and have given *Prometheus* to Rameau. That would have been in the nature of things. I foresee that it will be impossible to work with Rameau. He is good only to listen to, not to live with. I repeat that his kind of music is not suitable for mixed plays like mine.[32]

[32] Letter to Charles Augustin Feriol, Comte d'Argental (August 1744), in *Select Letters of Voltaire*, 86ff.

Finally, there is this comment on man's generally disinterested taste for entertainment.

Madam, as you know, all spectacles amuse mankind. We go equally to the marionettes, to the bonfire on the eve of St. John's, to the Comic Opera, to high mass, to a burial.[33]

[33] Letter to Suzanne Necker (June 1770), in Ibid., 168.

There are in Voltaire's poem, "The Maid of Orleans," additional instances of functional music, such as music used to greet nobles. These vary considerably in tone, from, "When citizens engaged with wine and dance, Extolled their prince, by songs and couplets graced . . . ,"[34] to, "with joyous hymns, their sire's return they hailed," and "twenty trumpets then were heard to sound" in a welcome at a great palace.[35]

[34] Ibid., Canto XV.

[35] Ibid., Canto IV.

This same poem also contains a reference to a rabbit "roused by the echo of the hunting horn."[36]

In view of the military adventures which characterized the period of Frederick the Great, we are not surprised to find numerous references to military music in Voltaire's poems. Several of these center on the "shrill" sound of the military trumpet, including, "To the King of Prussia," which mentions the military "trumpet's shrill sound,"[37] and the epic poem, "The Henriade," where again we find "the shrill trumpet."[38] In this same poem we find,

> The shrillness of the cheering horn provokes
> Their rage, and echoes from the distant rocks.[39]

A somewhat different mood is portrayed where we read,

> Paris, the king, the army, heaven, and hell
> Witnessed the combat—at the trumpets' swell
> On to the field the ready warriors came,
> Conscious of valor, and a thirst for fame.[40]

A similar use of the trumpet to inspire the soldiers is found in an allegorical description:[41]

> The air though roaring cannons rend
> While warriors with fierce rage contend,
> The thoughtless French drink, laugh, and sing,
> And with their mirth the heavens ring ...
> The Phantom, which we Glory name,
> Spurs them to the pursuit of fame;
> With threatening eye, and front all over
> Bedusted, marching still before,
> She holds a trumpet in her hand
> To sound to arms, and cheer the band,
> And loudly sings, with voice sonorous,
> Catches, which they repeat in chorus.
> Oh! people brilliant, gay, and vain,
> Who drag with patience glory's chain,
> 'Tis great, an honorable grave
> To seek, Eugene and death to brave.
> But what will be your mighty prize?[42]

Another, and rather darker, allegorical reference to the trumpet and battle is found in Voltaire's "The Heinriade."

[36] Ibid.

[37] "To the King of Prussia," in *The Works of Voltaire*, XXXVI, 196.

[38] "The Henriade," Canto VIII, in Ibid., XXXVIII, 119.

[39] Ibid., Canto VIII, 126.

[40] Ibid., Canto X, 147ff.

[41] We remind the reader that in the Old Testament the trumpet is blown by real people and in some cases we are given their names. In the New Testament all references to the trumpet are in allegory. No live person plays the trumpet in the New Testament.

[42] "In Camp before Philippsburg, July 3, 1734," in *The Works of Voltaire*, XXXVI, 178ff.

Hark! a loud peal comes thundering from afar,
'Tis Discord blows afresh the flames of war,
To thwart the monarch's virtue, with new fires
His fainting foes the bedlam fiend inspires;
She blows her fatal trumpet, the woods around
And mountains tremble at the infernal sound.
Swift to d'Aumale the baleful notes impart
Their power, he feels the summons at his heart.[43]

[43] Ibid., Canto VIII, 125ff.

4 Mersenne on Performance

MARIN MERSENNE (1588–1648) studied mathematics, physics, the classics and metaphysics at the Jesuit College of Le Mans and later at the college at La Fleche, where one of his classmates, and life-long friend, was René Descartes. After becoming a Jesuit priest, and a member of the Minorite friars, Mersenne began teaching Hebrew, philosophy and theology at the Sorbonne in Paris in 1619. His residence became a required stopping place for every intellectual visiting Paris, which, together with his correspondence with persons throughout Europe, including Galilei, Huygens and Descartes, made him a virtual one-man academy.

As we have pointed out in Chapter Two, his studies and experimentation in music resulted in his *Harmonie universelle* (1636), a work of encyclopedic proportion organized in five treatises. They are,

I *Traitez de la nature des sons, et des mouvements de toutes sortes de corps.*

II *Traité de mechanique.*

III *Traitez de la voix, et des chants.*

IV *Traitez des consonances, des dissonances, des genres, des modes, et de la composition.*

V *Traité des instruments.*

The first two treatises deal with mathematics-based music theory and acoustics. The final three deal with vocal production, composition and instruments.

Since Mersenne's primary interest in music was in song, he comments in several places on the essential qualities of a good singer. In a brief outline of the principles of teaching sight-singing, the focus of which is the ear, Mersenne also makes a brief appeal for the importance of quality of voice, one that is,

> beautiful, full, pleasant and mellow, borne and guided in a beautiful way ... [created by the] rollings of air in the canal or pipe of the throat, without the pit of the stomach, the nose, the roof of the mouth, nor the movement of the jaws ... It seems, however, that the present fashion is only to delicacy and affectation.[1]

Additional qualities of a good voice are the ability to hold a steady tone and "pleasantness and a certain harmoniousness upon which depend the charms which delight the listeners," which is encountered quite rarely. Still another quality needed is that it be "full and solid, which increases its harmoniousness."

> This can be explained by the comparison with a canal which is always full of water when it flows, or by that of a body and a face well filled-out and in good condition, whereas voices which are deprived of this quality are like a thin trickle of water which runs in a large canal, or a lean and gaunt face.[2]

Donnington cites additional vocal qualities mentioned by Mersenne.

> A solid sostenuto without pitch wobble; flexibility in passage work; accurate intonation; sweetness and a certain harmoniousness, on which depends the charms which ravish the hearers, for voices which are hard do not please, however accurate they may be, and possessed of the other qualities I have mentioned, for they have too much sharpness [*aigreur*] and glitter [*esclat*], which hurts sensitive ears, and which hinders their gliding pleasantly enough into their hearers' spirit to win them, and to carry them whither so ever you desire.[3]

---

[1] Marin Mersenne: *Fourth Treatise of the Harmonie universelle*, ed. Robert Williams (Rochester: Eastman School of Music, unpublished dissertation, 1972), IV, vi, 1. As hereafter, these numbers represent: Treatise, Book, and Proposition. [All translations from the Fourth Treatise are taken from this source.]

[2] IV, vi, 5.

[3] Quoted in Robert Donnington, *The Interpretation of Early Music* (New York, 1964), 517.

As with his views on composers, Mersenne concludes that to some degree the beautiful singer is born and not made.

> This should be ascribed to the order of Divine Providence, which makes use of all kinds of conditions, as it does of as many voices, to compose the great concert of this universe, whose beauties and charms we will never understand except in Heaven.[4]

With regard to that which could be taught, Mersenne was critical of most singing teachers for not having good enough voices to demonstrate well for their students. Also, he notes,

> In addition, they should have traveled in foreign countries, particularly in Italy, where they pride themselves on singing well, and on knowing music much better than the French. For although all which they do is perhaps not to be approved of, nevertheless, it is certain that they have something excellent in their solos, which they animate much more powerfully than do our singers, who surpass them in affectation, but not in vigor.[5]

This reference to Italian singers reflects the fact that the spreading popularity of Italian opera was making Italian singers an inevitable model for all of Europe. Above all, the Italian singers were known for their emotional delivery.

> As to the Italians, they ... represent as much as they can the passions and the feelings of the soul and spirit; for example, anger, fury, spleen, rage, faintheartedness, and many other passions, with a violence so strange, that one judges them as if they were touched with the same affects as they represent in singing; in place of which our Frenchmen are content to caress the ear, and use nothing but a perpetual sweetness in their songs; which hinders their energy.[6]

Mersenne also admired the freedom of interpretation enjoyed by the Italian singers.

> Italian musicians do not make as many difficulties as we do, however, for they are given much more freedom than the French are, as much in the inflection and intervals of simple solos, as in duos and ensemble pieces. I do not find fault with them for this, since they find it good, and there is no legislator who forbids them the opposite, or who forces them to our customs and our imaginations.[7]

[4] IV, vi, 6.

[5] Ibid.

[6] Marin Mersenne, *Harmonie universelle*, II, vi, 356. The English translation is taken from John Egan (Bloomington: Indiana University, unpublished dissertation, 1962). [All translations from the Second Treatise are taken from this source.]

[7] IV, iv, 23.

In another place he mentions these qualities but now adds the characteristics he admires in the French tradition.

> Therefore I am able to speak to our advantage, since we in many things, particularly politeness, delicacy, and in the way in which we perform them. For as to the quality of the voice, or its force, the Italians can dispute with all other nations, since they have many fine traits, and many inventions in which our songs are destitute.[8]

Having said here that French singers are destitute in their improvisation, in another place Mersenne seems to feel a need to find a way to compliment the French vocal style.

> Every nation imparting a knowledge of singing, and that makes passages in the throat, and the Italians themselves who make a particular profession of music, avow that the French perform the best passages, whose beauty and sweetness it is not possible to explain, whether with the eye or ear, for the trickling and murmuring of waters and the singing of nightingales is not as agreeable. And I find nothing in nature whose analogy can make us understand these passages, being more ravishing than divisions, for they are the quintessence of music.[9]

At a time when the opportunity to actually hear music was much more rare than today, Mersenne concluded that it was impossible to judge, regarding the best voice, unless one could hear singers from all countries, including Asia.

> If one wants to judge what the best method of singing is and in what the best quality of the voice consists, it is necessary to establish the rules that are accepted by all singers and proven by reason. And then he who executes them the best in singing surpasses all other voices ... will be the best.[10]

In the meantime, however, he concludes that French singers are the best.

Mersenne wrote an entire treatise on instrumental music, much of which is, again, mathematically based. He goes into considerable detail, finding, for example, that a harpsichord has more than 1500 separate parts.[11] He also discusses problems in pitch and especially the need for some means of

---

[8] Marin Mersenne, *Treatise Three, Book Two ("Second Book of Songs") of the Traitez de la Voix et des Chants ...*, trans. Wilbur F. Russell (Princeton: Westminster Choir College, unpublished dissertation, 1952), III, ii, 3. [All translations from Treatise Three, Book Two, are from this source.]

[9] III, i, 32. Mersenne makes the interesting observation that the ancient Greek writers never mention ornaments.

[10] III, i, 34.

[11] Marin Mersenne, *Treatise Five, Traité des instruments,* trans. Roger Chapman (The Hague: Nijhoff, 1957), V, iii, 20. [All translations from Treatise Five, are from this source.]

establishing a standardized pitch. His recommendation for a solution to this problem was to write next to the bass part in every composition the number of vibrations of the first pitch in the bass. Thus, musicians in all countries would perform the work at the same pitch![12]

[12] V, iii, 18.

As he progressed, writing about each of the families of instruments, Mersenne was frustrated at his inability to find factual information regarding the history of the development of the instruments and their manufacture.

> One almost always has trouble and difficulty in noting the primary inventors of artifices and things used for pleasure or the usefulness to man, whether our predecessors were so negligent that they have left us no clue or they were ignorant of letters and did not know how to read or write, as is experienced now among the Canadians and other savages.[13]

[13] V, vii, 2.

Mersenne includes among his general comments on instruments some discussion of the aesthetic qualities of the various families of instruments.[14] How does one establish which instruments have the most agreeable sound? This, says Mersenne, is a very difficult question and he finds professional musicians have a great diversity of opinion. For one thing, no one has heard all the instruments, especially those in foreign countries. Another reason has to do with the temperament of the observer.

[14] V, i, 4.

> The difference of temperaments which are found in men similarly causes the sound of some to seem more agreeable to that one than the others, so that these reasons ... can hinder the sincerity of the judgment.

Familiarity also affects the judgment, thus,

> soldiers and those who have a warlike temperament and stirring blood find the sound of the trumpet more agreeable than that of the lute or the other instruments, and hunters are more fond of the sound the horn makes than of the others, because they are accustomed to hear it; for what is familiar to us often pleases us more.

Well, says Mersenne, these kinds of difficulties are found in all worldly things, but man must exercise his Reason and make judgments. Therefore he generalizes that the sound of the lute is most charming; the German flute is more agreeable than other flutes and that the violin is the most ravishing of the strings. More interesting to us are some of his comments which reflect on ensemble quality.

> As to those which are produced by the wind, one can say in general that all the tones which are made by interrupted air alone are sweeter than the tone of the other wind instruments and any other which could be produced by the string, but they are not so agreeable as those which are made by the vibration of a reed, for although they seem rough, they have a natural gaiety which makes them preferable to the dismal and somber sweetness of the flute, although the gloomy sounds produce a concert of many parts more agreeable than that which is made of gayer tones ...
>
> Now in speaking of sounds more generally, we can say that the sweet ones are gloomy, choked and shut up, like those of the stopped flutes, and that the gay ones are more open, like those of the reeds and of flutes that the organ makers call in resonance. The tones are almost all the same provided that they are not so weak that the ear cannot perceive them or so violent that it would be offensive. What makes them more pleasant is the variety with which one embellishes them, either successively or simultaneously with other sounds.

In conclusion, Mersenne offers three additional aesthetic principles with regard to judging the various instruments. First, he concludes that variety is an important factor for the listener.

> Choose whatever tone you wish and listen continually: it will put you to sleep or give you a headache. The tone of a flute, placed on a windchest, being continued is amazingly tiresome and displeasing, and that of a lute will be even more ... Then it is the variety that makes the tone agreeable; and if it is not varied, it deserves mostly to be called noise rather than harmonic sound.

Second, he concludes the judgment of individual instruments will depend in part on the "temperament" of the listener.

> If the sound of the flutes, among which can be placed the trumpet, has more power over the mind, it is because of

the greater impression it makes in the air, or because of its particular quality. And actually in addition to that reason, experience shows that those who have a more delicate ear and more refined and subtle minds, are pleased more in the sounds of the string instruments. And those with grosser and heavier spirits take a greater pleasure in the sound of the trumpet and flutes, although this may not perhaps be so general that the contrary cannot occur.

Finally, Mersenne recognizes an analogy with color, with the single instrument being like a simple color such as black or white and a concert being like a colored painting. This, in turn, has a relationship with acoustics.

> Some [paintings] are made of such skill that they must be seen in the distance and the others close by, since the pictures which have the thickest colors which are cracked, as the painters say, who have much more skill, demand to be seen from the distance, are loved, cherished, and esteemed by the sons of Art. The others on the contrary, which are very much softened and finished, require to be viewed from very close, and are much esteemed by those who are nearsighted and who are unable to consider of what skill consists. In the same way, the music of the lutes is for those who do not wish to hear the music so much as the voice, and that of the viols is for those who by pushing farther away prefer to hear rather than to see. Now this resemblance will make us note in passing that the low tone, which approaches silence is comparable to black, and the higher to white.

Turning to the string instrument family, Mersenne finds the violin has greatest "effect on the passions and affections of the body and soul" of any string instrument, for reasons of "the great tension of their strings and their high sounds."

> Those who have heard the Twenty-four Violins of the King avow that they have never heard anything more ravishing or more powerful. Thus it comes that this instrument is the most proper of all for playing for dancing as is experienced in the ballet and everywhere else.[15]

Later, he observes,

> Now the violin has this above all the other instruments aside from the song of animals, both winged and terrestrial, that it

[15] V, iv, 1, replacing the wind band of the sixteenth century. In IV, iv, he gives the instrumentation of the famous Twenty-four Violins of the King as 6 treble, 6 bass, 4 contratenors, 4 alto and 4 "of a fifth part."

imitates and counterfeits all sorts of instruments, such as the voice, the organ, the hurdy-gurdy, the bagpipe, the fife, etc., so that it can suggest the sadness, as the lute does, and can become animated like the trumpet.[16]

[16] IV, iv.

Above all, Mersenne seems to place a high aesthetic value on the string instruments in part because of the ease with which one can hear their overtones. While he could not offer the correct explanation of what the overtones were, physically,[17] he could find in them a metaphor for moral action.

[17] Even though Mersenne understood the tones of the natural trumpet corresponded to the overtone principle, he did not understand that the sounds heard above a string tone were based on the same principle. His best guess: "It is more probable that these different sounds come from the different movements of the exterior air."

If the tone of each string is more harmonious and agreeable as it makes a greater number of different tones heard in the same time, and if one may be permitted to compare moral actions to natural, and to translate Physics into human actions, one can say that each action is as much more agreeable and harmonious to God, as it is accompanied by a greater number of motives, provided that they all be good.[18]

[18] V, iv, 10.

Regarding the brass instrument family, Mersenne was most fascinated by the trumpet, in part by its range, which in his time exceeded even the organ!

As to the range of the trumpet, it is marvelously great ... It surpasses all the keyboards of the spinets and organs.[19]

[19] V, v, 11.

His most interesting comment relative to the trumpet is with regard to its tone, especially if one remembers that in nearly all early literature the trumpet tone is described as "harsh" or "powerful."

[Those who play well can] imitate the softest echo and take away boredom and the desire to hear the softness of the lute and other instruments in those who love harmony.[20]

[20] V, v, 18.

We also find interesting Mersenne's comments on the fact that this instrument, being limited to the overtone series, could not play all the notes. In the following he offers his charming natural explanation for a familiar problem, the out of tune B/Bb in the third octave and the subsequent gap from G to the C above.

But because it is neither consonance nor difference of consonances, Nature rejects it and prefers to break the course of its intervals and its melodies, rather than to pass through an interval which is only of value to wound the ear and mind ... It can still be said that Nature, having given the [first] six tones, as the six days on which she rests, that she imitates her Author Who reposed at the end of the six days.[21]

[21] V, v, 13.

Turning to Mersenne's comments on performance practice, we find particularly interesting his comment that the trombone performed the same diminutions as the other wind instruments.[22]

[22] V, v, 22.

Related by the type of mouthpiece was the cornett family, a family of instruments which reached its artistic highpoint in the sixteenth century. A gap in the handed-down oral tradition of teaching has left us with insufficient information regarding the performance practice of this instrument, especially with regard to the embouchure on the side of the mouth and how that together with syllabification created articulation. No modern player can exemplify this famous description of the cornett by Mersenne.

> As to the characteristic quality of sound that they produce, it is similar to the brilliance of a sun's ray, which appears in the shadow or in the darkness, when one hears it among the voices in the cathedrals or chapels.[23]

[23] V, v, 23.

There were astonishing virtuosi of the cornett known to Mersenne, including one who could play eighty measures, and another one hundred measures, in one breath.

> Still this seems to surpass all credence, since one cannot live without very often drawing a breath, even if he uses no part of the breath for singing or for making any instrument sound ...
> From this it can be concluded that the cornett helps in conserving the wind, and in dispensing less at a time than one would do with the mouth in ordinary respiration.[24]

[24] Ibid.

The bass of the cornett family was the serpent, which Mersenne characterizes in another often quoted sentence.

> The true bass of the cornett is performed with the serpent, so that one can say that one without the other is a body without soul.[25]

[25] Ibid.

In a different treatise, Mersenne says a serpent is capable of sustaining twenty of the most powerful voices or can be so sweet as to play chamber music. The instrument, he says, is so easy a child of fifteen can master it.[26]

The most surprising comments by Mersenne regarding the familiar wind instruments are associated with the oboe [shawm]. Whereas today we think of a conical bore instrument as being more moderate in sound than a cylinder bore instrument, Mersenne, astonishingly enough, found the opposite. Of conical bores in general he explains,

> This renders their tones more violent than those of the instruments which are drilled with a single thickness from the beginning to the end.[27]

Thus, he finds the oboe also "violent" and nearly as powerful as a trumpet!

> As to their music, it is suitable for the large ensemble, such as the Ballets, although the violins are now used in their place, for weddings, for village festivals, and for other public celebrations, because of the great noise that they make and the great harmony that they render, for they have the strongest and most violent tone of all the instruments, except for the trumpet.[28]

One also finds in Mersenne's fifth treatise an engraving of the *Hautbois du Poitou*,[29] an instrument active in the court of Louis XIV, but for which little technical information is known. Mersenne pictures it as an oboe-type instrument with a capped reed.

Another instrument popular in the court was the musette. While actually a bagpipe, the court oboists regarded this instrument as a part of the oboe family, because the chanter is in fact a little oboe and sometimes was played as such, without the air bag. The court oboists were the performers of the musette at court, as Mersenne confirms.

> When one has heard the musette in the hands of those who play it perfectly, as does Mr. des Touches, one of the Royal oboists, it must be admitted that it yields to none of the other instruments, and that there is a singular pleasure in hearing it.[30]

[26] II, v, 278.

[27] V, v, 32.

[28] V, v, 33. Raguenet in 1702 speaks of the new oboe as being as mellow as a violin. See Donnington, *The Interpretation of Early Music*, 557ff.

[29] V, v, 34.

[30] V, v, 28.

As a churchman, Mersenne gives special attention to the organ. Two of his observations are particularly interesting in terms of aesthetics. First, Mersenne endorses Giovanni Doni's[31] suggestions of a correspondence between the modes and the color of specific organ pipes.

[31] Giovanni Battista Doni, *Compendio del trattato de' generi e de' modi* (Rome, 1635).

> The organ can be used to express each mode because of the great number of its stops, of which the one of tin is proper for the Dorian, and the others composed of pipes more or less large at the top than at the bottom, closed and open, for example, the narrow ones are suitable for the Phrygian, and the wider ones for the Lydian; and then he says that the pipes which imitate the block flutes are good to express the Dorian; those which imitate the fife and the flageolet for the Phrygian; and the cornett and the pipes which make the German flute for the Lydian. The boxwood is proper to make the Dorian pipes; the regals are good for the Lydian, and the brass pipes for the Phrygian.[32]

[32] V, vii, 30.

We also find enlightening Mersenne's personal criteria for what makes a good organist. Of particular interest here is his documentation of the practice of improvisation by organists.

> One can observe that the organist is best who makes the plain chant or subject heard better, who makes the other parts of the counterpoint sing, and performs the cadences best.
>   Some make a great fact of those who can make three or four hundred measures of good counterpoint figured against an organ point; the others of those who have a great velocity and dexterity, as happens when they make thirty-second notes in the binary measure, which lasts only a second; and still others of those who make a very great number of passages, of diminutions, and variations against some subject given them. To this can be added that those who play with a beautiful movement and good grace, and who are exact in their measure are the most perfect of all.[33]

[33] V, vi, 41.

Mersenne included under percussion instruments which were to be considered musical, only those which produced a pitch—pitch, but not "noise," being describable by the mathematics of his generation.

> All the bodies which make noise and which produce a sensible sound when they are struck can be placed in the rank of percussion instruments.[34]

[34] V, vii, 1.

The most interesting discussion which Mersenne engages in on this subject is relative to popular myths associated with church bells. He relates a number of superstitions believed by the public regarding the disturbances in the air caused by the ringing of the great cathedral bells. Among these, some believed it could cause the death of the fetus in the womb. Mersenne adds,

> Since it is experienced that the drum, the thunder, and the trumpet make more effect on the mind or the senses than the sound of other instruments, it is easy to conclude that the great effects of music or other sounds can happen only through great movements, which are made of a lot of air, or that the violence must make up for the size of the air when there is little air which serves the noise.[35]

[35] V, vii, 28.

Mersenne does not concern himself with the rules of performing ornaments in his treatises. Occasionally he mentions them in passing, as for example that the trill must begin on the upper note and this note must be more elongated than the principal note.[36] One comment we find of particular interest with regard to aesthetics.

[36] IV, vi, 7.

> Trilled cadences are the most difficult part of all that has to be done in singing, because it is necessary simply to beat the air in the throat [*battre l'air de la gorge*] which must make a series of repercussions [*tremblemens*] without the help of the tongue. But they are as much more pleasing as they are more difficult, for if the other progressions are the colors and the shadings, the cadences can be called the rays and the light.[37]

[37] II, vi, 355. Mersenne adds,
> As for ornaments from the lips, they are not agreeable, nor permitted, any more than those which seem to be drawn from the stomach.

Finally, Mersenne makes two interesting observations on the subject of conducting. First, in his mathematical style he defines the "beat."

> The *beat* is the space of time used to lift and lower the hand. Since we can make these two opposing movements swifter or slower, he who conducts the ensemble determines the swiftness according to the kind of music and the material it employs, or according to his wish. I shall, however, henceforth take one beat, whether it is binary or ternary, for one second, that is, for 1/3600 of an hour, inasmuch as the slowest vibration of the pulse of the heart which I have been able to

encounter lasts exactly one second and beats 3600 times in an hour. Thus the systole, or the contraction of the heart, will correspond to the lifting, and the diastole, or the dilation, to the lowering of the hand, so that the masters of music speak truly when singing the praises of God, *My heart and my body will rejoice in the living God*.[38]

[38] IV, iv, 20.

Second, he offers a few comments on conducting technique.

The semibrevis ordinarily lasts one lifting and one lowering of the hand, which can be made as well with the foot.[39]

[39] IV, v, 11.

In the case of a ternary beat, Mersenne recommends "two white notes in striking, and a single one in lifting." Those accompanying singers can also conduct with the fingerboard of a lute, etc. And he notices that where there are those singers who "have a delicate and exact ears and a well-ruled imagination" they can keep the beat even without a conductor.

Mersenne mentions in passing, and unfortunately without details, the practice of improvisation in the performance of chant, something which is mentioned in a number of other sources. He says only,

I reserve several other examples for the song book of the church, which can be enriched with a thousand wonderful inventions.[40]

[40] III, ii, 4ff.

In a brief discussion of the church modes here, Mersenne concludes,

I add only that the fifth, sixth, and the twelfth seem most beautiful to me, but each one can choose that which pleases him most for his particular consolation, and even add as much new as he wishes.

But it is certain that when several songs of the church are sung, with attention and required devotion, one will receive a great contentment, for there are few more beautiful.

In his most interesting discussion of Church music, Mersenne presents a lengthy argument which attempts to establish the aesthetic superiority of the unison,[41] the point of

[41] II, ii, 4.

which was a thinly disguised defense of traditional Church chant. It is appropriate to conclude with this discussion, for it also characterizes the struggle which a seventeenth century Church philosopher such as Mersenne faced. His education and perspective was rather narrow, being defined at every turn by the Catholic Church and its traditional tenets. And yet, all around him knowledge was making rapid strides in every field, surging toward the Enlightenment. How was such a traditional Church philosopher to respond to this new environment? One response was literary productions such as this one of Mersenne which are virtual encyclopedias in their field, like modern equivalents of the massive medieval *summa* of Thomas Aquinas. It was as if there was a desire to expand the Church's message to encompass every new idea. We can also see Mersenne, although he argues for the aesthetic value of the unison, making a final attempt to argue for the aesthetic value of the old unison Church music in preference to Baroque polyphony. Thus we find here a personal involvement, even a passion, expressed in his language that we did not find in much of his earlier commentary. First he argues that the unison is,

> more pleasing than the octave because it flatters the ear more, and it is understood more easily by the imagination, which is the principal seat of pleasure.[42]

He adds that he finds in the unison, but not the octave, an equality that one also finds in many equations of science and in the equilibrium which characterizes the science of mechanics.

Next, he finds virtue in the fact that "experiment shows that all the consonances tend towards the unison." One reason for the powerful impression which Church chant makes is that "the mind is not distracted by the variety of the consonances and dissonances." Another argument for the unison, over the octave, reminds the reader how much longer the church services were in the seventeenth century.

> Now one of the strongest reasons that persuade us that the unison is more pleasing and more natural than the octave is

[42] The English translations for this Proposition are taken from Edward Lippman, *Musical Aesthetics: A Historical Reader* (New York: Pendragon Press, 1986), 107ff.

drawn from the experience that shows that we become bored much more in hearing singing at the octave than in unison, which one hears in churches with pleasure for a period of several hours: and although children sing naturally at the octave with men, nevertheless their intention [!] is to sing in unison.

Why, then, he asks "since all music exists only for the sake of the unison which is its end, do we not value it more highly than all the other harmonies?" Clearly describing himself, he answers,

> As to those who have risen above all that is created, and who have experienced a thousand times the aversion that one has towards all the truths of mathematics and of physics when they have been discovered, from which one receives almost no contentment except in the labor one undergoes in searching for them, they receive no contentment from concerts, and love to hear singing at the unison more than in several parts, as much as the unison represents to them the abode of the blessed, and the perfect union of the three divine persons who are in the unison of a perfect equality.

Some people, intent on contemplation, would rather hear no singing at all than be distracted. Those who do not understand all this must be extended pity.

> I estimate then that the unison is more pleasing than the consonances, and that we must show compassion for the fragility and inconstancy of men who do not have this feeling, and who think more highly of diversity and inequality than of unity and equality, inasmuch as they do not judge things because they possess more simplicity and more excellence, but by what contributes best to their appetite and to their phantasy.

Now Mersenne borrows from geometry the notion that lines, figures and bodies derive all meaning from the point. Thus, consonances depend on the unison, like lines on the point,

> and that is why they are the sweeter the more they approach it, for they have nothing sweet nor pleasing except what they borrow from the unison of their tones.

But does not the need for variety speak against the aesthetic virtue of the unison? Mersenne agrees we cannot be content for a long time without the variety of "different actions and passions, of which each tires us, and at once displeases us." For example, he says, if we are weary, we desire to sit. But after sitting "two or three hours," one is as weary as before. From this he concludes,

> Now that state of variety in which we are, is the reason that we avoid the unison as much as we can, because it is too sweet and too excellent for this life. Thence it comes that we prefer to finish music with the octave, the fifth, the third ...

And does not the diversity we find in Nature argue against the aesthetic primacy of the unison? After a long discussion, he concludes it is the imperfect state of men that blinds them from seeing clearly "the great union of all creatures." And in a flash of eloquence, Mersenne suggests it is all a matter of perspective.

> As to the greater knowledge that comes from the other consonances, one may compare it to the light of several little candles, or to that of glow-worms: but that of unity and the unison is similar to the light of the sun, which obscures all the others by its presence, as the grace and the excellence of the unison makes that of the other consonances vanish.

After still another attempt to prove that "the unison is more excellent than the other consonances," by astrology, Mersenne offers his final conclusion on this subject.

> Now all these considerations bring us to recognize that the unison is the most perfect and the most pleasing consonance of music, since it participates more abundantly in that which renders it sweet and pleasing; and since there is only a single imperfection of the variety that preoccupies us, and that makes us prefer what is more similar to our frailty and our misery, which is not able to subsist here without diversity, which is the mother of corruption, although we would aspire to the unison and to unity.

From all this, Mersenne is moved to make a final observation on the educational and moral purpose of music.

Now if music serves for something in this world, one should particularly make use of it to recall the memory of one part of these considerations, so that it not be said in eternity that men who make a profession of reason, and who should make use of recreations and of speculations for the end to which God destined them, have abused the chaste and rational pleasure of music, and have imitated some musicians, who do not at all raise themselves higher than to the passion and the action of the senses, and to the pleasure of the ear, which should serve solely as a channel to provide free entrance to the contemplation of eternal things, and to the pleasure that comes from the thought of the final end, of which true philosophers should converse incessantly.

5 French Philosophers on Music

THE ENLIGHTENMENT IN FRANCE brought an atmosphere in which there was an almost Aristotelian drive to find and explain objectively the truth of all forms of human activity. Consequently, there is no other period of music history which produced such a prolific outpouring of philosophical thought. In the fields of painting, sculpture and the theater, this thought centered on defining, using the example of painting, "What are the characteristics which one associates with a great painting and how does one reduce these principles to a set of rules for young artists to follow?"

In fields such as painting, sculpture and the theater, where the observer first contemplates an art object en route to arriving at his own impressions, this philosophical activity produced much valuable information. But this approach was not so successful with the subject of music, because rational and objective reasoning do not arrive at the important truths of music. The important truths of music are experiential and they are gained by the listener's direct, personal association with the great composer. The listener does not, as is the case in painting, sculpture and theater, have to look elsewhere first. Ironically, therefore, these philosophers would have arrived at more important truths by studying the listener, and not composition. Nevertheless, they have left very valuable philosophical discussions on music and observations on the state of music in seventeenth century France.

In contemplating music, these philosophers had an additional complication. It seems clear in their writing that most of them had come to accept the fact that music cannot be separated from the emotions. While they lacked our modern knowledge of the physical separation of rational and emotional thought in the brain, they were aware from common experience that the emotions are not easily subjected to rational thought. In spite of this problem, they apparently felt that one could still isolate aesthetic principles in music and determine the "rules" by which music could be judged. For example, Jean-Baptiste Du Bos, writing in 1719, attempts to equate music with other arts.

> The basic principles that govern music are thus similar to those that govern poetry and painting. Like poetry and painting, music is an imitation. Music cannot be good unless it conforms to the general rules that apply to the other arts on such matters as choice of subject and exactness of representation.[1]

One can immediately see here the kinds of problems which arise in trying to force music into the molds of the other arts. Music, in fact, is *not* an imitation as the other arts are, music is the *real thing*.

Yves Marie André, in his *L'Essai sur le beau* (1741), presents an extended defense of why music is a higher art than painting. He primarily points to both the fact that music is heard live, while a painting is frozen in time, and that sounds are more expressive than colors.[2] André also makes some observations on the aesthetic qualities of the conceptual aspects of music. Consonance becomes distasteful with too frequent repetition. Dissonance he describes as both a kind of "harmonic spice" but also the agent for communicating certain specific emotions, including wild anger, troublous dissension, the horrors of battle and tempestuous storms.[3] André also attempts to explain the nature of unity in music, an aesthetic principle so valued in the other arts. In music he finds this expressed most clearly in the rules of harmony.

Five years later Charles Batteux attempts to define in more concrete terms the requirements which expressive music and dance must have to be successful. These might be summarized as follows:

[1] Jean-Baptiste Du Bos (1670–1742), *Réflexions critiques sur la poésie et sur la peinture* [Paris, 1719], quoted in Peter le Huray and James Day, *Music and Aesthetics in the Eighteenth and Early-Nineteenth Centuries* (Cambridge: Cambridge University Press, 1981), 21. Du Bos served the government in Foreign Affairs and as secretary of the Academie française.

[2] Yves Marie André (1675–1764), *L'Essai sur le beau* [1741], quoted in Peter le Huray and James Day, *Music and Aesthetics in the Eighteenth and Early-Nineteenth Centuries* (Cambridge: Cambridge University Press, 1981), 34ff. André was a professor of mathematics at Caen.

[3] Ibid., 32.

1. Every expression must conform to the thing that it expresses, as a dress is tailored for the body.

2. The fundamental character of the subject will determine the expression.

3. Clarity is of prime importance.

4. Each mood must be exactly right. It is the same with feelings as with color.

5. The expression must be lively, and frequently fine and delicate. Everyone is to some extent familiar with the passions. If we only paint the passions halfheartedly, we are no better than the historian or the person who slavishly imitates.

6. The expression must be straightforward and simple; everything that smacks of effort is painful and tiring.

7. The expression must be fresh, especially in music. Here he quotes, without source, a Latin expression, "We are led to melody by natural instinct."[4]

[4] Charles Batteux (1713–1780), *Les beaux arts réduits à un même principe* [Paris,1746], quoted in Peter le Huray and James Day, *Music and Aesthetics*, 50ff.

Modern clinical research demonstrates that Batteux was quite accurate in the last statement. Not only man, but lower animals appear to be born with some melodic patterns genetically in place.

Finally, Batteux adds that even though music is highly controlled, by conventions of writing time, melody and harmony, these structures do not "alter or destroy the natural meaning of sounds." Measure [meaning movement through time] and movement [meaning moving the emotions], he finds, are what give life to a composition.

On Beauty in Music

ANDRÉ IS THE ONLY ONE of these French philosophers who attempts a detailed analysis of Beauty specifically in music. His purpose appears to have been to attempt to counter the influence of the humanists, with their emphasis on the emotions, by returning to the old focus on Reason. He begins by reflecting on the great reputation of music among the ancient Greeks, but observes that the opinion of some moderns is much more reserved.

> I am aware that some philosophers do not have such an exalted respect for music. Some even hold opinions that are quite to the contrary, claiming that feeling is the sole judge of harmony and that the pleasure of the ear is the only beauty that music affords. They argue moreover, that this pleasure is far too dependent on opinion, prejudice, convention and acquired habit to be the object of firm rules. And, they ask, is not the proof of this obvious enough? Are there any two nations whose musical tastes are the same? Europeans and Orientals, French, Italians, Germans, Spaniards and Englishmen, Turks and Tartars even, has not each race its own particular music which it unquestioningly values above all others? Since each nation is evidently charmed and satisfied by its own music, what more is to be said? Nothing indeed, so far as those peoples are concerned who only conduct their lives and their thoughts in a haphazard way. But for thinking people—for men—something more is needed, namely that in all pleasures reason must at least be on an equal footing with the senses.[5]

[5] Ibid., 28.

André proposes to "place reason on an equal footing with the senses" by proposing that beauty in music exists on three levels, which he lists as,

1. There is an essential musical beauty that is absolute, wholly independent of human institutions and even divine.

2. There is a natural beauty which comes from the Creator and is not connected to human taste or opinion.

3. There is an artificial musical beauty that is to some degree arbitrary but which none the less is dependent on the eternal laws of harmony.[6]

[6] Ibid.

To attempt to explain the first of these, André imagines a conversation with a person who has just left a concert, while still filled with the impressions of the music. André asks the listener what exactly pleased him in the concert. In the end all the listener can put into words is that he listened to the ordering of the sounds, the propriety of the progressions, the regularity of the flow of time, the tempo, the balance of the ensemble, etc. We would regard this answer as a "left-brained" one, for the listener only mentions conceptual aspects of the performance. But for André it was apparently not conceptual enough, for he proposes there must be,

> a purer pleasure than the sweetness of the actual sounds, and a beauty that does not have its roots in the senses, a particular beauty that charms the mind and which the mind alone perceives and judges.[7]

[7] Ibid., 29ff.

What this purer pleasure is, in André's view, is a connection between the music and some innate form of rational understanding within the listener.

> In other words, sir, during the time that this large ensemble of sonorous instruments was impressing your ear with pleasurable sounds, you experienced deep down within you a master of music who beat time, if I may put it thus, to show how right the music was, and who revealed its principles by means of a light that was superior to that of the senses. These principles are grounded in order, in the structural beauty of the piece, in harmonic numbers, in the rule of proportion and harmonious progression, and in the idea of propriety, a sacred law that allots each part its position, its conclusion and the right path by which to reach its end. Thus while all those who took part in the concert were reading their individual parts, you were also reading yours, written in eternal and ineffaceable notes from the great book of reason which is open to all receptive minds.

By the second form of beauty, that which comes from the Creator, André means natural things, beginning with the physics of music and in particular the overtone series. But also he has in mind the body of the listener, which has a kind of receptive harmony: the nerves stretched over bones like strings of an instrument, arteries which beat time and especially the physical components of the ear, throat and mouth.

Thus he finds a natural sympathy between the vibrations of music and the body, although he cannot explain how it works. Further, he regards this relationship as the key to understanding emotions in music.

> There is a natural sympathy between certain sounds and the emotions of the soul. There is no question here of explaining how this comes about; all that we need to know is this indubitable fact. There are sounds which have a secret understanding with the heart, and this we cannot deny. Lively sounds inspire courage, languishing sounds appease, laughing sounds cheer, mournful sounds sadden, majestic sounds uplift the soul, harsh sounds irritate, gentle sounds soften.[8]

[8] Ibid., 31.

The third kind of beauty in music, André finds, is that which belongs to the human contribution, including the conventions of art and taste in composition and performance.

On Taste in Music

A SEVENTEENTH CENTURY French dictionary of music by Sebastien de Brossard, while it is not addressed to Taste as such, is interesting in its documentation of the wide variety of styles which were generally recognized as early as 1703. His final sentence also implies an aesthetic ranking of these styles.

> Style means, in general, the particular manner or fashion of expressing ideas, of writing, or of doing some other thing. In music, it signifies the manner in which every individual composes, plays or teaches, and all this is very diversified according to the genius of the authors, the country and the nation: as well as according to the materials, the places, the times, the subjects, the expressions, etc. Thus one is wont to say the style of Carissimi, of Lully, of Lambert, etc.; the style of the Italians, of the French, of the Spaniards, etc. The style of gay and joyful music is very different from the style of grave and serious music ... therefore we have different epithets in order to distinguish among all these different characters, such as ancient and modern style, Italian, French, and German style, ecclesiastic, dramatic, and chamber style, etc ... The

Italians have expressions for all that we have mentioned, and
we shall explain them in the order of their importance.[9]

The most important publication which attempted to define taste in music was by Jean Laurent le Cerf de La Viéville (1647–1710), a French aristocrat who was a strong supporter of Lully and who published a response to Raguenet's "Parallèle des Italiens et des Français" in 1704, called "*Comparaison de la musique italienne et de la musique française*." The second part of this publication is an interesting discussion on "Good Taste in Music," set in the form of an imaginary discussion between two anonymous noble ladies and the author, who is called a Chevalier. First, the "Countess du B" asks if the Chevalier will teach her "how to distinguish perfectly the beauties of music." The answer is, unwittingly, a reference to the left and right hemispheres of the brain, for he weighs the merits of judging by feeling versus "rules."

> There are two great ways of knowing good and bad things: by our inward feeling and by the rules. We know the good and the bad only by these means. What we see and what we hear pleases us or displeases us. If one listens only to the inward feeling, one will say, "It seems to me that that is good, or that it is not." On the other hand, the masters, the skilled, following the observations they have made, have established precepts in every craft. These comprised whatever had seemed to them to be the best and the surest. The established precepts are the rules, and if one consults them regarding what one sees and what one hears, one will say that this is good or is not good, according to such and such a rule, or for such and such a reason. These masters were men; were they incapable of being deceived? The authority of the rules is considerable, but after all it is not a law. Inward feeling is still less sure, because each should distrust his own, should distrust that it is what it should be. Who will dare flatter himself that he has a fortunate nature, endowed with sure and clear ideas of the good, the beautiful, the true? We have all brought into the world the foundation of these ideas, more or less clear and certain, but since our birth we have received, and this it is sad and painful to correct, a thousand false impressions, a thousand dangerous prejudices, which have weakened and stifled within us the voice of uncorrupted nature.

[9] Sebastien de Brossard (1654–1730), *Dictionnaire de Musique* [Paris, 1703], quoted in Paul Henry Lang, "Musical Thought of the Baroque: The Doctrine of Temperaments and Affections," in *Twentieth-Century Views of Music History*, ed. William Hays (New York: Scribner's, 1972), 197.

I think that in this uncertainty and confusion the remedy is to lend to the inward feeling the support of the rules, that our policy should be correct and strengthen the one by the other, and that it is this union of the rules and the feeling which forms good taste. To listen attentively to the inward feeling, to disentangle it, and then to purify it by the application of the rules; there is the art of judging with certainty, and therefore I am persuaded that good taste is the most natural feeling, corrected or confirmed by the best rules.[10]

[10] Le Cerf de la Viéville, "Traite du bon gout en musique," in Oliver Strunk, *Source Readings in Music History* (New York: Norton, 1950), 491ff.

The Countess now begs the Chevalier to please teach her the rules for judging music.

There are little rules and great rules, madame, and we have touched upon both sorts in our conversation. The little rules are those of composition, on which twenty treatises have been written, of which I do not cite a single one, because I am waiting for somebody to write a twenty-first one that will be good.[11]

[11] Ibid., 492.

It is a remarkable condemnation of music theory when he says he has ignored the first twenty treatises on the subject and is still waiting for a good one!

The Chevalier gives, as an example of a "little" rule, the formula that low or high notes should accompany low or lofty concepts. As for the great rules,

A piece of music should be natural, expressive, harmonious. In the first place, natural, or rather, simple, for simplicity is the first part, the first sign of the natural, which is almost equally an ingredient in these three qualities. In the second place, expressive. In the third place, harmonious, melodious, pleasing—take your choice. These are the three great, the three important rules which one must apply to the melodies that the inward feeling has approved, and it is they which in the last resort decide.[12]

[12] Ibid., 493.

As an afterthought the Chevalier adds another rule, "always to abhor excess. Let us make it a habit and a merit to have contempt, distaste, and aversion without quarter for all that contains anything superfluous."

The Countess, still not satisfied, wants a simple rule to test whether her judgments were correct. She says, for example,

Am I not justified in saying that my heart, my ear, and all the rules agree in persuading me that "*Bois epais*" is a charming melody. And it is by Lully, a new pledge of the correctness of my taste. This other melody does not flatter my ear, nor does it touch me; it has neither sweetness nor expression. And it is by Charpentier. Yes, I am judging it rightly; it is bad. Would that be bad reasoning, Chevalier?[13]

[13] Ibid., 495.

The Chevalier cautions the Countess on the dangers of judging on the basis of the composer's name or reputation and, finally, offers her a practical means of judging music.

You will need to carry in your head two melodies representing the two qualities, one good and one bad; that is, good and bad by almost unanimous consent, and two symphonies, one good and one bad, and you must have all their beauties and all their faults at the tip of your fingers. You must have the knowledge of the least of the beauties and faults of these two melodies and these two symphonies ever at command and thoroughly familiar, and compare with these models the melodies and symphonies you hear.

These latter you will esteem in proportion to their resemblance to the others, and the idea of this resemblance alone, accordingly as it strikes you more or less forcibly, will cause you to say, with greater or less force, "I like that melody; that symphony does not please me." I am convinced that the ablest connoisseur should not neglect to combine with the judgments based on reasoning these judgments by comparison, from which will be derived an additional clearness, will adapted to confirm our feelings.[14]

[14] Ibid., 495ff.

The Countess says that if she understands correctly, "the more perfectly a melody complies with the rules the better it is, and the further it departs from them the worse." In his response, the Chevalier touches on the important aesthetic principle of universality. To put it in the form of a question, can one trust the judgment of the masses?

There are precepts with regard to this matter. First, infringements of the little rules are as nothing in comparison with violations of the great ones. Listen to a lesson of Holy Week which begins with a sixth, but go out when one begins with a roulade. In the second place, the pleasures of the heart being, by the principles we have established, superior to those of the ear, a melody which offends against the laws that are directed toward touching the heart offends more than one which disregards merely those which aim to satisfy the ear. Let us forgive two similar cadences which are too near to each other, or a poor thorough bass, but let us never forgive a melody which is cold and forced ...

In the third place, the most beautiful thing is that which is equally admired by the people and by the learned or by all the connoisseurs. Then, after this, I should admire more that which is generally admired by all the people. Finally, that which is admired by all the learned. The learned are the masters of music, the musicians by profession, stubborn about rules. The people are the multitude, the great mass, which has not risen to special knowledge and has only its natural feeling as its guide and as the warrant for its judgments. The connoisseurs are those who are neither altogether of the people nor altogether learned, half the one and half the other, a shade less learned than of the people, that is to say, crediting the rules a shade less than natural feeling ...

As to the half-learned, they are in music what they are in any art, in anything whatever, the most contemptible and the most insupportable of all men.[15]

[15] Ibid., 496ff.

The other noble lady present, the "Marquis des E," contributes an interesting observation on universality, as measured by the response of the public, and the recommendation of a system for using that judgment.

That characterization of the people, the connoisseurs, and the learned makes me realize that we must listen to the reasoning of the learned, defer to the feeling of the connoisseurs, and study how the people are moved by theatrical representations can infinitely clarify and facilitate our judgments and help us to make them true. At the first three representations of an opera, let us concern ourselves only with ourselves; it will keep us sufficiently occupied ... But at the fourth and later performances let us apply ourselves to studying in what manner and how greatly the people are touched. The value and the degree of value of pieces will certainly be revealed by the impression which they make on the heart of the people and by the vivacity of that impression. When Armida works herself up to stab Rinaldo in the last scene of the second act, I have twenty times seen everybody seized by terror, holding his breath, motionless, all the soul in the ears and eyes, until the melody of the violin which ends the scene gave leave to breathe, then at that point breathing again with a murmur of delight and admiration. I had no need to reason. That unanimous response of the people told me with certainty that the scene was of overpowering beauty.[16]

[16] Ibid., 499.

When the noble lady suggests that perhaps one should form one's taste after that of the highest nobles, the Chevalier makes a comment which clearly reflects the beginning of the Enlightenment and the coming Revolution.

In the matter of taste, mademoiselle, great nobles are only men like ourselves, whose name proves little. Each has his voice and the voices are equal, or at least it is not their quality which will determine their weight.[17]

[17] Ibid., 505.

Another issue which arises in this discussion is whether good taste demands that one give praise where praise is due the performer. The Chevalier adds,

That is not enough; the degree of praise must correspond to the degree of value of the work. To praise more or less than this is bad taste, and I am persuaded that here is the reef on which the greatest number of people are wrecked. He who can praise with reason and in due proportion will be of a perfect connoisseur.[18]

[18] Ibid., 504.

On the Perception of Music

It is surprising that so few early philosophers concerned themselves with the nature of the perception of music, for it is here that music is so different from the other arts. By this we mean that while the other arts are only a representation of something, music is real, a direct present tense communication between composer and listener. Batteux, the only one of these French writers to discuss perception at all, does not refer to this distinction, but he does touch on a very valid and important point: we do not understand music, as listeners, in anything remotely near the conceptual aspects of it that we study in school.

If I were to say that I could derive no pleasure from a lecture that I did not understand, my confession would in no way seem strange. But if I ventured to say the same of a piece of music, people would ask whether I considered myself enough of a connoisseur to appreciate the merits of so carefully constructed and fine a composition. I would dare to reply yes, for it is a matter of feeling [and not conceptual knowledge]. I do not [while listening to music] pretend in any way to calculate the sounds, their interrelationships or their connection with the ear. I am speaking here neither of oscillations, string vibrations, nor mathematical proportions. I leave such speculations to learned theorists; these are akin to the grammar and dialectic of a lecture which I can appreciate without going into such details. Music speaks to me in tones: this language is natural to me. If I do not understand it, art has corrupted nature rather than perfected her.[19]

[19] Batteux, *Les beaux arts réduits à un même principe*, 48ff.

This is perfectly correct, but as he continues, returning to the error of including music and painting in the same category, he seems to lose touch with the importance of what he has just written.

> A musical composition must be judged in the same way as a picture. In the picture I find shapes and colors that I can comprehend; it charms and touches me. What would we think of a painter who was content to throw on the canvas bold shapes and masses of the liveliest color without reference to any known object? The same argument can be applied to music. There is no disparity here, and if there were it would strengthen my argument. The ear is said to be much finer than the eye.[20] I am therefore much more capable of judging a musical composition than a painting.

[20] All ancient and medieval philosophers argued just the reverse.

Curiously, he inserts a footnote here which is entirely inaccurate and is a primary contradiction to his point about listening to feeling in music and not conceptual detail. In the footnote he says a simple song has meaning, but is addressed to the common man, whereas multi-part harmonized music requires "some kind of musical erudition" to understand its meaning. This is wrong, of course, as abundant evidence all over the earth daily proves people can appreciate music while knowing nothing about it.

Finally, we find some particularly curious observations by Montesquieu on the perception of music under the influence of climate. Under the title, "Of the Difference of Men in different climates," he contends,

> Cold air constringes the extremities of the external fibres of the body; this increases their elasticity, and favors the return of the blood from the extreme parts of the heart. It contracts those very fibres; consequently it increases also their force. On the contrary, warm air relaxes and lengthens the extremes of the fibres; of course it diminishes their force and elasticity.
>
> People are therefore more vigorous in cold climates. Here the action of the heart and the reaction of the extremities of the fibres are better performed, the temperature of the humors is greater, the blood moves more freely towards the heart, and reciprocally the heart has more power.

As an example of the influence of climate on music, he observes,

> As climates are distinguished by degrees of latitude, we might distinguish them also in some measure by those of sensibility. I have been at the opera in England and in Italy, where I have seen the same pieces and the same performers: and yet the same music produces such different effects on the two nations: one is so cold and phlegmatic, and the other so lively and enraptured, that it seems almost inconceivable.[21]

On the Purposes of Music

DURING THE EARLY EIGHTEENTH CENTURY, in part as a reflection of the Enlightenment, one rarely finds the older purpose for music as being associated with God. But that is what came to mind for André Maugars, in his report of his visit to Rome in 1639, when he recalled a famous Italian singer, Leonora Baroni.

> When she passes from one note to another, she sometimes makes you feel the divisions between the enharmonic and the chromatic modes with such skill and artistry that there is no one who is not greatly pleased by this beautiful and difficult method of singing. She does not need to ask the help of a theorbo player or a violinist, without one of which her singing would be imperfect, for she herself plays these instruments

[21] Charles de Secondat, Baron de Montesquieu (1689–1755), *The Spirit of Laws* [1748], trans. Thomas Nugent in *Great Books*, XXXVIII (Chicago: Encyclopedia Britannica, 1952), 102ff. He also concludes that the English have a "disrelish of everything" and an "impatience of temper" which makes concentration difficult.

perfectly. Finally, I had the good fortune to hear her sing several times, more than thirty different songs, with second and third verses, which she had composed herself. I must tell you that she did me the special favor of singing with her mother and her sister, her mother playing the lyre, her sister the harp, and she the theorbo. This concert, composed of three beautiful voices and three different instruments, so affected my senses and so ravished my spirit that I forgot my mortal condition and thought I was among the angels enjoying the delights of the blessed. So to address you as a Christian, the purpose of music is, by touching our hearts, to raise them to God, because it is a sample in this world of the eternal joy, and its purpose is not by lascivious gestures to lead us to vice, toward which we are only too much inclined by nature.[22]

On the Communication of Feeling

THE MORE COMMON PURPOSE OF MUSIC given by these French writers was relative to the communication of feeling, a topic which is a hallmark of the Baroque itself. We see this already very early in the seventeenth century. David de Flurance Rivault, chief tutor to the young Louis XIII, wrote a treatise, *L'art d'embellir* (1702), which touches briefly on music and includes his belief in the power of music to affect man. He speaks of a certain kind of music which has a tranquilizing effect, and later,

> A well-measured voice can rejoice an afflicted person ...
> The voice can sometimes bring forth contentment and love;
> sometimes it can carry away the minds of the hearers to
> rage and fury: and then again quieten these fumes and calm
> impassioned souls.[23]

In another place in this same treatise, Rivault provides the memorable phrase, "The way to grow beautiful is to grow wise, for the wisdom of the soul is a cosmetic for the face."[24]

Raguenet gives enthusiastic praise for the expression of emotions in Italian music.

> As the Italians are much more brisk than the French, so
> are they more sensible of the passions and consequently

[22] André Maugars, "Response faite à un curieux sur le sentiment de la musique d'Italie, écrite à Rome le premier Octobre 1639," quoted in Carol MacClintock, *Readings in the History of Music in Performance* (Bloomington: Indiana University Press, 1979), 122ff.

[23] "L'art d'embellir," quoted in Frances Yates, *The French Academies of the Sixteenth Century* (Nendeln: Kraus, 1968), 280, fn. 5.

[24] Ibid., 279.

express them more lively in all their productions. If a storm or rage is to be described in a symphony, their notes give us so natural an idea of it that our souls can hardly receive a stronger impression from the reality than they do from the description; everything is so brisk and piercing, so impetuous and affecting, that the imagination, the senses, the soul, and the body itself are all betrayed into a general transport; it is impossible not to be borne down with the rapidity of these movements. A symphony of furies shakes the soul; it undermines and overthrows it in spite of all its care; the artist himself, whilst he is performing it, is seized with an unavoidable agony; he tortures his violin; he racks his body; he is no longer master of himself, but is agitated like one possessed with an irresistible motion.

If, on the other side, the symphony is to express a calm and tranquility, which requires a quite different style, they however execute it with an equal success. Here the notes descend so low that the soul is swallowed with them in the profound abyss. Every string of the bow is of an infinite length, lingering on a dying sound which decays gradually until at last it absolutely expires. Their symphonies of sleep insensibly steal the soul from the body and so suspend its faculties and operations that, being bound up, as it were, in the harmony that entirely possesses and enchants it, it is as dead to everything else as if all its powers were captivated by a real sleep ...

But there is one thing beyond all this which neither the French nor any other nation besides the Italians in the world ever attempted; for they will sometimes unite in a most surprising manner the tender with the sprightly, as may be instanced in that celebrated air, "*Mai non si vidde ancor piu bella fedelta*," which is the softest and most tender of any in the world, and yet its accompaniment is as lively and piercing as ever was composed. These different characters are they able to unite so artfully that, far from destroying a contrary by its contrary, they make the one serve to embellish the other.[25]

[25] François Raguenet, "Parallèle des Italiens et des Français," [1702], quoted in Strunk, *Source Readings in Music History*, 478ff.

Philosophically speaking, the most impressive French writer, among the group we have been examining here, is Jean-Baptiste Du Bos. His thinking was very perceptive and everything he writes on the subject of the expression of emotions in music stands up very well today. Du Bos, an avid opera fan, viewed everything from the aesthetic perspective of Nature. He finds music the most effective of all the arts in speaking directly to the feelings of the observer. It follows, therefore, that he places vocal music above instrumental music, since the latter lacks the verbal precision to exactly determine the emotion being expressed. He did, however, admit the contribution of the orchestral accompaniment in strengthening emotions.

> Do we not perceive that these symphonies enflame us, calm us, soften us, and in short, operate upon us, as effectually almost as Corneille's or Racine's verses.[26]

[26] Du Bos, *Réflexions critiques*, 18.

It is a particularly accurate and important point he makes when he reminds his readers that spoken words are mere symbols of emotion, but carry no actual emotional content in themselves. Sung words, on the other hand, carry the direct emotional meaning of the music. His placing this in the context of Nature is also interesting, for all philologists today consider sung utterances reflecting emotions to precede speech in early man by a considerable period of time. Thus this primitive, emotional communication might well be thought of as "the work of nature herself."

> Just as the painter imitates the forms and colors of nature so the musician imitates the tones of the voice—its accents, sighs and inflections. He imitates in short all the sounds that nature herself uses to express the feelings and passions. All these sounds, as we have already shown, have a wonderful power to move us because they are the signs of the passions that are the work of nature herself, from whence they have derived their energy. Spoken words, on the other hand are only arbitrary symbols of the passions. The spoken word only derives its meaning and value from man-made conventions and it has only limited geographical currency.[27]

[27] Ibid.,18.

He adds that the additional "energy" which words have when sung is what led to the recitative style and hence opera.[28]

[28] Ibid.,19.

Another very important aesthetic point which Du Bos makes is his clarification that the importance of music is not in its external, conceptual features.

Just as some people are more attracted to the color of pictures than to the expression of passions, so others are only sensible to the pleasures of melody or even to the richness of harmony, and pay not the slightest attention to whether the melody is an effective imitation, or care whether it is consonant with the words to which it is set. Such people do not require the composer to match his melodic lines to the feelings that the words suggest, but are content that his melodies should be pleasing, and even singular. As far as they are concerned it is enough that the occasional word in a recitative shall be treated expressively. There are far too many musicians who are of this mind, and who act as though music were incapable of anything more ...

Musical compositions that fail to move us can unequivocally be equated with pictures that have no merit other than their coloring, or with poems that are no more than well-constructed verses. In poetry and painting, technical excellence must serve to express the insights of genius, and to reveal those imaginative beauties that constitute the imitation of nature. In the same way, harmonic richness and variety, ornamentation and melodic originality must be used solely to create and embellish the musical imitation of the language of nature and the passions. The science of composition is, so to speak, the servant which the genius of the musician must keep under his thumb, just as the poet of genius must control his talent for writing verse ... Genius is essential to expression, whereas even without genius, it is still possible to compose scholarly music and to produce excellent rhymes.[29]

In Part III of his *Les beaux arts réduits à un même principe*, Batteux presents a brilliant discussion of man's forms of communication. He begins with the definition, "Men have three means of expressing their ideas and their feelings: speech, the tone of the voice, and gesture."[30] In defining how these three differ, he begins with two extraordinary deductions, which have since been confirmed in clinical research: that emotions are genetic and that they speak directly "without detour" through Reason, which is to say, the left hemisphere of the brain.

Speech expresses passion only by means of the ideas to which the feelings are tied, and as though by reflection. Music and gesture reach the heart directly and without any detour.

[29] Ibid., 21ff.

[30] Batteux, *Les beaux arts*, 260.

> In a word, speech is a language of institution, which men have formed for communicating their ideas more distinctly: gestures and music are like the dictionary of plain nature; they contain a language that we all know upon being born and of which we make use to announce everything that is related to our needs and to the conservation of our being: also they are vivid, short, energetic. What better basis for the arts whose object is to move the soul, than a language all of whose expressions are rather those of humanity itself than those of men![31]

[31] Ibid., 260ff.

Batteux next proposes that there are three levels of sophistication to these forms of communication. The most elemental level, of speech, tone and gesture, express simple nature, "the naive portrait of our thoughts and feelings." The second level is when "nature is polished by the help of art, to add embellishment to utility." In the third level, "one has in view only pleasure," which is to say, Art.

> From which I conclude first: That the principal object of music and of dance should be the imitation of feeling or of passions: instead of which that of poetry is principally the imitation of actions. But as passions and actions are almost always united in nature, and as they should also be together in the arts, there will be this difference of poetry from music and dance: that in poetry the passions will be employed as means or motives that prepare the action and produce it; and in music and dance the actions will be only a sort of canvas destined to carry, sustain, conduct, and connect the different passions that the artist wishes to express.

From our perspective he has defined correctly here the very essence of music: to express feelings. He elaborates on these distinctions, making the important point that poetry is still "the language of the mind" whereas music is [a language] of feelings and passions. We would say today, poetry is tied by language to the left hemisphere of the brain, as language, while music belongs to the province of the right hemisphere, which also contains the emotions. They are *both* languages of the mind.

> Actions and passions are nearly always united and mixed together in everything men do. They are produced and

announced reciprocally. They should therefore nearly always be together in the arts. When artists present an action, it should be animated by some passion; similarly when they present passions, they should be sustained by an action. That does not need to be verified by examples. But as the arts, considering the means they employ to express, may be appropriate to express one part of nature rather than another, it follows that the part that should dominate in them is that which is related most to this means of expression.

Thus poetry having chosen speech, which is most particularly the language of the mind, and music and dance having taken for themselves, the one the tones of the voice, and the other the movements of the body, and these two sorts of expressions being dedicated above all to feeling, true poets have had to attach themselves above all to actions and to discourse, and true musicians to feelings and to passions.[32]

[32] Ibid., 262.

May we point out that the third sentence above might also be described as the central duty and purpose of the conductor.

Regarding opera, therefore, he says it is the communication of feelings, not the plot, we are interested in. Furthermore, any complex idea depending on language, such as metaphors, plays on words, etc., "resists music so strongly." In contrast, he says, "that which is an expression of feeling seems to be disposed to it of itself. Tones are half-formed in words; it demands only a little art to draw them out."

It is with dance as with music. Declamation necessarily languishes when the soul is not moved, and when there is a question only of instructing: because then all the movements of the body signifying almost nothing, they give no pleasure to those who see them. A gesture is beautiful only when it portrays grief, tenderness, pride; the soul, in a word: if we are dealing with a logical argument, it is ridiculous of itself, because it is useless to the thing one is saying: one reasons in cold blood: and if in quiet reasoning there is a small gesture and a certain natural tone that accompany it, this is to make visible that the soul of the one who is reasoning desires that the truth he is teaching persuade the heart while he is trying to convince the mind of it. Thus it is always feeling which produces that expression.[33]

[33] Ibid., 263.

Batteux does make one fundamental mistake, one often made, by including music in the same category with the other arts. Music is fundamentally different from the other arts in its capacity as a live expressive art form, in which the communication from composer to listener is direct. Arts such as painting and sculpture are representative arts and Batteux is thoroughly incorrect in the way he associates music with them.

> There is no need to repeat here that melodic lines and dance movements are only imitations, artificial structures of tones and poetic gestures that are merely realistic. The passions are here as imaginary as are actions in poetry. They are equally and wholly the creation of genius and taste: nothing about them is true, everything is artificial. And if it sometimes happens that the musician or dancer is involved in the actual passion that he is expressing this is entirely accidental and it has nothing to do with the purpose of the art; it is like a painting which ought to be on canvas, but which is found to be on a living skin. Art is only created to deceive.[34]

[34] Ibid., 48.

Batteux concludes this particular discussion with another curious juxtaposition of thought. He begins with a marvelous testimonial to the fact that the importance of music, the feelings, cannot be communicated in words. Here he appears to have been one of a number of early philosophers who seemed to understand, through either intuition or deduction, that the feelings and music of the right hemisphere of the brain are entirely separate from the words and language of the left hemisphere. But, precisely because he was not privileged to know the findings of modern brain research—that this is exactly how the two hemisphere are organized and that, while separate, each is valid, and because he mistakenly associated music with painting and sculpture, he unfortunately failed to understand the true significance of his own first two paragraphs.

> It is true, you may say, that a melodic line can express certain passions: love, for instance, or joy, or sadness. But for every passion that can be identified there are a thousand others that cannot be put into words.

That is indeed so, but does it follow that these are pointless? It is enough that they are felt; they do not have to be named. The heart has its own understanding that is independent of words. When it is touched it has understood everything. Moreover, just as there are great things that words cannot reach, so there are subtle things that words cannot capture, above all things that concern the feelings.

We may conclude then that although music may be the most exactly calculated art in respect of its tones, and the most geometrically structured in respect of its consonances, even with these qualities it may well have no significance whatever. The analogy might be with a prism, which produces the finest colors but no picture, or with a color keyboard the colors and color sequences of which might amuse the eye, but which would certainly weary the mind.[35]

[35] Ibid., 50

Finally, he makes another deduction, which is confirmed by modern clinical research, that it is the specific choice of notes for the melody which allow music "to take on the character of the various passions."[36] It is in this respect that he finds justification for dissonance in music.

[36] Ibid., 53.

Not only does dissonance add salt and seasoning, but it serves in a particular way to characterize the musical expression. Nothing is so irregular as the course of the passions of love, anger and discord. The voice becomes shrill and then suddenly it takes on an explosive quality, in order to express them. Should art not soften such natural asperities, the truthfulness of the expression will compensate for its roughness. It is the composer's task to use dissonance with care, restraint and intelligence.

On the Role of Music in Society

DURING THE EARLY YEARS of the eighteenth century there are some interesting discussions on the proper role music should play in society. First, however, it might be interesting to read some descriptions of how La Bruyère found music in society during the immediately previous period.

At a sermon, at a concert, or in a picture gallery, you may hear precisely contrary opinions uttered to right and to left of you, about precisely the same thing. This inclines me to think that in any sort of work one may venture to include what is good and what is bad; some will like the good things and some the bad.[37]

......

> A man who knows five or six technical terms and nothing more can profess to be a connoisseur in music, in painting, in architecture or in good food; he thinks he gets more pleasure than others do from hearing, seeing and eating; he takes in his fellows, and he is taken in himself.[38]

Even at court, he found little sophistication.

> It is a long-established custom at Court to give pensions and grant favors to a musician, a dancing-master, a comedian, a flute-player, a flatterer, a time-server; they have their accepted merits, their unquestioned and recognized talents, which amuse the great and allow them to relax from their greatness; everyone knows that Favier is a fine dancer and that Lorenzani composes fine motets.[39]

Although the noble should have more taste, La Bruyère found only contentment with the status quo.

> Princes, without being instructed in the rules of art, have a natural sense of comparison: they are born and brought up amidst the finest things, and as it were in the very center of these; and they compare with these whatever they read and see or hear. Anything that is too much unlike Lully, Racine and Le Brun stands condemned.[40]

One comment, however, seems to reflect the concerns of the coming generation, as La Bruyère seems to understand that music should have a higher purpose.

> Men of noble nature seem moved by entertainments, plays and music to a closer and deeper sympathy with the distress of their kindred or friends.[41]

As the discussion of the role of music in society began to attract more serious philosophic interest, we find the discussion once again centered in the practice of ancient Greece, as we can see in Fenlon's letter to the Academy in 1716.

[37] La Bruyère, *Characters*, trans. Jean Stewart (Baltimore: Penguin Books, 1970), 220ff. Jean de La Bruyère (1645–1696) was born to a bourgeois family, studied law and in 1673 became Treasurer-General of Finance in Caen.

[38] Ibid., 146.

[39] Ibid., 263.

[40] Ibid., 160.

[41] Ibid., 199.

I turn to the pagans themselves for a judgment on this question. Plato permits no music with the effeminate tones of the Lydians in his Republic. Further, the Lacedaemonians excluded from theirs all complicated instruments which could soften the heart. Music intended only to soothe the ear is merely an amusement for weak and lazy people and is unworthy of a well-regulated republic. Music is good only insofar as it agrees with the sense of the words and as the words themselves inspire virtuous sentiments. Painting, sculpture, and other fine arts should have the same end. Eloquence should also be a part of a design wherein pleasure exists only to counterbalance evil passions and to make virtue attractive...

Poetry is more serious and useful than common people believe. Since the origin of mankind, religion has consecrated poetry to its own use. Before men had a revealed text, the sacred songs they knew by heart preserved the memory of creation and the tradition of God's miracles.[42]

In his *Dialogues on Eloquence*, Fénelon discusses the role of music in ancient and contemporary societies at some length. Here it seems clear that he regards some form of education to be an important necessity for the arts.

A. You would wish citizens to dislike idleness and to be occupied with very serious matters and to strive always towards the public good?
B. Yes indeed.

......

A. You would not permit any of the sciences or any of the arts which serve only for pleasure, for amusement, and for curiosity? What would become of those which belonged neither to the tasks of domestic life nor to the duties of public life?
B. I would banish them from my republic...
A. But what would you do with musicians? Would you not agree with those ancient Greeks who never separated the useful from the pleasant? The Greeks, who developed music and poetry, united as one, to so high a perfection, intended that these should serve to ennoble the heart and to inspire great passions. It was by music and poetry that they prepared themselves for battle; they took musicians and musical instruments to war. In line with this came

[42] *Fénelon's Letter to the French Academy* [1716], trans. Barbara Warnick (New York: University Press of America, 1984), 66ff.

also the trumpets and drums to stir them to an enthusiasm and a sort of madness which they called divine. It was by music and the cadence of verse that they softened ferocious tribes. It was by this harmony that they instilled wisdom along with pleasure into the depths of their children's hearts. They made them sing Homer's verse in order to inspire them in an agreeable way with a contempt for death, for riches, and for the pleasures which weaken the soul; and to stir them to the love of glory, liberty, and native land. Even their dances had a serious aim in their way, and it is certain that they did not dance solely for pleasure. We see by the example of David that oriental peoples regarded dancing as a serious art, analogous to music and poetry. A thousand precepts were mingled in their fables and poems; thus the gravest and most austere philosophy showed itself only with a laughing face. This appeared again in the priest's mysterious dances, which the pagans mingled with their ceremonies for the festivals of the gods. All the arts which consist in melodious sounds, or in movements of the body, or in the use of language—in a word, music, dancing, eloquence, poetry—were devised only to express the passions and to inspire them in the very act of expressing them. By such means as these, mankind wished to impress great thoughts upon the human soul and to bring to men lively and striking pictures of the beauty of virtue and the ugliness of evil. Thus all these arts appeared to be for pleasure, but were in reality among the ancients a part of their deepest striving for morality and religion. Even the chase was an apprenticeship for war. Pleasures the most attractive contained some virtuous lesson. From that source there came to Greece so many heroic virtues, admired by all ages. This first system of education was changed, it is true, and it had indeed its own extreme defects. Its essential defect was that it was founded upon a false and dangerous religion.

C. You just said that this first system of education was changed. Please do not forget to explain that to us.

A. Yes, it was changed. Virtue gives true refinement. But soon, if you do not guard against it, refinement degenerates little by little. The Asiatic Greeks were the first to be corrupted; the Ionians became effeminate; all that coast of Asia became a playhouse of luxury ... All Greece was infected with it. Pleasure, which ought only to be the means to inculcate wisdom, usurped the place of wisdom

herself. The philosophers protested. Socrates arose and
demonstrated to his misled fellow citizens that the pleasure
which they made their goal ought only to be the highway
to virtue. Plato, his disciple, ... excludes from his republic
every note of music, every appeal of tragedy, every recital
of poems, and even the passages of Homer, that did not
go to inspire the love of good laws. There you have the
judgment which Socrates and Plato pronounce upon the
poets and musicians. Are you not of their opinions?

B. I share their sentiments exactly. Man should not tolerate
anything that is useless. Since he can find pleasure in
serious things, he does not have to seek it elsewhere. If
anything can assist the cause of virtue, the identification of
virtue with pleasure can do so. On the contrary, when you
separate them, you strongly invite men to abandon virtue.
Besides, everything that pleases without instructing merely
beguiles and softens.[43]

[43] *Fénelon's Dialogues on Eloquence*, trans. Wilbur Howell (Princeton: Princeton University Press, 1951), 67ff.

Later he observes that he would also ban tragedy, if it does not have the purpose of instruction while giving pleasure.

Montesquieu, under a heading "Explanation of a Paradox of the Ancients in respect to Manners," discusses some of these same issues, although he betrays some fundamental misconceptions about ancient musical practice.

On Performance Practice

MAUGARS, IN HIS REPORT of his visit to Rome in 1639, gives a vivid account of the importance and expectation of improvisation. First he observes that the Italians prefer instrumental music to vocal because "a single man can produce more beautiful inventions than four voices together, and that it has a charm and freedom which the vocal music does not have." Then he reports having played for a private audience on his viol, after which he was challenged to return and improvise—the Italians not believing a Frenchman could do this.

> After the esteem of these good people, it was not yet enough to win absolutely that of the professionals, who are a little

too refined and much too reluctant to applaud foreigners. I was informed that they admitted that I played very well alone and that they had never heard anyone play so many parts on the viol, but they had doubts, since I was French, that I was capable of treating and diversifying a subject impromptu. You know, Sir, that that is where I succeed best. Since these words were told to me on the eve of St. Louis's day in the French church, where I was listening to the fine music that was being played, it made me resolve the next morning, emboldened by the holy name of Louis, by national honor, and by the presence of twenty-three Cardinals who were present at the Mass, to mount a pulpit, where having been greeted with applause, they gave me fifteen or twenty notes on a small organ after the third *Kyrie eleison*, which I played with so many variations that they were eminently satisfied, and asked me on behalf of the Cardinals to play once more after the *Agnus Dei*. I counted myself lucky to render this small service to such an eminent company. They sent me another subject, gayer than the first one, which I diversified with so many inventions, with different movements and different speeds, that they were astonished, and came immediately to compliment me, but I retired to my room to rest.[44]

[44] Maugars, "Response faite à un curieux sur le sentiment de la musique d'Italie, écrite à Rome le premier Octobre 1639," 123ff.

After mention that he also performed for the pope, Maugars continued with some remarks of a more aesthetic nature on improvisation.

The friendship which you have for me, persuades me, Monsieur, that you will not accuse me of too much vanity in this digression, which I have made only to inform you that it is necessary for a Frenchman who wants to acquire a reputation in Rome to be very well versed in his subject, the more so because they do not think that we are capable of treating a subject impromptu. And certainly no man who plays an instrument deserves to be thought excellent unless he knows how to improvise, and especially on the viol, which being a different instrument because of the small number of strings and the difficulty that exists in fingering all the parts, its true talent is to play around the given subject and to produce fine inventions and agreeable diminutions. But two essential and natural qualities are necessary for this result: to have a lively and strong imagination and quickness of the hand to execute one's ideas promptly; that is why people cold and slow by nature will never succeed well.

In view of some modern theories that Italian music in the Baroque was played without ornamentation, Bonnet-Bourdelot's criticism of the excessive ornamentation is quite revealing.

> In general one hears in Italian music only a *Basso continuo* always ornamented, which is often a kind of *batterie*, with chords and arpeggios, which casts dust in the eyes of those who are not connoisseurs, and which, reduced to its simplest form, is equivalent to ours. The B. C. are only good to show off the swiftness of hand of those who accompany, either the clavecin or the viol. Also, to outdo these basses already too much ornamented, they vary them again, and the one who ornaments the most wins. Thus one no longer hears the subject, which appears all too naked in the midst of this great brilliance and remains buried under a jolting of very fast and sparkling sounds, which, passing too lightly, cannot make any harmony against the subject ... The voice should dominate and attract the chief attention, but the contrary happens here: one hears only the B. C., which bubbles so loudly that the voice is smothered. There is also a disadvantage in having the basses in batteries and ornamenting *ad lib.*, for it is difficult for a clavecin, a viol, and a theorbo to be able to play together accurately in the same style of ornamentation, no more than can many string instruments or winds; one takes one passage, another the next, which causes an extraordinary cacophony, such that a composer no longer recognizes his work, which appears disfigured; and in the midst of it all, one contents one's self with admiring the rapidity of the hand that is executing the passage! However, there you have the style of execution of the Italian music that is so much extolled.
>
> But this is not the case with Sieur de Lully, great disciple of the beautiful and the true, who would have banished from his orchestra a violin who had spoiled his harmony by some diminution, or a cat's cry badly placed, in imitation of those rigid Grecian inspectors of public spectacles. Can one not compel himself to play music the way it is written? Is it the Italian style to make false harmonies at every turn? ...
>
> If this [ornamentation] is suitable to Italian and Latin words, why does one wish to subject the French language to it? Does an Italian control his affairs like a Frenchman? Their tastes, their dress, their customs, their manners, their pleasures, are they not all different? Why does one not wish them to be so in their vocal music as well, and in the playing

of instruments? Does an Italian sing like a Frenchman? Why does one want the Frenchman to sing like the Italian? Each nation has different customs; why wish to dress French music in disguise and make her extravagant, she whose language is so wise and so unaffected and cannot bear the least violence, being an enemy of the frequent repetitions and the long fermatas that one tolerates in Italian, or Latin [church], music which do not suit ours at all?

Here one can compare French music to a beautiful woman whose simple natural beauty, without art, draws to her the hearts of all who see her, who has only to appear to please, without fearing defeat by the affected airs of an extravagant coquette who seeks to draw people to her side at any price.[45]

That judicious writer, Polybius, informs us that music was necessary to soften the manners of the Arcadians, who lived in a cold, gloomy country; that the inhabitants of Cynete, who slighted music, were the cruelest of all the Greeks, and that no other town was so immersed in luxury and debauchery. Plato is not afraid to affirm that there is no possibility of making a change in music without altering the frame of government. Aristotle, who seems to have written his *Politics* only in order to contradict Plato, agrees with him, notwithstanding, in regard to the power and influence of music over the manners of the people. This was also the opinion of Theophrastus, of Plutarch, and of all the ancients—an opinion grounded on mature reflection; being one of the principles of their politics. Thus it was they enacted laws, and thus they required that cities should be governed.

This I fancy must be explained in the following manner. It is observable that in the cities of Greece, especially those whose principal object was war, all lucrative arts and professions were considered unworthy of a freeman. "Most arts," say Xenophon [*Memorabilia*, V], "corrupt and enervate the bodies of those that exercise them; they oblige them to sit in the shade, or near the fire. They can find no leisure, either for their friends or for the republic." It was only by the corruption of some democracies that artisans became freemen. This we learn from Aristotle, who maintains that a well-regulated republic will never give them the right and freedom of the city ...

Thus in the Greek republics the magistrates were extremely embarrassed. They would not have the citizens apply themselves to trade, to agriculture, or to the arts, and yet they would not have them idle. They found, therefore, employment

[45] Jacques Bonnet-Bourdelot, *Histoire de la musique, et de ses effets, depuis son origine jusqu'à présent* [Paris, 1715], quoted in MacClintock, *Readings in the History of Music in Performance*, 243ff.

for them in gymnastics and military exercises; and none else were allowed by their institution. Hence the Greeks must be considered as a society of wrestlers and boxers. Now, these exercises having a natural tendency to render people hardy and fierce, there was a necessity for tempering them with others that might soften their manners. For this purpose, music, which influences the mind by means of the corporeal organs, was extremely proper. It is a kind of medium between manly exercises, which harden the body, and speculative sciences, which are apt to render us unsociable and sour. It cannot be said that music inspired virtue, for this would be inconceivable: but it prevented the effects of a savage institution, and enabled the soul to have such a share in the education as it could never have had without the assistance of harmony.

Let us suppose among ourselves a society of men so passionately fond of hunting as to make it their sole employment; they would doubtless contract thereby a kind of rusticity and fierceness. But if they happen to imbibe a taste for music, we should quickly perceive a sensible difference in their customs and manners. In short, the exercises used by the Greeks could raise but one kind of passions, viz., fierceness, indignation, and cruelty. But music excites all these; and is likewise able to inspire the soul with a sense of pity, lenity, tenderness, and love. Our moral writers, who declaim so vehemently against the stage, sufficiently demonstrate the power of music over the mind.

If the society above mentioned were to have no other music than that of drums, and the sound of the trumpet, would it not be more difficult to accomplish this end than by the more melting tones of softer harmony? The ancients were therefore in the right when, under particular circumstances, they preferred one mode to another in regard to manners.

But some will ask, why should music be preferable to any other entertainment? It is because of all sensible pleasures there is none that less corrupts the soul.[46]

[46] Montesquieu, *The Spirit of Laws*, 17ff.

6 French Philosophers on the Character of French Musicians

THE ENLIGHTENMENT IN FRANCE brought an atmosphere in which there was an almost Aristotelian drive to find and explain objectively the truth of all forms of human activity. Consequently, there is no other period of music history which produced such a prolific outpouring of philosophical thought. Since one of the great hallmarks of the seventeenth century was the origin and spread of Italian opera, much commentary was generated on the difference between French and Italian music. This discussion was taken very seriously and participants included not only philosophers, but musicians and members of the aristocracy. One of the supreme ironies of French criticism, and music history, was the fact that most of the court took as official representative French music, the compositions by Lully—seemingly forgetting that he was Italian. Held in less respect was Rameau, because his music sounded too Italian—seemingly forgetting that he was French.

On French versus Italian Music

IN THE DEBATE which engaged French philosophers on the relative virtues of French and Italian music several found it a disadvantage that the French composers were too academic in their approach, too bound to the ancient rules of composition. One of these writers was André Maugars, a violist and secretary attached to Cardinal Richelieu, who was sent to Rome in 1639 on a diplomatic mission. Reporting back that "I have listened carefully to the most celebrated concerts in Rome," he goes on to compare several aspects of French and Italian music. Among these is the subject of the French composers' dedication to their "stubbornness in following the rules." Following his visit to Italy, Maugars observed,

> In the first place, I find that their composers of church music have more artistry, more knowledge, and more variety than ours; but also that they have more freedom. And for me, since I could not disapprove of this freedom, when it is used discreetly and with skill, which insensibly deceives our feelings, so I cannot approve of the stubbornness of our composers who keep themselves religiously limited in pedantic categories and who feel that they would commit solecisms against the rules of the art if they wrote two successive fifths or if they departed even a little bit from their modes. No doubt it is in these very agreeable departures that the secret of the art consists—since music has figures of speech just like rhetoric, which all tend to charm the listener and deceive him insensibly. To tell the truth, it is not so necessary to amuse ourselves by observing the rules so rigorously that it makes us lose track of a fugue or the beauty of a song, in view of the fact these rules have been invented only to keep young schoolboys under control and prevent them from emancipating themselves before they have reached years of discretion. That is why a judicious man, with full knowledge of the science, is not condemned, by absolute fiat, to stay eternally in this narrow prison and can always soar according as his caprice carries him into some fine experiment, wherever the power of the words and the beauty of the parts shall lead him. This is what the Italians practice to perfection, and as they are much more refined than we in musical matters, they sneer at our musical regularity, and thus they write their Motets with more art, more knowledge, more variety, and more skill than we do ours ...
>
> As for our composers, if they were willing to emancipate themselves a little more from their pedantic rules and take a few journeys to observe foreign music, my feeling is that they would succeed much better than they are doing now. It is not because I am not aware that we have many who are very

capable in France, and among others that illustrious Intendant of the King's music [Antoine Boesset], who can play such lovely chords in his charming motets, in his ravishing songs, and in his manner of singing. All the Italian music will never be powerful enough to make me lose the esteem that I have for his merit and his virtue.

In general, we sin in omission and the Italians in commission. It seems to me that it would be easy for a smart man to write compositions that would have their variety without their extravagances.[1]

A similarly strong complaint against his contemporaries' absorption with the rules was made by François Raguenet, in his famous *Parallèle des Italiens et des Français*, of 1702.

It is not to be wondered that the Italians think our music dull and stupefying, that according to their taste it appears flat and insipid, if we consider the nature of the French melodies compared to those of the Italian. The French, in their melodies, aim at the soft, the easy, the flowing and coherent; the whole melody is of the same key, or, if sometimes they venture to vary it, they do it with so many preparations, they so qualify it, that still the melody seems to be as natural and consistent as if they had attempted no change at all; there is nothing bold and adventurous in it; it is all equal and of one piece. But the Italians pass boldly and in an instant from B-natural to B-flat to B-natural; they venture the boldest cadences and the most irregular dissonance; and their melodies are so out of the way that they resemble the compositions of no other nation in the world.

The French would think themselves undone if they offended in the least against the rules; they flatter, tickle, and court the ear and are still doubtful of success, though everything be done with an exact regularity. The more hardy Italian changes the tone and the mode without any awe or hesitation; he makes double or treble cadences of seven or eight bars together upon tones we should think incapable of the least division. He will make a swelling of so prodigious a length that they who are unacquainted with it can't choose but be offended at first to see him so adventurous, but before he has done it they will think they can't sufficiently admire him. He will have passages of such an extent as will perfectly confound his auditors at first, and upon such irregular tones as shall instill a terror as well as surprise into the audience, who

[1] André Maugars, "*Response faite à un curieux sur le sentiment de la musique d'Italie, écrite à Rome le premier Octobre 1639,*" quoted in Carol MacClintock, *Readings in the History of Music in Performance* (Bloomington: Indiana University Press, 1979), 117ff, 124ff.

will immediately conclude that the whole concert is degenerating into a dreadful dissonance; and betraying them by that means into a concern for the music, which seems to be upon the brink of ruin, he immediately reconciles them by such regular cadences that everyone is surprised to see harmony rising again, in a manner, out of discord itself and owing its greatest beauties to those irregularities which seemed to threaten it with destruction. The Italians venture at everything that is harsh and out of the way, but then they do it like people that have a right to venture and are sure of success. Under a notion of being the greatest and most absolute masters of music in the world, like despotic sovereigns they dispense with its rules in hardy but fortunate sallies; they exert themselves above the art, but, like masters of that art whose laws they follow or transgress at pleasure, they insult the niceness of the ear which others court; they master and conquer it with charms which owe their irresistible force to the boldness of the adventurous composer.[2]

[2] François Raguenet, "Parallèle des Italiens et des Français," (1702), quoted in Oliver Strunk, *Source Readings in Music History* (New York: Norton, 1950), 477ff.

In the writings of Jacques Bonnet-Bourdelot we have a perspective of the French–Italian debate at its height in Paris in 1715.

You know then, as I do, Monsieur, that there are presently two parties formed on the subject of music; one, the rabid admirers of Italian music, sustained by a small sect of *demi-savants* in this art; nevertheless they are persons of fairly high standing who royally decide and proscribe absolutely French music as being stale and tasteless or entirely insipid. The other party, faithful to the taste of the country and better grounded in the art of music, are unable to suffer without indignation that the good taste of French music is scorned in Paris, and they treat Italian music as bizarre and capricious and as a rebel against the rules of the art.[3]

[3] Jacques Bonnet-Bourdelot, *Histoire de la musique, et de ses effets, depuis son origine jusqu'à présent* [Paris, 1715], quoted in Carol MacClintock, *Readings in the History of Music in Performance*, 241. Bonnet-Bourdelot (d. 1724) was a nephew of Pierre Bourdelot, an historian who died before finishing his history of music. Jacques' brother, Pierre, took up the project, but he also died before finishing. Jacques took their work, to which he added his own observations, and finished the project.

Bonnet-Bourdelot himself admits that everything about Italian music in general is learned and refined and that the French owe to the Italians the greater part of the practice of ornamentation. On the other hand, he questions Italian taste.

If we cede to them science and invention, should they not cede to us with the same impartiality the good natural taste we possess, and the tender and noble execution in which we excel: above all, the harmony of our instruments? The enrichments we have added from our own store, should they not be accepted? ... Can one not say without offending the partisans of Italian music that their too frequent and misplaced ornaments stifle expression, that they do not sufficiently distinguish their works, being in that like to Gothic architecture, which, too heavily adorned with ornaments, is obscured by them, so that one can no longer distinguish the body of the work?

Ten years later, Le Cerf de la Viéville also made a general criticism of Italian music.

> The Italians find no music good, if it is not difficult, they can scarcely bring themselves to look at it when there are only quarter- and eighth-notes.[4]

[4] Le Cerf de La Viéville, *Histoire de la musique* (Amsterdam, 1725), I, 307.

For Charles de Brosses, writing in 1739, this entire debate was based mostly on mutual ignorance, that is, the lack of sufficient first-hand experience by either the French or Italians in hearing each other's music.

> It is only up to me to challenge you as an incompetent judge, as every Frenchman would be who tries to pass judgment on Italian music without having heard it in its native country. The French cannot know better the effect that *Artaxerxes* can produce on the stage than the Italians can feel the effects of *Armide*. I have heard the second and last act of this French opera sung in Rome, at the house of Cardinal Ottoboni; it was the best possible choice of Lully's music; the Italians yawned and we shrugged our shoulders.
>
> Nothing could be more ridiculous; then too, we felt that no voice is capable of singing well any other music than that of its own country. Italian music which we sing in France should not appear more ridiculous than ours does in Rome; be careful not to pass any judgment on it, and certainly, to judge it, almost as much as to sing it, you must know the language perfectly and penetrate the feeling of the words.[5]

As a practical example, De Brosses offers the following anecdote.

> The other day in the Paglianini Bookstore I found a treatise on [French and Italian music] written by a Frenchman named Bonnet ... As soon as he comes to Italian music, nothing could be more absurd than everything he says; there is not

[5] Charles de Brosses, "Lettres familières écrites d'Italie en 1739 et 1740" [Paris, 1885], quoted in MacClintock, *Readings in the History of Music in Performance*, 268. De Brosses (1707–1777) a magistrate and president of the Parliament of Dijon, was a highly educated man in the fields of art, literature, music and the study of antiquities.

a shadow of truth nor any appearance of common sense; he cannot endure it; he reveals in a moment that he has never been in Italy, that he does not know a word of the language, and what is worse, that he has never heard real Italian songs . . .

The [Italian] musician Menicuccio, having found this book on my table, began to read a few pages, and was astonished at this height of unreason. I took the occasion to remonstrate with him that he was himself unjust in his antipathy for our French music, which he scarcely knows better in spite of the short stay he has made in France; for the Italians are more unjust toward us than the greatest partisans of French music can be toward Italian music.[6]

[6] Ibid., 269.

On French versus Italian Singers

FOR RAGUENET, IN 1702, the essential advantage the Italian singers had was a very extrovert and passionate style, which he attributed to their greater experience in singing more complicated music.

> The Italians are more bold and hardy in their melodies than the French; they carry their point farther, both in their tender songs and those that are more sprightly as well as in their other compositions; nay, they often unite styles which the French think incompatible. The French, in those compositions that consist of many parts, seldom regard more than that which is principal, whereas the Italians usually study to make all the parts equally shining and beautiful. In short, the invention of the one is inexhaustible, but the genius of the other is narrow and constrained . . .[7]

[7] Raguenet, "Parallèle des Italiens et des Français," 476ff.

. . . . . .

Sometimes we meet with a swelling to which the first notes of the thorough bass jar so harshly as the ear is highly offended with it, but the bass, continuing to play on, returns at last to the swelling with such beautiful intervals that we quickly discover the composer's design, in the choice of those discords, was to give the hearer a more true and perfect relish of the ravishing notes that on a sudden restore the whole harmony.

> Let a Frenchman be set to sing one of these dissonances, and he will lack courage enough to support it with that resolution wherewith it must be sustained to make it succeed; his ear, being accustomed to the most soft and natural intervals, is startled at such an irregularity; he trembles and is in a sweat whilst he attempts to sing it. Whereas the Italians, who are inured from their youth to these dissonances, sing the most irregular notes with the same assurance they would the most beautiful and perform everything with a confidence that secures them of success.
>
> Music is become exceedingly common in Italy; the Italians sing from their cradles, they sing at all times and places, a natural uniform song is too vulgar for their ears. Such melodies are to them like things tasteless and decayed.[8]

[8] Ibid., 478.

Jean Laurent le Cerf de La Viéville, in his treatise on "Good Taste in Music" (1704), touches on the comparison of French and Italian styles in the context of a discussion on the aesthetic characteristics of a good singer.

> A perfect voice should be sonorous, of wide range, sweet, exact [nette], lively, flexible. These six qualities, which nature combines only once in a century, are ordinarily present in half measure. A voice of wide range and of a beautiful tone, a touching tone, is a great, a beautiful voice, and the sweeter it is, in addition, a thing rarer in great voices than in others, the more beautiful I believe it to be. A lively and flexible voice is a pretty voice, a pleasing voice, and the more exact it is, in addition, the frequent drawbacks of pretty voices, and the more I shall esteem it ...
>
> I reduce the merit of a singer to three things: accuracy, expression, neatness [proprete] ...
>
> Expression on the part of a singer consists in entering, in a spirited and appropriate manner, into the feeling of the verses he sings, to inform them with passion is the term, as one who understand them and is the first to feel them. On the whole the recitative and the smaller melodies should be sung lightly, the great airs more consciously, bringing out the full force of each note. It is noticeable that the fault of beginners is to sing too fast, that of the good provincial singers to go a little too slowly. Neatness [proprete] is that great mass of little observations, unknown to the Italians but so well known to our own masters, and which by their combined effect afford great pleasure, I assure you. To open the mouth, to produce

the tones in the right way, to prepare, ornament, and finish a cadence gracefully, etc.[9]

Robert Donnington also quotes Le Cerf de La Viéville as having written,

> The Italian singers pronounce badly ... because ... they close all their teeth and do not open the mouth enough: except in the florid passages, where they hold it open for a quarter of an hour at a time, without moving the tongue, or the lips ... [10]

The greatest distinction between French and Italian vocal traditions was, of course, the wide use of castrati by the Italians. De Brosses, visiting Italy in 1739, offers some interesting information on these singers.

> The operation is performed about the age of seven or eight years of age; the child must ask for it himself; the police have imposed this condition to render tolerance for it a little less intolerable. They usually become large and fat like capons, with thighs, buttocks, arms, breast, and neck round and plump like women. When one meets them in a crowd one is astonished when they speak to hear such a tiny child's voice from these colossi ...
>
> One must grow accustomed to these castrato voices to enjoy them. Their timbre is as clear and piercing as that of choir boys, and much stronger. It seems to me that they sing an octave above the natural women's voice. Their voices always have a dry and thin quality, far distant from the young and velvety quality of women's voices; but they are brilliant, light, full of *Eclat*, very strong, and with a wide range.[11]

Later, he adds,

> The Italians admire the cadences [cadenzas] that occur in the finale of every solo song. For me, they do not please me at all; in addition to being very frequent they always say the same thing. I want to laugh when I see a fat eunuch blow himself up like a balloon, to show the range of his voice for a quarter of an hour without taking a breath in twenty elaborate passages, one after the other.[12]

Regarding the comparison of normal French and Italian voices, De Brosses writes,

[9] Le Cerf de la Viéville, *Histoire de la musique*, 501ff.

[10] Quoted in Robert Donnington, *The Interpretation of Early Music* (New York, 1964), 525.

[11] Charles de Brosses, "Lettres familières," 275ff.

[12] Ibid., 281.

> Do not talk to the Italians of the admirable tones of our French music, spun out, sustained tones gradually increased or diminished on the same degree; they would not be capable of understanding you any more than they could provide such sounds. The Italians nevertheless distinguish two kinds of voices: one they call *voce di testa*, which is quite light and suited to the charming little turns they can give to the musical ornaments; the other the chest voice, *voce di petto*, which has sounds more open, more natural, and fuller. In a word, the voices of Italy are agreeable, flexible, seductive to the last degree, but, if all them were put into the beaker, one would not get from all their voices joined together any voice comparable to or approaching that of Catherine Lemaure.

In another place, De Brosses criticizes the Italian tradition for producing singers limited to the theater.

> If you ask a singer to sing a drawing room song, she will not sing without going to the piano to accompany herself, playing the bass with her left hand and the melody, not the chords, with her right hand ... So in spite of the small esteem they have for our songs, they praise our gay vaudevilles, our duets and *chansonettes de table*; that is all they like of our music.

Finally, after praising the vocal compositions of Pergolesi, Bernasconi, Scarlatti, Jomelli and Vinci, he adds this interesting note.

> Handel has a great reputation in England; his works are not much known in Italy, and, from what I have seen of his vocal music, I would think him to be inferior to all those whom I have named to you.[13]

[13] Ibid., 285.

On French versus Italian Instrumental Music

DURING ANDRÉ MAUGAR'S VISIT to Rome in 1639 he was particularly surprised by an abundance of fine harpists, an instrument rarely reported in literature of this period. He also found the organ performances lacking by French standards, which he attributed to their fewer registers. He then makes a brief summary of national styles of instrumental music.

We play the lute well and the Italians the archlute. We play the organ agreeably and the Italians learnedly. We play the spinet admirably, and the English play the viol perfectly. I admit that I owe them something and that I have imitated them in their tunings, but not in other things; our French birth and training give us this advantage over all the other nations in that they will never be able to equal us in fine movements, in agreeable diminutions, and particularly in the natural melodies of Courantes and Ballets.[14]

Quite a different impression was given by Raguenet in 1702, after his visit to Italy. In a report which demonstrates his rather detailed knowledge of the instruments in use in both countries, he seemed almost shocked by the aggressive and emotional style of the Italian instrumentalists.

> As to the instruments, our masters touch the violin much finer and with a greater nicety than they do in Italy. Every stroke of their bow sounds harsh, if broken, and disagreeable, if continued ...[15]

......

> [The Italian] violins are mounted with strings much larger than ours; their bows are longer, and they can make their instruments sound as loud again as we do ours. The first time I heard our orchestra in the Opera after my return from Italy, my ears had been so used to the loudness of the Italian violins that I thought ours had all been bridled ... Their bass-viols are as large again as the French, and all ours put together don't sound so loud in our operas as two or three of those basses do in Italy. This is certainly an instrument much wanted in France; it is the basis on which the Italians in a manner build the whole consort; it is a sure foundation, equally firm as it is deep and low; it has a full mellow sound, filling the air with an agreeable harmony in a sphere of activity extending itself to the utmost bounds of the most spacious places.[16]

......

Moreover, besides all the instruments that are common to us as well as the Italians, we have the oboes, which, by their sounds, equally mellow and piercing, have infinitely the advantage of the violins in all brisk, lively airs, and the flutes,

[14] André Maugars, "Response faite à un curieux sur le sentiment de la musique d'Italie," 120, 125.

[15] Raguenet, "Parallèle des Italiens et des Français," 475.

[16] Ibid., 486.

which so many of our great artists have taught to groan after so moving a manner in our mournful melodies, and sigh so amorously in those that are tender.[17]

[17] Ibid., 475.

On the other hand, Raguenet was much more impressed with the actual scoring heard in the Italian ensembles.

As for the accompaniments of the violin [in France], they are, for the most part, nothing but single strokes of the bow, heard by intervals, without any uniform coherent music, serving only to express, from time to time, a few chords. Whereas in Italy, the first and second upper part, the thorough bass, and all the other parts that concur to the composition of the fullest pieces, are equally finished. The parts for the violins are usually as beautiful as the melody itself. So that after we have been entertained with something very charming in the melody, we are insensibly captivated by the parts that accompany it, which are equally engaging and make us quit the subject to listen to them. Everything is so exactly beautiful that it is difficult to find out the principal part ... It is too much for one soul to taste the several beauties of so many parts. She must multiply herself before she can relish and digest three or four delights at once which are all beautiful alike; it is transport, enchantment, and ecstasy of pleasure; her faculties are upon so great a stretch, she is forced to ease herself by exclamations; she waits impatiently for the end of the melody that she may have a breathing space ...

To conclude, the Italians are inexhaustible in their productions of such pieces as are composed of several parts, in which on the other side the French are extremely limited. In France, the composer thinks he has done his business if he can diversify the subject; as for the accompaniments you find nothing like it in them; without any variety or surprise. The French composers steal from one another or copy from their own works so that all their compositions are much alike.[18]

[18] Ibid., 480ff.

Raguenet at this point pays tribute to Lully as one who has surpassed all musicians and admits, somewhat in embarrassment, that Lully is an Italian. As for the native French musicians, Raguenet paints a rather dismal portrait of their social recognition.

I have seen Corelli, Pasquini, and Gaetani play all together in the same opera at Rome, and they are allowed to be the greatest masters in the world on the violin, the harpsichord, and theorbo or archlute, and as such they are generally paid 300 or 400 *pistoles* apiece for a month, or six weeks at the most. This is the commonest pay in Italy, and this encouragement is one reason why they have more masters there than we have with us. We despise them in France as people of a mean profession; in Italy they are esteemed as men of note and distinction. There they raise very considerable fortunes, whereas with us they get but a bare livelihood. From hence it is that ten times more people apply themselves to music in Italy than France. Nothing is more common in Italy than performers, singers and music.[19]

[19] Ibid., 487.

Le Cerf de la Viéville, writing in 1705, had the same impression as Raguenet regarding the vigorous Italian ensemble sound. This is mentioned in his treatise on "Good Taste in Music," where we also find a brief discussion on the aesthetic characteristics of good instrumental music.

> Of the three qualities to which I reduce the merit of a player, exactness is the principal one, especially for the players of instruments which are played directly by the fingers, without a bow ... Without exactness, what is a piece for the lute or the harpsichord? A noise, a jangling of harmonies in which one understands nothing. I would sooner listen to a hurdy-gurdy. After this precious exactness comes delicacy. It is in instruments what neatness [*proprete*] is in singing ...
>
> In truth, [the] Italians carry too far a certain desire to elicit sound from their instruments. My intelligence, my heart, my ears tell me, all at once, that they produce a sound excessively shrill and violent. I am always afraid that the first stroke of the bow will make the violin fly into splinters, they use so much pressure.[20]

[20] Le Cerf de la Viéville, *Histoire de la musique*, 502ff.

The most enlightening comments on Italian instrumental music are found in the record of Charles de Brosses' travel to Italy in 1739. In general, he found a much higher level of orchestral discipline in Italy.

> These people have notions of precision much different from ours and they say much worse things about our playing than about our music.[21]

[21] Charles de Brosses, "Lettres familières," 279ff.

His most interesting description of Italian instrumental music is of church concerti and he provides many interesting details of their style. His account is another acknowledgment of the superior concepts of orchestration in Italy.

> In a sacred concert performed on Christmas Eve in the Papal chamber of Monte Cavallo, I judged that there were about two hundred instruments; I expected a prodigious noise. In the performance the effect did not seem to me any greater than if there had been only fifty; from this I conjecture that a certain number of violins suffices to give to the melody all the sound it is capable of enduring, and that a thousand additional ones would not make it louder. As the entire orchestra plays accompaniments, it must take care not to drown out the voices. While the parts of the *ripieno* play harmonic chords, the first violin almost everywhere plays the same melody as the voice; this unison sustains and accompanies it very well. I do not know why we do not play the same way. They have a method of accompanying that we do not understand, which it would be easy for us to introduce into our playing and which greatly increases the power of their music; it is the art of augmenting or diminishing the sound, which I might call the art of shadings or of *chiaroscuro*. This is applied either gradually by degrees, or all at once. In addition to loud and soft, they use also a *mezzo piano* and a *mezzo forte*. These are reflections, half-tints, which give incredible pleasure to the sound color ...
>
> They understand how to vary the sound by the variety of the instruments they use, violins, horns, trumpets, oboes, flutes, harps, viols d'amore, archlutes, mandolins, etc. We do not have sufficient diversity in our instruments, which contributes to the monotony of which our music is accused. Their ritornellos are ravishing, and the chorus that follows them is so prettily turned out, so flattering and so surprising, that beside them our French songs are only sing-song; it is madness to want to compare them.

In summary, De Brosses gives the impression that the Italian music was generally more sophisticated.

> I have heard it said a thousand times in France that Italian instrumental music is better than ours, but that we excel in vocal music. It seems to me to be just the contrary and that the Italians think just as I do. For instrumental, they have concerts, with large choirs, or mixed concerts of choirs and solo violins much better than anything we can do in this genre ...

> Not long ago I took a rather good [French] violinist to a concert at Cardinal Bichi's house, and I had him play the sixth sonata in C minor from Leclair's third book, to see if those people would have the nerve not to find it beautiful; they were not so stupid, but they did not care much for the performer, who really did not play badly. I do not know, but I find French playing dull and insipid compared with theirs; it is not that our hands are not as good on the fingerboard of the violin, we lack the bow hand; they have a thousand delicate turns, a thousand sallies, in a word, an articulation that we are not able to acquire.[22]

Charles de Brosses concludes his discussion of French and Italian music with a brief, but interesting, reference to Italian church music.

> I might add a couple of words on church music; we hear it often, for every time there is a service in a church there is music, and there are so many churches here, each of which has so many feasts! They perform not only motets but also concertos, sometimes with two choirs, which answer each other from two lofts, from one side of the church to the other.
> There was a superb instance of this sort of music at the Gesu on New Year's Day, but still inferior than that at Saint Cecilia, where a Spaniard gave a motet of his own composition, the most beautiful I have heard in Italy. The choirs of their motets are admirable, but the songs are lacking in the nobility and gravity suitable to their subjects. I would praise their knowledge and their harmony but not their taste. Our motets by Lalande are more beautiful and better constructed than theirs. The music in Latin does not have the same popularity as that in the vulgar tongue; little of it is performed outside the church. I would have trouble in telling you which are the most celebrated composers. As to the old Carissimi... for heaven's sake, do not speak of him in Italy for fear of being looked upon as a sugarloaf hat; those who succeeded him have gone out of fashion a long while ago. For a long time in Venice they praised the psalms in the vulgar tongue of a certain Benedetto Marcello; they are in three or four voices with basso continuo, without an orchestra. Those that I have heard appeared learned to me, but sad and devoid of a singing quality.[23]

---

[22] Ibid., 282. De Brosses adds a note here that the Italians admit French excel in dancing and that when they give a ball they use French or German minuets, rather than their own music.

[23] Ibid., 286ff.

7 Descartes on Music

RENÉ DESCARTES (1596–1650), after losing his mother at an early age, received from his father a financial inheritance which allowed him to spend his life in contemplation, free from the necessity of employment. His education was in Jesuit schools, centered primarily in mathematics, a background which inspired him to attempt to apply the same step by step process to philosophy. In the course of so doing, he felt the necessity to rid himself of possible error in all prior learning by starting over, educating himself from the beginning. In setting out on this course, he wanted to find some universal beginning point which could not be questioned and thus he formulated the most single famous sentence in philosophy, *Cogito ergo sum* [I think, therefore I am]. This concept of starting with the individual, conscious self was in itself a revolution. Even though the humanists of the Renaissance had helped rediscover the individual, in the Catholic countries such as France there was still preserved in the universities a Scholastic tradition a thousand years old which emphasized God before self.

From the perspective of self, Descartes concentrates on knowing. How do we know anything? How do we know anything is real? It is fun to follow him around in circles: since we sense things while dreaming that are evidently not real, how do we know what the senses perceive when we are awake are real and how do we distinguish between states of sleep and being awake? But in the end, since his arguments are mixed together with so much weird science, for the modern reader he becomes a bore. Particularly so since the real object of his thinking was in trying to prove there is a God.[1] He retreads a thousand years of Church dialog and ends up where they did: if you wish to believe God is real, you must believe it on Faith, not on the basis of the evidence of the senses or of indisputable conclusions of the intellect.

Cartesian philosophy began to be taught in universities in the Low Countries while Descartes was still living in that area. Some professors were very critical of his work and in these cases Descartes responded as a person rather than a philosopher. One of these squabbles caught our attention because Descartes mentions one of the most remarkable women of the Baroque.[2] Descartes is complaining here about Voetius, a professor of theology at the University of Utrecht.

> This Voetius has also spoilt Mlle de Schuurman: she had excellent gifts for poetry, painting and other gentle arts, but these last five or six years he has taken her over completely so that she cares for nothing but theological controversies, and all decent people shun her.[3]

At the very beginning of his "Rules for the Direction of the Mind," Descartes points out that the arts differ from other intellectual pursuits in several significant ways. First, no one man can excel in them all and to excel in even one requires concentration on one. Further, the hand trained for harp playing, cannot be used for other pursuits, such as agriculture. All this is by way of introducing his observation that it was the arts which convinced the other intellectual disciplines that one must be a specialist in only one subject, devoting his entire life to that alone. Descartes, on the other hand, thought everyone should study all known knowledge, in all fields, at least once in their lives. Further, he believed that since all sciences were so closely interconnected, it made more sense to study them all rather than to isolate one.

An increasing number of philosophers were arriving, through deduction or intuition, at the understanding that man has a bicameral brain. While their labels would differ (modern medicine made the official names "left" and

[1] In a Letter to Marin Mersene, April 15, 1630, quoted in *Descartes Philosophical Letters*, trans. Anthony Kenny (Oxford: Clarendon Press, 1970), 10ff.

[2] Maria Schuurman (1607–1678) was so talented she was known as the "Minerva of Holland." She was a talented artist and sculptor, but also active in mathematics and philosophy. During her lifetime she was particularly known for her ability in languages, reading eleven and speaking seven. One of her contemporaries paid her the generous compliment, "If all the languages of the earth should cease to exist, she herself would give them birth anew."

[3] Letter to Mersenne, November 11, 1640, quoted in *Descartes Philosophical Letters*, 81.

"right"), it was becoming increasing clear that there was more than one way of knowing. Descartes begins,

> There are two ways of arriving at a knowledge of things—through experience and through deduction.[4]

But this did not mean that he believed these two to be equal, in fact he felt that our experience only made things deceptive. Descartes found only two subjects so pure and simple that "nothing of experience can render them uncertain." It followed that it was the step-by-step teaching principle of these two, arithmetic and geometry, which he attempted to turn into a method for the study of all subjects.

By 1641, in a letter to Henricus Regius, a professor of medicine at Utrecht and one of the philosopher's supporters, Descartes offers a view every bit as narrow as a medieval Church philosopher.

> There is only one soul in man, the rational soul; for no actions can be reckoned human unless they depend on reason.[5]

That is the firm stand of a philosopher. But as a man Descartes could, if the occasion made it in his interest, suddenly say something quite the opposite. In 1645, for example, the Princess, Elizabeth of Bohemia, was suffering from "a slow fever and a dry cough." Descartes wrote her that the commonest cause of slow fever was sadness and its cure was the mastery of Reason over the passions.[6] But when Elizabeth challenged Descartes, pointing out that she found it necessary to make decisions on the basis of her experience, and not on Reason, Descartes quickly retreated.

> I do not doubt that your Highness' maxim is the best of all, namely that it is better to guide oneself by experience in these matters than by reason. It is rarely that we have to do with people who are as perfectly reasonable as men ought to be, so that one cannot judge what they will do simply by considering what they ought to do; and often the soundest advice is not the most successful.[7]

For one who believed that man consisted only of a rational soul, the reader will foresee that the entire subject of the

[4] "Rules for the Direction of the Mind," [1628], Rule Two. Unless otherwise indicated the translations are taken from *The Philosophical Writings of Descartes*, trans. John Cottingham, Robert Stoothoff and Dugald Murdoch (Cambridge: Cambridge University Press, 1985).

[5] Letter to Regius, May, 1641, quoted in *Descartes Philosophical Letters*, 102.

[6] *Descartes Philosophical Letters*, 161.

[7] Letter to Elizabeth, May, 1646, quoted in Ibid., 195. Elizabeth (1618–1680) was a Princess Palatine of Bohemia.

emotions, so fundamental to music, was one which gave Descartes great problems in explanation. It is interesting that on one occasion Descartes used the organ as a metaphor for the basic body mechanism which results in the perception of the emotions.

> You can think of our machine's heart and arteries, which push the animal spirits into the cavities of its brain, as being like the bellows of an organ, which push air into the wind-chests; and you can think of external objects, which stimulate certain nerves and cause spirits contained in the cavities to pass into some of the pores, as being like the fingers of the organist, which press certain keys and cause the air to pass from the wind-chests into certain pipes. Now the harmony of an organ does not depend on the externally visible arrangement of the pipes or on the shape of the wind-chests or other parts. The functions we are concerned with here does not depend at all on the external shape of the visible parts which anatomists distinguish in the substance of the brain, or on the shape of the brain's cavities, but solely on three factors: the spirits which come from the heart, the pores of the brain through which they pass, and the way in which the spirits are distributed in these pores.[8]

The "animal spirits" referred to here, Descartes defines as,

> The parts of the blood which penetrate as far as the brain serve not only to nourish and sustain its substance, but also and primarily to produce in it a certain very fine wind, or rather a very lively and pure flame, which is called the *animal spirits*.[9]

For a time, Descartes seems to have struggled with the question of where the emotions are actually located. We get a hint of this, perhaps, in a letter to Henricus Regius.

> To say of the passions that their seat is in the brain is very paradoxical ... For although the spirits which move the muscles comes from the brain, the seat of the passions must be taken to be part of the body which is most affected by them, which is undoubtedly the heart. So I would say: "The principal seat of the passions in so far as they are corporeal, is the heart, since that is principally affected by them; but in so far as they affect also the mind, their seat is in the brain, since only the brain can directly act upon the mind."[10]

[8] "Treatise on Man," 166.

[9] Ibid., 129.

[10] Letter to Regius, May, 1641, quoted in *Descartes Philosophical Letters*, 103.

By 1644, however, he had worked out a much detailed explanation for the physiology of the emotions. Unfortunately, from here on, as the reader will discover, his thinking included much "weird science." In his "Principles of Philosophy," Descartes explains that emotional awareness comes through small nerves, scattered throughout the body.

> The nerves which go to the stomach, esophagus, throat, and other internal parts whose function is to keep our natural wants supplied, produce one kind of internal sensation, which is called "natural appetite." The nerves which go to the heart and the surrounding area, despite their very small size, produce another kind of internal sensation which comprises all the disturbances or passions and emotions of the mind such as joy, sorrow, love, hate and so on. For example, when the blood has the right consistency so that it expands in the heart more readily than usual, it relaxes the nerves scattered around the openings, and sets up a movement which leads to a subsequent movement in the brain producing a natural feeling of joy in the mind; and other causes produce the same sort of movement in these tiny nerves, thereby giving the same feeling of joy. Thus, if we imagine ourselves enjoying some good, the act of imagination does not itself contain the feeling of joy, but it causes the animal spirits to travel from the brain to the muscles in which these nerves are embedded. This causes the openings of the heart to expand, and this in turn produces the movement in the tiny nerves of the heart which must result in the feeling of joy ... Or again, if the blood is too thick and flows sluggishly into the ventricles of the heart and does not expand enough inside it, it produces a different movement in the same small nerves around the heart; when this movement is transmitted to the brain it produces a feeling of sadness in the mind, although the mind itself may perhaps not know of any reason why it should be sad. And there are several other causes capable of producing the same feeling. Other movements in these tiny nerves produce different emotions such as love, hatred, fear, anger and so on; I am here thinking of these simply as emotions or passions of the soul, that is, as confused thoughts, which the mind does not derive from itself alone but experiences as a result of something happening to the body with which it is closely conjoined. These emotions are quite different in kind from the distinct thoughts which we have concerning what is to be embraced or desired or shunned.[11]

[11] "Principles of Philosophy," IV, 316ff.

The real centerpiece of all this weird science is the pineal gland, a small gland in the brain, to which Descartes assigned nearly everything for which he could not otherwise discover a physical location. To be fair to Descartes, we must note that the medical profession, after two thousand years of research, still has no idea what function this gland performs. But, on the other hand, research has proven that several of the functions which Descartes attributes to this gland are incorrect. In various treatises he says this gland is the seat of the imagination and the common sense,[12] the passions as well as the seat of the soul.[13] With regard to the latter, this gland being the seat of the soul, Descartes gives a very precise description of his theory in a letter of 1640 to Lazare Meysonnier, a professor, doctor and astrologer at Lyons. One can see here that Descartes was evidently bothered by the question, that since we have two eyes, two ears, etc., how *two* senses could feed information to the brain which would result in *one* understanding?

> I will answer the question you asked me about the function of the little gland called [pineal]. My view is that this gland is the principal seat of the soul, and the place in which all our thoughts are formed. The reason I believe this is that I cannot find any part of the brain, except for this, which is not double. Since we see only one thing with two eyes, and hear only one voice with two ears, and altogether have only one thought at a time, it must necessarily be the case that the impressions which enter by the two eyes or by the two ears, and so on, unite with each other in some part of the body before being considered by the soul. Now it is impossible to find any such place, in the whole head, except this gland; moreover it is situated in the most suitable possible place for this purpose, in the middle of all the concavities; and it is supported and surrounded by the little branches of the carotid arteries which bring the spirits into the brain.[14]

After presenting the definition of human passions as "something which moves the soul to want the things for which they prepare the body,"[15] Descartes concludes there are only six principal ["primitive"] passions: wonder, love,

[12] "Treatise on Man," 129 and "Meditations on First Philosophy," VI.

[13] "Principles of Philosophy," IV, 316ff.

[14] Letter to Meyssonnier, January 29, 1640, quoted in *Descartes Philosophical Letters*, 69ff. He discusses this again at some length in a letter to Mersenne of December 24, 1640.

[15] Ibid., xl, li.

hatred, desire, joy and sadness. All others are contained in these, or composed of them.[16]

[16] Ibid., lxixff.

Wonder, is a "sudden surprise of the soul" which causes it to devote unusual attention to objects that "seem to it unusual and extraordinary." Since this passion is concerned primarily with knowledge, it is not accompanied by changes in the heart or blood. A stronger form of Wonder, astonishment, has an added element of surprise which "causes the spirits in the cavities of the brain to make their way to the place where the impression of the object of wonder is located." Descartes observes,

> Although it is only the dull and stupid who are not naturally disposed to wonder, this does not mean that those with the best minds are always the most inclined to it.

Excessive Wonder may become a habit, he notes, when we fail to correct it.

Regarding Love and Hatred,[17]

[17] Ibid., lxxixff.

> Love is an emotion of the soul caused by a movement of the [animal] spirits, which impels the soul to join itself willingly to objects that appear to be agreeable to it. And hatred is an emotion caused by the spirits, which impels the soul to want to be separated from objects which are presented to it as harmful.

Descartes distinguishes between benevolent love (a wish for the well-being of the object) and concupiscent love (to desire the object) and notes that there is an abundance of passions which are also associated with love: the desire of the ambitious for glory, the miser for money, the drunkard for wine, etc. He also associates affection, friendship and devotion with whether we esteem the object as less, equal or more than ourselves.

Desire is a passion in which an agitation of the soul caused by the animal spirits disposes the soul to wish, in the future, for something agreeable.[18] Descartes finds there is no opposite for Desire, but that of it there are many kinds: curiosity for knowledge, desire for glory, desire for vengeance, etc.

[18] Ibid., lxxxviff.

Joy and Sadness,[19] he defines as follows:

> Joy is a pleasant emotion which the soul has when it enjoys a good,[20] which impression in the brain represent to it as its own ... Sadness is an unpleasant listlessness which affects the soul when it suffers discomfort from an evil or deficiency which impressions in the brain represent to it as its own.

Next Descartes explains the physical manifestation associated with these basic passions,[21] excepting Wonder which is located only in the brain. In the case of Love,

> the pulse has a regular beat, but is much fuller and stronger than normal; we feel a gentle heat in the chest; and the digestion of food takes place very quickly in the stomach. In this way this passion is conducive to good health.

He continues in this manner with Hatred, Joy, Sadness and Desire.

Descartes now elaborates on the physical manifestations associated with the passions.[22] We will cite, as an example, only those associated with Love.

> These observations, and many others that would take too long to report, have led me to conclude that when the understanding thinks of some object of love, this thought forms an impression in the brain which directs the animal spirits through the nerves of the sixth pair to the muscles surrounding the intestines and stomach, where they act in such a way that the alimentary juices (which are changing into new blood) flow rapidly to the heart without stopping in the liver. Driven there with greater force than the blood from other parts of the body, these juices enter the heart in greater abundance and produce a stronger heat there because they are coarser than the blood which has already been rarefied many times as it passes again and again through the heart. As a result the spirits sent by the heart to the brain have parts which are coarser and more agitated than usual; and as they strengthen the impression formed by the first thought of the loved object, these spirits compel the soul to dwell upon this thought. This is what the passion of love consists in.

We have subjected the reader to all this nonsense to help the reader understand that music was, to a real degree,

---

[19] Ibid., xciff.

[20] In a letter to Princess Elizabeth, November, 1646, quoted in John Blom, *Descartes* (New York: New York University Press, 1978), 197, Descartes observes,

> I also even dare to believe that interior joy has some secret force to render fortune more favorable.

[21] "The Passions of the Soul," xcviff.

[22] Ibid., ciiff.

a victim of the "Age of Reason." Professors are quick to "explain" music as a manifestation of Reason, but no listener believes them. Their common sense tells them otherwise. Today the world of medicine clearly understands that music is not of the world of reason. The public understands that. Only the music theory professor continues to describe music in irrelevant terms.

Curiously enough, long before Descartes began publishing his nonsense about the importance of the emotions he actually wrote a treatise on music. His "Compendium of Music," was his earliest treatise and appears to have been written during lulls while he was serving in the army of Prince Maurice of Nassau in 1617. In spite of this early demonstration of his interest in music, he would never mention it again in his treatises, except in passing or when in need of a metaphor. It is particularly odd that he never mentions music in his treatise on the passions, for this subject was closely associated with music in all similar European treatises. Of course, we must assume that Descartes had discovered in the subsequent years of writing that music was a subject which did not lend itself easily to the kind of rational thought process which he had advocated.

It is also interesting that for all of his later doubts about non-rational subjects, Descartes' definition of music was also its purpose, to communicate emotions to the soul of the listener.

> The basis of music is sound; its aim is to please and to arouse various emotions in us. Melodies can be at the same time sad and enjoyable; nor is this so unique, for in the same way writers of elegies and tragedies please us most the more sorrow they awaken in us ...
>
> The human voice seems most pleasing to us because it is most directly attuned to our souls.[23]

In his treatise, "The Passions of the Soul" Descartes contends that every passion of the soul is usually accompanied by an action in the body.[24] In the "Compendium of Music," he appears to have this in mind when he offers some obser-

[23] "Compendium of Music," trans. Walter Robert (American Institute of Musicology, 1961).

[24] "The Passions of the Soul," ii.

vations on the physical manifestations of musicians while performing.

> Few are aware how in music with diminution [*musica valde diminuta*], employing many voices, this time division is brought to the listener's attention without the use of a beat [*battuta*]; this, I say, is accomplished in vocal music by stronger breathing and on instruments by stronger pressure, so that at the beginning of each measure the sound is produced more distinctly; singers and instrumentalists observe this instinctively, especially in connection with tunes to which we are accustomed to dance and sway. Here we accompany each beat of the music by a corresponding motion of our body; we are quite naturally impelled to do this by the music. For it is undoubtedly true that sound strikes all bodies on all sides, as one can observe in the case of bells and thunder ... Since this is so, and since, as we have said, the sound is emitted more strongly and clearly at the beginning of each measure, we must conclude that it has greater impact on our spirits, and that we are thus roused to motion. It follows that even animals can dance to rhythm if they are taught and trained, for it takes only a physical stimulus to achieve this reaction.[25]

[25] "Compendium of Music," 14ff.

Descartes adds a few more observations on the relationship of tempo and the communication of emotions. Slower tempi, he suggests, "arouse in us quieter feelings such as languor, sadness, fear and pride." Faster tempi arouse "faster emotions, such as joy."[26]

[26] Ibid., 15.

The most intriguing comment by Descartes is that he would like to "discuss the various powers which the consonances possess of evoking emotions," but that the topic exceeds the scope of his treatise. We may have been disappointed if he wrote more on this subject, however, for when he addresses this topic in a letter to Mersenne he seems to abandon any meaningful hope to establish aesthetic principles.

> It is one thing to say that a consonance is sweeter than another, another to say it is more pleasing. Everyone knows that honey is sweeter than olives, yet many would prefer to eat olives, not honey. Thus, everyone knows that the fifth is sweeter than the fourth, the fourth sweeter than the major third, this in turn sweeter than the minor third. Yet there are

places in which the minor third is more pleasing than the fifth, others, indeed, where a dissonance is more pleasing than a consonance.[27]

[27] Quoted in Lorenzo Bianconi, *Music in the Seventeenth Century* (Cambridge: Cambridge University Press, 1989), 56.

Descartes, with his predilection to systematic thought, devotes the greater part of his treatise to the perception of music. He begins with a series of propositions, called "Preliminaries,"[28] for which he provides little further discussion.

[28] "Compendium of Music," 11ff.

1. All senses are capable of experiencing pleasure.

2. For this pleasure a proportional relation of some kind between the object and the sense itself must be present. For example, the noise of guns or thunder is not fit for music, because it injures the ears ...

3. The object must be such that it does not fall on the sense in too complicated or confused a fashion ...

4. An object is perceived more easily by the senses when the difference of the parts is smaller.

5. We may say that the parts of a whole object are less different when there is greater proportion between them.

6. This proportion must be arithmetic, not geometric, the reason being that in the former there is less to perceive, as all differences are the same throughout.

In the last three of these, Descartes appears to have been thinking primarily of time, for later he contends,

> Time in sound must consist of equal parts, for these are perceived most easily according to point 4 above, or it must consist of parts which are in a proportion of 1:2 or 1:3; this progression cannot be extended, for only these relations can be easily distinguished by the ear, according to points 5 and 6. If time values were of greater inequality, the ear would not be able to recognize their differences without great effort, as experience shows; for should I, for example, place five even notes against one, it would be almost impossible to sing.[29]

[29] Ibid., 13.

7. The most pleasing sense-objects are neither those which are most easy to perceive nor those which are most difficult; but those which are not so easy as to fail to satisfy the natural desire of the senses to operate on their objects nor yet so difficult as to tire the senses.

8. Finally, it must be observed that variety is in all things most pleasing.

In a letter to Mersenne in 1630, Descartes makes a lengthy discussion of aesthetics, concluding that neither "beauty" nor "pleasure" can be given meaningful definitions in music since everything is a matter of individual preference.

> You ask whether one can discover the essence of beauty. This is the same as your earlier question, why one sound is more pleasant than another, except that the word "beauty" seems to have a special relation to the sense of sight. But in general "beautiful" and "pleasant" signify simply a relation between our judgment and an object; and because the judgments of men differ so much from each other neither beauty nor pleasantness can be said to have any definite measure. I cannot give any better explanation that the one I have long ago in my treatise on music; I will quote it word for word, since I have the book before me.
>
>> The most pleasing sense-objects are neither those which are most easy to perceive nor those which are most difficult; but those which are not so easy as to fail to satisfy the natural desire of the senses to operate on their objects nor yet so difficult as to tire the senses.
>
> To explain what I meant by difficult or easy perception I instanced the divisions of a flower bed. If there are only one or two types of shape arranged in the same pattern, they will be taken in more easily than if there are ten or twelve arranged in different ways. But this does not mean that one design can be called absolutely more beautiful than another; to some men's fancy one with three shapes will be the most beautiful, to others it will be one with four or five and so on. But whatever will please most men could be called the most beautiful without qualification; but what this is cannot be determined.
>
> Secondly, what makes one man want to dance may make another want to cry. This is because it evokes ideas in our

memory: for instance those who have in the past enjoyed dancing to a certain tune feel a fresh wish to dance when they hear a similar one; on the other hand, if a man never heard a galliard without some affliction befalling him, he would certainly grow sad when he heard it again. This is so certain that I reckon that if you whipped a dog five or six times to the sound of a violin, he would begin to howl and run away as soon as he heard that music again.[30]

Descartes makes only a few additional observations on the perception of music. He discusses the aesthetic nature of various intervals, the most interesting observation being that the fifth "sounds neither as sharp to the ear as the major third nor as languid as the octave; it is the most pleasing of all consonances."[31]

His comment regarding the bass voice, "it must strike the ear more forcibly in order to be heard distinctly," is interesting as an early recognition of what we call the "pyramid principle," a means of balancing through performance the tendency of the brain to boost the perception of upper partials.[32]

Descartes believed some form of memory in the musical performer resided in the actual fingers, hands and arms. This first appears in a letter of January, 1640, to Lazare Meysonnier.

I think also that some of the impressions which serve the memory can be in various other parts of the body: for instance the skill of a lute player is not only in his head, but also partly in the muscles of his hands and so on.[33]

Descartes mentions this again in a letter to Mersenne in March of the same year with more detail

I think that it is the other parts of the brain, especially the interior parts, which most serve memory. I think that all the nerves and muscles can serve it, too, so that a lute player, for instance, has a part of his memory in his hands: for the ease of bending and disposing his fingers in various ways, which he as acquired by practice, helps him to remember the passages which need these dispositions when they are played.[34]

[30] Letter to Mersene, March 18, 1630, quoted in *Descartes Philosophical Letters*, 7ff.

[31] "Compendium of Music," 23.

[32] Ibid., 48.

[33] Letter to Meyssonnier, January 29, 1640, quoted in *Descartes Philosophical Letters*, 70.

[34] Letter to Mersenne, April 1, 1640, quoted in Ibid., 71.

This idea falls under a very new and interesting topic being studied by some today, molecular memory.

8 On Court Music in the French Baroque

THE BAROQUE ARRIVED IN FRANCE under the reign of Louis XIII, a weak man who suffered in equal measure from physical problems and doctors, who in a single year bled him forty-seven times and gave him two hundred and fifteen enemas! As he was inclined toward the male sex, when the worried government officials pointed out that he had not visited the bed of his wife in thirteen years, he relented and produced his greatest contribution to France—Louis XIV.

Louis XIII was remembered by his contemporaries as being very fond of music, for sometimes joining his singers and for having actually composed a *ballet de cour*.[1] Under his *Chapelle* there were only fourteen singers, two choirboys, a cornettist and a lute instructor engaged for the education of the choirboys. The musicians of the *Chambre* included another five singers, two lutanists, a spinet player and a flautist.

The larger instrumental ensembles were organized under the *Écurie*,[2] the most important of which were the *24 Violins du Roi* and the distinguished *Les Grands Hautbois*. The latter ensemble had been formed under François I and consisted of an expanded Hautboisten ensemble of two shawm and two cornett players playing *dessus* (treble), four alto or tenor shawms playing *haute-contre* and *taille* parts, two trombones playing *basse-taille*, and the bass shawms playing a *basse* part.[3] These larger ensembles provided the music for the *ballet de cour*, the principal large-scale musical entertainment of the early seventeenth century and a form similar to the

[1] Catherine Massip, "Paris, 1600–61," in *The Early Baroque Era* (Englewood Cliffs: Prentice Hall, 1994), 225.

[2] This was an ancient title meaning "stable," but now included not only musicians, but riding masters, heralds of arms, sword bearers and officers of the royal household. It might have been better named the Department of Ceremony.

[3] Jules Ecorchville, "Quelques documents sur la musique de la Grand-Écurie du Roi," in *Sammelbande des Internationalen Musikgesellschaft* (1903), III, 608ff.

English masque, and for Italian Opera when it reached the court in 1645.

Louis XIII also maintained a body of trumpet players for ceremonial and state occasions. For his marriage in 1612 they supplied several days worth of music for a series of horse ballets depicting a variety of Greek gods, the legends of Amadis of Gaul and Perseus, the Seasons and the Hours of the Day. The final day included a great procession which included Roman warriors leading captive kings of Africa and Asia, mounted on elephants, and a model palace exploding with fireworks.[4]

While aristocratic activities in France always were centered in Paris, some extant accounts suggest the regional lords also enjoyed similar festivities. La Ruelle's illustrated chronicle of the funeral ceremonies for Charles III, Duke of Lorraine, includes engravings showing wind bands. One pictures the singers in the church in a balcony together with shawm and trombone players. One of the shawms is a huge bass instrument with an up-turned bell, looking like a seven-foot bass clarinet. Another engraving shows the entire interior of the church during the principal funeral ceremony. Here we see a large balcony with some thirty musicians, of whom at least twelve are clearly wind players and the rest singers, while a separate balcony contains string players.[5]

Louis XIV developed a court bigger and richer than any in the history of modern Europe. Many German dukes sent their eldest son on a sabbatical to Versailles to learn how to do it right! When Frederick the Great in Potsdam once wondered why he was sitting on French furniture, in a French-styled palace, speaking French and eating French food, the answer was the influence of the court of Louis XIV.

Louis XIV himself was also an extraordinary man, as kings go. He was an effective and hard-working administrator, in addition to having strong personal qualities. He was described by one who knew him as follows:

> Never did a man give with better grace than Louis XIV ... Never did disobliging words escape him; and if he had to blame, to reprimand, or to correct, which was rare, it was

[4] Robert Isherwood, *Music in the Service of the King* (Cornell University Press), 95.

[5] La Ruelle, *Obsequies of Charles III* (Nancy, 1608).

nearly always with goodness, never ... with anger or severity. Never was a man so naturally polite ... Never did he pass the humblest petticoat without raising his hat.[6]

[6] Louis de Rouvroy Saint-Simon, *Memoirs of Louis XIV and the Regency* (London, 1901), II, 369.

He created the most extensive musical establishment known until his time, organized under four separate administrative branches: the *Écurie*, the *Chapelle*, the *Chambre* and the *Maison Militaire*.

The musicians of the *Écurie* enjoyed high prestige, having the right of *commensaux* (meal companions of the king), exemption from many taxes and obligations to church-wardens and civic officials. They received gifts of food, clothing and financial bonuses and they were allowed to live and do extra work in Paris. At this time the members appear to have been hired more on the basis of recommendation, than by audition. It follows that study with a current member was the most promising route to success for a young musician. The importance of such teacher–pupil relationships can be seen in a typical contract drawn up between Jean Baptiste Desjardins, a member of the *Les Grands Hautbois*, and a student named François Gillotot. The modern teacher might feel reluctant to assume some of the responsibilities expected of the seventeenth century teacher.

> Today it has appeared in front of the notary of Paris that the undersigned Jean B. Desjardins ... is obligated to François Gillotot, a servant of M. the Abbey Bouchart ... to show him how to play the oboe, flute and instrumental music which this entails. Gillotot may be free to obtain this goal and do his profession without being obligated. Mr. Desjardins will furnish him with instruments. This contract entails the sum of 185 livres ... [The final payment] is made when Mr. Desjardins succeeds in placing Gillotot in a quality position as an oboist. Desjardins must try to place Gillotot ... Gillotot must go precisely all the days to take his lessons with Desjardins.[7]

[7] Dated October 3, 1701, quoted in "Documents du Minutier Central," in *Recherches sur la musique française classique* (Paris, 1968), 245.

The best known performance ensemble under Louis XIV was the *Les Grands Hautbois*, a twelve-member wind band. Formed by the reign of François I, it was first an ensemble of six oboes and (Italian) trombones with a separate ensemble of six violins. By the second half of the sixteenth century the violins began to be listed apart and the wind band became twelve in number. It is clear that by the seventeenth century they were actively doubling on other instruments as well. In the case of one member, Jacques Danican Philidor, the inventory taken after his death in 1708 revealed that he owned fourteen oboes [shawms] (*dessus, quintes* and *tailles*), twenty-one flutes (*dessus, quintes, tailles* and bass), two bassoons, two flageolets, a violin, a tambour and a pair of timpani.[8]

[8] Marcelle Benoit, *Versailles et les musiciens du roi* (Paris, 1971), 360.

It was this ensemble which introduced the modern oboe during the second half of the seventeenth century. A fascinating report by one listener, who heard the ensemble in about 1665, appears to have heard the players at the time they were still struggling with learning to control the new instrument.

> The oboes, whom one can now hear at the king's palace and in Paris, have stately repertoire and style. Their cadences [cadenzas] are correct, their vibrato is sweet, their ornaments are just as correct as the more educated vocal ones and those of the most perfect instruments. We have seen their success in the theater, especially in certain entrées. They had a marvelous effect in one Pastorale. But one can never be confident of the air; the shortness of breath, the thickening of the lungs, the fatigue of the stomach and finally, one is conscious of a notable difference in beginnings and endings; here one could discover more exactness.[9]

[9] Abbe des Pures, quoted in J. Ecorcheville, *Vignt suites d'orchestre* (Paris, 1906), I, 92.

For the larger productions, such as those organized by Lully, these wind players often joined the strings, doubling their parts. The famous French philosopher, Jean-Jacques Rousseau, who had once been a professional music copyist, recalled this tradition and reveals further details of the modern oboe in its first generation.

> The parts for the oboe that one extracts from the violin of the grand orchestra can not be exactly copied as they are in the original, since the tessitura is less than the violin and there are soft notes it can not produce; it is also not as agile at slow speeds: the force of the oboe must be handled gently so as not to obscure the accents of the music. If I had to judge a symphonic copyist ... I would give him the task of extracting an oboe part from the violin. Every copyist should know how to do it.[10]

[10] Jean-Jacques Rousseau, "Copiste," in *Dictionnaire de Musique* (Paris, 1767), 130.

Another separate ensemble under the *Écurie* was the six-member *Musettes et Hautbois du Poitou*.[11] The musette was a small, highly decorated, bagpipe, but what was the *Hautbois du Poitou*? The instrument was used in three sizes in this ensemble (alto, tenor and bass), but as there no surviving specimens, no one is entirely sure how we should classify this instrument. An early French treatise on instruments implies that it, like the new oboe, was related to the family of shawms but that it looked more like a recorder.[12] A seventeenth century French dictionary says it differed from the oboe only in length, in the placement of holes and in having a windcap.[13] The famous Diderot *Encyclopedie* calls it a type of old-fashioned shawm with only minor differences with the oboe. They were played by regular oboists of the *Écurie* and are mentioned as being present in all the large *divertissements*.

A court flautist, Michel de La Barre, was asked in 1730 by the Grand Ecuyer to investigate the history of this ensemble. Unfortunately his report contains nothing of historical substance. The positions, that is to say the line-items in the court budget appear until 1784, but these positions were being filled by flautists.

Similarly, another ensemble in the *Écurie*, *Les Cromornes*, employed an instrument for which there are no survivors. While it is tempting to think of this as a crumhorn ensemble,[14] the evidence points rather to some member of the bassoon family.[15] A treatise by Borjon, *Traité de la Musette* (Lyon, 1672) tells us that the cromornes were being made in complete consorts by 1672 and the court records speak of two *dessus*, one *quinte*, one *taille* and a *basse*.

One newspaper review mentions their appearance in 1702; a reference to the Chapel music which suggests a confusion with the bassoon.

> They all have their livery and are sometimes used in balls, ballets, comedies in the King's household and elsewhere where they are required. There are also two of them in the Chapel Music.[16]

The instrument is mentioned specifically in the accounts of the funeral of Louis XIV.

[11] Marcelle Benoit, in "Paris, 1661–87: the Age of Lully," in *The Early Baroque Era* (Englewood Cliffs: Prentice Hall, 1994), 253, curiously reduces this to "Poitevin bagpipes," which neither describes accurately the musette, nor is reflected in court documents in the National Archives.

[12] Pierre Trichet, *Traité des instruments de musique* (Bordeaux, c. 1640).

[13] Antoine Furetière, *Dictionnaire universel* (The Hague, 1690). Mersenne, in his *Treatise on Instruments* [V, xxxiv], includes an illustration which pictures this instrument as differing with the oboe primarily in having a capped reed.

[14] A mistake made by Benoit, "Paris, 1661–87."

[15] As a matter of fact, in Walther's *Musikalisches Lexikon* (Leipzig, 1732), 193, one finds,

> Cromorne (gall.) s.m. bedeutet (1) einen Basson.

[16] *État de la France* (1702).

Full suits of mourning with crepe bands for the trumpets, drums and fifes of the Chamber, oboes, musettes, and cromornes.[17]

[17] Marcelle Benoit, *Musiques de Cour* (Paris, 1971), 273.

Finally, there were two ensembles, the *Les Fifres et Tambours* and *Les Trompettes*, which supplied ceremonial duties and accompanied the king everywhere he went.

Another administrative wing, the *Musique de la Chambre*, was organized under two *surintendants*, one of whom was the famous Jean-Baptiste Lully. Lully's success in organizing the large-scale musical entertainments of the king was the source of his eventual control of the musical activities at Versailles, as well as the stage productions in Paris. It was under this administrative unit that Couperin begrudgingly made his trips to the palace. Speaking of one of his publications, he says,

> I have composed them for the little chamber concerts where Louis Quatorze made me come every Sunday in the year.[18]

[18] François Couperin, *Concerts Royaux* (Paris, 1722), Preface.

Under this wing also was a Master in charge of the education, in both music and grammar, of the children of the court as well as the vocal teacher, Michel Lambert. The quality of singing greatly improved at this time and led to the performance of art songs, in addition to the *ballets du cour*. Women singers begin to appear during the reign of Louis XIV and their role in singing art songs seems to have followed the king's preference. A court document of 1661 observes,

> When, having withdrawn privately into his Closet, [the king] wishes to hear French or Italian songs no one else can please him more agreeably than [Anna Bergerotti].[19]

[19] Quoted in Benoit, in "Paris, 1661–87," 250.

Also employed in the *Chambre* were a number of lute, theorbo and wind players, as well as keyboard performers. The positions for string players were expanded to now include both the 24 *Violins du Roi* and a separate 21 *Petits Violins*.

The Chapelle was administered by a *sous-maitre*, who organized and rehearsed the daily services and supervised the education of the children of the choirs. This area was also greatly expanded under Louis XIV and by the 1670s there were some sixty singers. To these were added cornett, bassoon, sackbut and serpent players independent of the other administrative areas.

Finally the administrative section called *Maison Militaire*, which was the military guard protecting the king, maintained not only the usual fifes, trumpets and drums, but also two four-member Hautboisten bands, which is to say oboes and bassoons. These two often combined and are found in pay records as "8 *hautbois des Mousquetaires*." We have pointed out above the practice of such players doubling the string parts when needed. On one interesting occasion, in 1698, the king and much of his musical establishment were in Fontainebleau. For some reason, the king and the string players had to make an early return to Versailles and the final performance of the comedy, *Bourgeois gentilhomme*, in Fontainebleau was performed by the Hautboisten of the Mousquetaires alone![20] We must also mention a very interesting reference to their performance at a court funeral service:

> The oboes of the army began a lugubrious concert, which was marvelously suited to the funeral ceremony.[21]

These various ensembles performed, often combined as larger groups, for every kind of state occasion. Foremost among these state events were national celebrations honoring the birth of royal children. Since these celebrations lasted one year, often a new child was born before the year was concluded and everything had to begin all over again.

One separate administrative staff existed solely to organize every moment of Louis XIV's day. The king was not permitted to even take a walk through the formal gardens behind Versailles without elaborate organization in advance. The walk would, of course, be scheduled for a specific time and the royal trumpets would be positioned by the door through which the king exited the palace. As the king took his walk, he heard constant music. An Hautboisten ensemble may have been placed in some bushes, for example, and played until the king passed. Then this ensemble ran ahead to a new

[20] National Archives, Paris (MS.Bundle 01/2830, Nr. 86, 88).

[21] Isherwood, *Music in the Service of the King*, 299.

hiding place, while perhaps a string ensemble hiding behind trees played in the interval, before it also repositioned itself, and so it continued.

But the entire court lived at Versailles—hundreds of people—and some entertainment had to be offered them all. This often took the form of *carrousels*, relics of the age of armed tournaments, or *divertissements*, which were allegorical in character.[22] The largest of the latter were known as *grands divertissement*. One of these, given in 1664 in honor of Anne of Austria and Marie-Therese, was called *Les plaisirs de l' ile enchantée,* the principal events of which lasted three days before six hundred official guests. We may imagine that many of the noble guests also came with their own ceremonial musicians. The Duke of Noaille, for example, brought four trumpeters and two timpani players "dressed in flame colored satin and silver, their plumes of the same livery."[23]

On the first day the king appeared in a carrousel as the character, Roger. Other allegorical figures included the Centuries, the Twelve Hours, the Signs of the Zodiac. After an allegorical presentation of the Brass Age, the Silver Age, the Golden Age and the Iron Age, and before another pageant with the theme of the Four Seasons, there was a concert under the direction of Lully.

> Thirty-four musicians very well dressed, who were to precede the Seasons, and made the most agreeable Consort in the World.

Another allegorical pageant on a pastoral theme, and also before the four Seasons, included more rural music.

> Fourteen musicians of Pan and Diana preceded those two Deities, with an agreeable Harmony of flutes and bag-pipes.

Following a dance by the Four Seasons (riding a horse, an elephant, a camel and a bear!), one account indicates that Lully conducted a concert of "oboes and flutes." Next, a machine-operated forest of artificial trees lifted twenty-four dancers into the air. This day ended with a great banquet with music by "36 violins, very well dressed, behind on a little stage."

[22] Benoit, "Paris, 1661–87," 240ff, gives a nice summary of a number of these performances.

[23] Much of the official speeches, lyrics for songs, and translations of contemporary newspaper articles which described these events are reprinted in *The Works of Mr. de Moliere* (New York: Benjamin Blom, 1967), Volumes I and II.

The second day featured a play by Molière, *La princesse d'Elide*. However, before the play, and between the acts, there was an independent Intermezzo with music by Lully. The text was no doubt also by Molière, for he personally played a role in these intermezzi. Apparently everything began with some kind of overture, for we read "So soon as the curtain was drawn, a great Consort of Instrumental Music was heard."

Scene One of the Intermezzo consisted of a song by Aurora. Scene Two is entitled "Huntsmen and Musicians." Here were four Huntsmen asleep on the grass, who were three singers of the king's chapel, with Molière himself playing Lyciscas. After some dialogue,

> several horns are heard, and in Consort with violins begin a Tune, to which six Huntsmen dance with a great deal of Exactness and Order.

Now the play itself begins, with another Intermezzo between each Act. In the Intermezzo before Act Three, the character Moron, who was also played by Molière, begs for a singing lesson. He proves to be a poor student, for in the Intermezzo before Act Four he complains,

> Why can't I sing? Damn'd Step-mother Nature, why did you not give me wherewithal to Sing like another? ... Why is it that I can't Sing? Have I not a stomach, a throat, and a tongue like another? Yes, yes; come then, I too will Sing, and show you that Love enables one to perform all things.

And this character played by Molière then did sing! Following the play, a final Intermezzo was given, consisting of some of the noble guests disguised as shepherds and shepherdesses who sang and danced. It was during this Intermezzo that we find the following extraordinary description

> While these amiable persons are dancing, there rises from under the stage the machine of a great tree, on which are sixteen fauns, eight of whom play on the flute, and the rest on the violin, with the most agreeable consort in the world. Thirty violins answer them from the pit, with six other instruments of harpsichords and theorbos.

The third day's activities were given near the artificial lakes behind the palace. Behind the lakes was a sizable artificial palace built for this performance.

> Their Majesties being arrived, had no sooner taken their places, than one of the two Islands that were by the sides of the first, was all covered with violins very well dressed. The other that was opposite to it was at the same time covered with trumpets and timpani, whose habits were no less rich.
>
> But what was more surprising, was to see *Alcina* issue from behind a rock, borne by a sea-monster of a prodigious bigness.

After a song of welcome by Alcina,

> A consort of violins is heard, while the frontispiece of the palace opens with wonderful art, and towers rise.

Now comes a ballet battle between dwarfs and giants. The day ended with the artificial palace disappearing in a blaze of fireworks.

> Then claps of thunder followed by several flares of lightning, portend the destruction of the palace, which is presently reduced to ashes by an artificial fire, which puts an end to this adventure, and to the diversions of the *Enchanted Island*.

A newspaper said nothing so magnificent had been seen for several centuries.

The formal three-day presentation of the *Les plaisirs de l'ile enchantée* was concluded, but not the entertainments. The following two days, Saturday and Sunday, there were several more horse tournaments. On Sunday evening Molière's comedy, *Impertinents*, was given, "intermixed with dancing."

On Monday, the king gave a lottery, through which all the noble ladies won "precious stones, furniture, plate and other like things." In the afternoon there was another tournament and in the evening another Molière play, *Tartuffe*.

> Although the king thought it very diverting, yet ... his extreme scrupulosity in point of religion could hardly bear that resemblance of Vice and Virtue; and though he did not doubt the good intentions of the author, yet he forbade the

acting of the comedy before the public, until it was entirely finished and examined by competent judges, that it might not deceive others, who were less capable to make a just discernment of it.

On Tuesday there were more tournaments and another play, *The Forced Marriage*, by Molière in the evening. Finally, on Wednesday, the festivities ended as the king left for Fontainebleau.

A contemporary account of another of these divertissements, the *Les fetes de l'Amour et de Bacchus* of 1668, leaves the impression that the music one heard might have been of a much higher aesthetic level than the allegorical themes might otherwise suggest.

> If one takes the Music, there is nothing which does not perfectly express all the passions, delighting the spirit of the Hearers. But what was never before seen is that pleasing harmony of voices, that symphony of instruments, that delightful union of different choruses, those sweet songs, those tender and amorous dialogues, those echoes, in short, that admirable conduct in every part, in which it might always be seen from the first words that the Music was increasing, and having begun with a single voice, it concluded with a concert of over one hundred persons, seen all at once upon the same Stage, uniting their instruments, their voices and their steps in a harmony and cadence that brings the Play to an end, leaving everyone in a state of admiration that cannot be adequately expressed.[24]

[24] Quoted in Ibid., 243.

The central figure in attempts to develop authentic French opera was Jean-Baptiste Lully, composer of ballet and instrumental music to the king, who had, from 1663 to 1671, collaborated with Molière. When Cardinal Mazarin, as part of his desire to bring Italian culture to Paris, sought to establish Italian opera, he turned to the famous Cavalli to stage a revival of *Xerse* for the wedding of Louis xiv. For *Xerse*, Lully was engaged to compose a number of *entrees de ballet* (featuring Spaniards, Basques, Iberian peasants, Scaramouche, Negroes, sailors, buffoons, satyrs, etc.) to be inserted into an opera which now required eight hours to perform. A following work by Cavalli, *Ercole amante*, had eighteen *entrees* by

Lully. These works were described not as operas, but "royal ballet, intertwined with a tragic poem sung to music." None of this resulted in popularizing Italian opera, but it appears to have popularized Lully, who was given the responsibility of creating genuine French opera, *tragedie lyrique*.

The king's instructions in 1672 to Lully acknowledges that "music occupies one of the foremost positions among the liberal arts, with the aim of encouraging its favorable development." Lully, "who has given, and continues to give, daily—and pleasurable—proof of his abilities," is instructed to establish a Royal Academy of Music for the establishment of "public performance of theatrical dramas in the manner of Italy, Germany and England." Lully was not only appointed for life, but after him one of his sons would be assigned to continue his duties. The following text indicates the extent of Lully's control, the reservation that aristocratic persons must be allowed to sing,[25] and the interesting suggestion that Lully apparently desired to establish an affiliated school of music.

[25] This stipulation reflects the change taking place everywhere since the Renaissance, by which it was becoming the custom for the servants, and no longer the gentlemen themselves, to perform music.

> And as compensation for the notable expenses which M. Lully shall inevitably be required to sustain in connection with the aforesaid representations (with regard to the scenes, costumes, machines, theater and all other necessities). We hereby grant him permission to give public performances of all his compositions, including those represented in Our presence, save that he shall not be permitted to make use of those musicians in Our personal employ for performances of the said dramas; he shall also be authorized to request such sums as he shall retain necessary and to station guards or other officials at the entrances of the venues where the aforesaid performances shall be given. At the same time, all persons of whatsoever quality or condition (including Our own court officials) are expressly forbidden to enter the venues in question without having paid; likewise, no person whatever may organize the performance of any wholly musical drama (in French or any other language) without the written consent of M. Lully, upon pain of a fine of ten thousand *livres* and confiscation of theaters, scenes, machines, costumes and other things—a third for Our own direct benefit, a third for the *hospital-general*, and a third for M. Lully, who shall also be empowered to establish private schools of music in Our city of Paris and wherever else he deems necessary for the good and well-being

of the aforesaid *Academie royale*. And since the said Academy shall be modeled upon these already in existence in Italy, where gentlemen may sing in public without contravening aristocratic decorum, We desire and hereby command that all gentlemen and *Mademoiselles* be permitted to sing in the aforesaid dramas and other entertainments in Our Royal Academy without prejudice to their titles of nobility, privileges, offices, rights and immunities.[26]

[26] Quoted in Lorenzo Bianconi, *Music in the Seventeenth Century*, trans. David Bryant (Cambridge: Cambridge University Press, 1989), 240.

Upon the death of Louis XIV, Philippe, Duke of Orleans, became regent until the young Louis XV came of age, thus much court activity was that designed for a child. Although all the court ensembles continued under the reign of Louis XV, his preference was for private concerts and the court no longer saw the great *divertissements*. Although he came from a musical family, Louis XV himself seemed little interested in art music of any kind. Perhaps his mind was elsewhere, for as one of the most famous womanizers in history he had established a cottage on the edge of Versailles called, *Parc aux Cerfs*, which was a stable of young girls for his enjoyment.

Nevertheless, the many separate ensembles founded by Louis XIV seem to still be present under the reign of Louis XV. They were all participating in his wedding in 1725 (at age 12!).[27] A *Te Deum* sung on this occasion was accompanied by the cromornes, trumpets and fifes and drums of the *Écurie*, and joined by three ensembles belonging to the City of Paris.[28]

[27] Benoit, *Versailles*, 48ff.

[28] National Archives, Paris (MS. Bundle 01/878, Nr. 401).

Neither was the cultural climate surrounding Louis XV conducive to the serious development of art forms such as opera. The fact that Louis XV preferred the French styles of the older Lully to that of the contemporary Rameau, while his queen was more inclined to Italian comic opera, led to entertaining reading in the press, but little important music.

The singers who traversed the stage in Paris may have been more interesting than the characters they played, if we can judge by the French soprano known as La Maupin. We first hear of her as being married to a young businessman and living in Paris. Soon after her marriage, she began an affair with a fencing master, with whom she also studied the art of the large and small sword. Upon the occasion of her husband being offered a position in Provence, La Maupin, not wishing to give up her life in Paris, moved in with the fencing master. When her husband began legal action against the lovers, they fled to Marseilles where they both apparently had sufficient voices to be employed by the local Opera.

Soon tiring of this lover, La Maupin developed a passion for, and seduced, a young woman. Alarmed friends of the young woman captured her and for her safety hid her in a convent in Avignon. La Maupin, however, soon discovered her location and, presenting herself as a novice, gained admission to the convent. La Maupin set fire to the convent and in the confusion carried off her young female lover. The young woman's friends rescued her once again and at this time La Maupin apparently lost interest and turned her attention toward Paris.

In 1695 she joined the Paris Opera, attracting immediate attention in the role of Pallas in *Cadmus*. Following this success she apparently enjoyed several years of extraordinary popularity. When a male singer in the Opera, named Dumesnil, managed in some fashion to slight her, La Maupin dressed in male attire and waited for him after the opera one evening in the *Place des Victoires*. When Dumesnil appeared, she insisted that he draw his sword and fight. When he refused, she gave him a sound beating and took from him his watch and snuffbox. The next day Dumesnil boasted to his friends of the Opera company that he successfully defended himself upon being attacked by three thieves. La Maupin, of course, humiliated him by immediately revealing that it was she alone who had beat him for his cowardice, producing his watch and snuffbox as evidence. On another occasion, a member of the company who similarly became the object of her wrath, hid from her for three weeks in the *Palais Royal* before finally making a public request for her pardon.

On the occasion of a great ball given by Monsieur, brother to Louis XIV, La Maupin appeared again dressed in a man's clothing. During the course of the ball she insulted a young lady, whereupon three of the lady's friends, supposing La

Maupin to be a man, demanded that she follow them outside where they proposed to defend the young lady's honor. While she could have easily avoided the fight by revealing herself to be a woman, she instead drew her sword and killed all three. She returned to the ball as if nothing had happened and explained the situation to Monsieur. He apparently found her story amusing and extended his pardon.

Some time later La Maupin turns up in Brussels, where she became the mistress of the Elector of Bavaria, who was in residence there. After a period of time the Elector tired of her and his passions turned to the Countess of Arcos. To rid himself of La Maupin, the Elector gave this lady's husband a large sum of money to deliver to La Maupin with an order to leave Brussels. La Maupin declared this a gesture worthy of a scoundrel, threw the purse in the Count's face and left for Paris.

Upon her arrival in Paris she resumed her success on the stage. In 1705 she announced her retirement from the Opera, surprised her friends by declaring her devotion to her husband and left Paris to join him in Provence. It is here with her husband that we last find mention of La Maupin, living out the rest of her life in a most pious manner, until her death at age thirty-four!

9 *Music in the French Dramatic Theater*

IN CATHOLIC FRANCE the influence of the Church had managed to suppress the dramatic arts until it was officially encouraged by Cardinal Richelieu. Although strong Church objections would continue throughout the seventeenth century, the remarkable talents of Corneille, Moliere and Racine made it popular with aristocratic society and thus establishing forever the theater in France.

The vigorous intellectual atmosphere in Paris, which resulted in so much discussion of opera and philosophy, also produced much commentary on the role of the future of French theater. Much of this discussion focused on the relationship of modern French theater to the writings of the ancient Greeks, in particular Aristotle. Here we shall consider the plays themselves only for their insights into the role of music in French society of the Baroque.

In the comedies of Molière there are two instances in which he provides a humorous record of the music making of amateurs. The *The Affected Ladies* (scene x), presents a nice satire of upper class dilettantes who compose music although they know nothing about it. The Marquis of Mascarille is discussing poetry, as a refinement of the upper class, with two ladies. He first reads his poem, a madrigal, and then announces he has also composed music for it.

> MASCARILLE. I must sing you the tune I made to it.
> CATHOS. Ah! you have learnt music?
> MASCARILLE. Not a bit of it!
> CATHOS. Then how can you have set it to music?

MASCARILLE. People of my position know everything without ever having learnt.
MADELON. Of course it is so, my dear.
MASCARILLE. Just listen, and see if the tune is to your taste [he warms up his voice]. The brutality of the season has greatly injured the delicacy of my voice; but it is of no consequence; permit me, without ceremony: *(he sings)*

Oh! oh! I was not taking care.
While thinking not of harm, I watch my fair.
Your lurking eye my heart doth steal away.
Stop thief! Stop thief! Stop thief! I say.

CATHOS. What soul-subduing music! One would willingly die while listening.
MADELON. What soft languor creeps over one's heart!
MASCARILLE. Do you not find the thought clearly expressed in the song? *Stop thief*, stop *thief*. And then as if one suddenly cried out *stop, stop, stop, stop,* stop thief. Then all a once, like a person out of breath—*Stop* thief!
MADELON. It shows a knowledge of perfect beauty, every part is inimitable, both the words and the melody enchant me.
CATHOS. I never yet met with anything worthy of being compared to it.
MASCARILLE. All I do comes naturally to me. I do it without study.
MADELON. Nature has treated you like a fond mother, you are her spoiled child.

In Molière's *Le Bourgeois Gentilhomme* we are given an extended view of the household music in the home of a socially aspiring businessman, named Mr. Jourdain. Although the treatment is satire, there is also much here that reflects on views of music in general. Act One begins with a music master, a dancing master, three singers, two violinists and four dancers on stage. The music master mentions that he has had his student compose a song while they all are waiting on the gentleman to wake up. The initial dialogue is concerned with describing what it is like for artists who work in such an environment.

MUSIC MASTER. We have found the very man we both wanted. He brings us in a comfortable little income, with his notions of gentility and gallantry which he has taken into his head; and it would be well for your dancing and my music if everybody were like him.

DANCING MASTER. No; not altogether. I wish, for his sake, that he would appreciate better than he does the things we give him.

MUSIC MASTER. He certainly understands them but little; but he pays well, and that is nowadays what our arts require above all things.

DANCING MASTER. I must confess, for my part, that I rather hunger after glory. Applause finds a very ready answer in my heart, and I think it mortifying enough that in the fine arts we should have to exhibit ourselves before fools, and submit our compositions to the vulgar taste of an ass. No! say what you will, there is a real pleasure in working for people who are able to appreciate the refinements of an art; who know how to yield a kind recognition to the beauties of a work, and who, by felicitous approbations, reward you for your labor ...

MUSIC MASTER. I grant it; and I relish them as much as you do. There is certainly nothing more refreshing than the applause you speak of; still we cannot live on this flattering acknowledgment of our talent. Undiluted praise does not give competence to a man; we must have something more solid to fall back on, and the best praise is the praise of the pocket. Our man, it is true, is a man of very limited capacity, who speaks at random upon all things, and only gives applause in the wrong place; but his money makes up for the errors of his judgment. He keeps his discernment in his purse, and his praises are golden. This ignorant, commonplace citizen is, as you see, better to us than that clever nobleman who introduced us here.

DANCING MASTER. There is some truth in what you say; still I think that you set a little too much value on money, and that it is in itself something so base that he who respects himself should never make a display of his love for it.

MUSIC MAN. Yet you receive readily enough the money our man gives you.

The businessman, Mr. Jourdain finally appears and, after soliciting compliments on the new dressing gown he has had made, he asks to see what "little drollery" the music and dancing masters have prepared.

MUSIC MASTER. I should like, first of all, for you to hear a song which [my student] has just composed for the serenade you asked of me. He is one of my pupils, who has an admirable talent for this kind of thing.
MR. JOURDAIN. Yes; but you should not have had it done by a pupil; you were not too good for the business yourself.
MUSIC MASTER. You must not be deceived, Sir, by the name of pupil. These kinds of pupils know sometimes as much as the greatest masters; and the song is as beautiful as possible. Only just listen to it.
MR. JOURDAIN. *(to his servants)* Hand me my dressing gown, so that I may hear better ...
THE PUPIL *(sings)*

> *All night and day I languish on; the sick man none can save*
> *Since those bright eyes have laid him low, to your stern laws a slave ...*

MR. JOURDAIN. This song seems to me rather dismal; it sends one to sleep; could you not enliven it a bit here and there?
MUSIC MASTER. We must, Sir, suit the music to the words.

This performance has reminded the businessman of a song which he now sings. At its conclusion, he asks "Now, isn't it pretty?"

MUSIC MASTER. The prettiest thing in the world.
DANCING MASTER. And you sing it very well.
MR. JOURDAIN. Do I? I have never learned music.
MUSIC MASTER. You ought to learn it, Sir, as you do dancing. These are two arts which are closely bound together.
DANCING MASTER. And which open the human mind to the beauty of things.
MR. JOURDAIN. Do people of rank learn music also?
MUSIC MASTER. Yes, Sir.

Upon hearing this, the businessman decides to study music. On second thought, he remembers he has also engaged a fencing teacher and a professor of philosophy and therefore fears he may not have time. The music and dancing masters, in response, begin to speak of the purposes and virtues of their arts.

MUSIC MASTER. Philosophy is something, no doubt; but music, Sir, music...

DANCING MASTER. Music and dancing, Sir; in music and dancing we have all that we need.

MUSIC MASTER. There is nothing so useful in a state as music... Without music no kingdom can exist... All the disorders, all the wars that happen in the world, are caused by nothing but the lack of music...

MR. JOURDAIN. How is that [possible]?

MUSIC MASTER. Does not war arise from a lack of concord between them?

MR. JOURDAIN. True.

MUSIC MASTER. And if all men learned music, would not this be the means of keeping them in better harmony, and of seeing universal peace reign in the world?

Mr. Jourdain accepts this idea and now the music master proposes that the businessman see the musical composition which the student has composed. A female and two male singers, dressed as shepherds, now prepare to sing the music, which the music master promises will "represent the different passions which can be expressed by music." Jourdain asks why such Intermezzi always involve shepherds. The interesting answer is one which was occasionally given as an objection to opera itself, that "normal" people do not discuss their affairs in singing.

> When we make people speak to music, we must, for the sake of probability, adopt the pastoral. Singing has always been affected by shepherds, and it is not very likely that our princes or citizens would sing their passions in dialogue.

During Act Two this dialogue between the music and dancing masters and the businessman continues, now focusing on music of a concert nature as the Music Master recommends that Mr. Jourdain establish his own salon.

MUSIC MASTER. But, Sir, this is not enough; a gentleman magnificent in all his ideas like you, and who has taste for doing things handsomely, should have a concert at his house every Wednesday or Thursday.

MR. JOURDAIN. But why should I? Do people of quality have concerts?

MUSIC MASTER. Yes, Sir.

MR. JOURDAIN. Oh! very well! Then I too must have some. It'll be fine?

MUSIC MASTER. Very. You must have three voices: a treble, a counter-tenor, and a bass; which must be accompanied by a bass-voil, a theorbo lute, and a harpsichord for the thorough-basses, with two violins to play the harmony.[1]

[1] In III, iii, Jourdain's wife complains there was a "regular din of violins and singers, that are a positive nuisance to all the neighborhood."

Mr. Jourdain requests that singers for the dinner table not be forgotten.

A fencing master comes on the scene and a brief argument ensues over the relative value of each of their arts. Now a professor of philosophy is introduced and speaks with disdain for the arguments at hand.

> Is there anything more base and more shameful than the passion which changes a man into a savage beast, and ought not Reason to govern all our actions?

Shortly the philosopher equates music and dancing with "the trades of prize-fighter, street-singer, and mountebank," which brings insults upon him from the music, dancing and fencing masters.

Another interesting view of music in contemporary seventeenth century France describes the public, which a character finds is a poor judge of music. In Molière's *The School for Wives Criticized* (scene v), the Chevalier Dorante comments on both the lower and upper class audience members at the theater, including a specific reference to musical concerts. Regarding the lower class he points to universality, which needs no instruction in the arts.

> Speaking generally, I would place considerable confidence in the approval of the pit, for, among those who frequent it, there are several who are capable of criticizing a play by the accepted canons, and the remainder form their opinion in the right way, which is to see things as they are, without blind prejudice, or affected compliance, or ridiculous refinement.

Regarding the upper class, he suggests they are less knowledgeable than the lower classes.

It angers me to see these people make themselves ridiculous, in spite of their rank; they are so conceited that they are continually talking boldly of everything, no matter how ignorant they may be. They shout applause at the worst passages of a play, and never cheer those that are good; and, when they see a picture, or hear a concert, blame and praise just in the same wrong-headed way.

The purpose of music most commonly given in early literature is to soothe the listener. Molière, exaggerating for the purpose of humor, carries this idea almost to the point of music therapy. In *Love the Best Physician* (III, vii), Clitander announces,

> I've brought several singers, musicians and dancers, to celebrate the feast and make merry. Call them in. These are people I brought with me, and which I use daily, to pacify by their harmony and dancing the disturbances of the mind.

In the *Monsieur de Pourceaugnac* (I, viii) two doctors recommend a series of draconian treatments for de Pourceaugnac, including bleeding (from a vein in the head) and that he should be "purged, de-obstructed, and evacuated by suitable purgatives." But first, one doctor recommends, before anything else,

> I think he ought to be cheered by pleasant conversation, songs, and instruments of music.

Indeed, in Scene Ten, a stage direction calls for two "Italian Musicians dressed as grotesque doctors,"[2] who sing to cheer up de Pourceaugnac.

[2] In II, xi, the stage direction calls for "Two singing lawyers."

> *Do not let yourself be killed*
> *By melancholic grief.*
> *Our harmonious song's for you,*
> *We have to make you laugh.*
> *We are only here to cure.*

Another purpose of music given in this repertoire is for the purpose of romance, for which, judging by one comment, music had become almost obligatory. In the Intermezzo given between the second and third acts during the first performance of Molière's *The Princess of Elis*, Moron observes,

Most women now are taken by the ear; they make everybody
learn music: and nobody succeeds with them, but by the
Sonnets and Verses they sing to them. I must learn to sing
that I may do like others.

A contrary opinion is found in Marivaux's *Double Infidelity* (Act Two), where Sylvia wonders why men go to all the trouble to court a girl who is not interested. She laments, "All this waste of concerts and plays."

There is a particularly clever scene which deals with the use of music for romance in Molière's *The Hypochondriac* (II, v). In addition, Molière takes the opportunity here to include some common contemporary complaints, including the reputed bad influence of the theater, poets who object to having to alter their verses to fit music and the frequency of pastoral scenes. This scene begins as Argan wants Cleante to prepare his daughter, Angelique, to sing before his guests. Cleante, who is secretly Angelique's lover, arranges for the two of them to improvise lyrics to the music of a previously composed chamber opera. The scene begins,

ARGAN. *(to Cleante)* Monsieur, just get my daughter to sing before the visitors.
CLEANTE. I was awaiting your commands, Monsieur. I thought we might entertain the company by singing with Mademoiselle a scene from a small opera that has recently been written. See, here is your part.
ANGELIQUE. I?
CLEANTE. Please do not make any objection, but allow me to explain to you the scene we have to sing. I have no voice for singing; but it will suffice here if I can make myself understood. You will be so kind as to make allowances for me, since I have to superintend the singing of the young lady.
ARGAN. Are the lines good?
CLEANTE. The opera is, strictly speaking, impromptu, and you will only hear rhythmical prose sung, or some sort of irregular verse, such as passion and necessity might suggest to two persons, who sing these things spontaneously, and speak on the spur of the moment.
ARGAN. Very good. We will listen.

As Angelique begins to sing her part as a shepherdess, the father remarks, "I did not think my daughter was clever enough to sing like this, at first sight, without making any mistakes." As the singing continues, and becomes rather heated in passion between the two lovers, the father becomes suspicious.

> ARGAN. No, no; we have heard enough. Your opera sets a very bad example. The shepherd Tireis is an impertinent fellow, and the shepherdess Philis an impudent minx, to talk like this in the presence of her father. Show me the score. Come, come where are the words you have sung? There is nothing but music here.
>
> CLEANTE. Are you not aware, Monsieur, that a method has recently been invented whereby the words and the notes are expressed by the same signs?

The most fundamental purpose of music is, of course, to communicate feelings. Again, Molière exaggerates this idea, reminding us of the German absorption with the "affections" at this time. In *The Sicilian* (Scene ii) a discussion of a potential serenade leads to an interesting discussion of tonality relative to feeling.

> ADRASTUS. Are the musicians here?
> HALY. Yes.
> ADRASTUS. Bid them come hither. I'll have them sing here 'till break of day, to see if their music will draw this charming creature to some window.
> HALY. Here they are. What shall they sing?
> ADRASTUS. What they think fit.
> HALY. It shall be a *Trio* then, which they sung to me the other day.
> ADRASTUS. No, no; I don't like that.
> HALY. Ah. Sir, 'tis a charming B sharp.
> ADRASTUS. What the Devil do you mean with your B sharp?
> HALY. Sir, I stand up for B sharp: You know I understand Music. B sharp charms me. No key is so harmonious as B sharp. Pray hear this *Trio*.
> ADRASTUS. No, I'll have something that's tender and soft, something that may put me into a gentle musing.
> HALY. I see you're for B flat; but there's a way to satisfy both of us. They shall sing you a certain scene of a little

> comedy which I have heard them rehearse. It is of two love-sick shepherds, full of languor, who upon B flat, come separately to make their complaints in a wood, afterwards they discover to each other the cruelty of their mistress; and, thereupon, comes a jovial shepherd, with an admirable B sharp, who rallies their weakness.
> ADRASTUS. Well, let's hear it.

Scene Three now begins with the lyrics for a song by three musicians, "*If, with the sad recital of my woes ...*"

There is one instance of the use of music for prophesy, found in fact in one of the few Racine plays which mentions music. *Athaliah*, not only has a singing chorus, but the appearance of unidentified "music" on stage to enhance the religious atmosphere. Referring to this scene in the Preface, Racine reflects on the use of music for prophesy in the Old Testament.

> This scene, which is a kind of episode, brings in music very naturally, by the custom which several prophets had of entering into their holy trances to the sound of instruments: witness that troop of prophets who came before Saul with the harps and lyres which were borne before them ...

Music in the Stage Directions

PERHAPS IN REBELLION to the competition of the popularity of opera, the French playwrights in general include very little music in their plays. The indication of musicians on stage is particularly rare, but certainly one of the more interesting examples is found in Molière's *Monsieur de Pourceaugnac*, which concludes with a stage direction reading "Several Masques of all kinds, some in the balconies and others in the street, enjoy themselves with diverse songs, dances and other innocent delights." The subsequent dialogue includes lyrics for a "Chorus of Singers." Another intriguing occasion is found in Molière's *The Compulsory Marriage* (Scene vi), where the stage direction calls for "Gypsies, furnished with tabors," who enter singing and dancing.

There are two plays in which we find indications of unusually large music ensembles present. The Intermezzo which begins Molière's *The Magnificent Lovers* begins with the stage direction, "The scene opens with the pleasant sound of a great many instruments." Similarly, Molière's *Le Bourgeois Gentilhomme* begins with a stage direction reading "The overture is played by a consort of many instruments."

Among the occasional references to the performances of art songs in these plays, there is one which is unusual because it involves a discussion of the failure of a performance. In Marivaux's one act play, *Money Makes the World Go Round*, Apollo enters with some singers and dancers. After a song, the lyrics for which are given, we find the following dialogue:

APOLLO. I'm afraid you were not too happy with this, Mr. Grangewell.
GRANGEWELL. Oh, don't pay any attention to me. I'm deaf to music.
SPINETTA. I was falling asleep.
APOLLO. And you, madam, were you disappointed too?
LYDIA. The music was elegant enough, but the performance seemed a little chilly to me.
PLUTUS. That's because the singers are hoarse. A little greasing of throats is what's needed.
APOLLO. Gently! You needn't pay my performers.
A SINGER. What? The gentleman makes us a present—why should you care? It won't prevent you from paying us. In fact, the sooner the better.

In Corneille's *The Liar* (I, v), Alcippe spreads the word that a serenade played in boats on the water has been given a young lady.

ALCIPPE. It's said That someone gave a concert for a girl.
DORANTE. On water?
ALCIPPE. Yes.
DORANTE. Water can fire love's flame.
PHILISTE. Sometimes.
DORANTE. And this was all last night?
ALCIPPE. It was...
DORANTE. The music?
ALCIPPE. Not at all to be disdained.

Later in this scene, Dorante explains that he organized the serenade, now providing more details.

> I'd hired five boats to make a better show;
> In each of four of them I placed a band
> Whose music would entrance the saddest heart.
> Violins in the first; voices and lutes
> Came next, then flutes, and oboes in the fourth,
> From which in turn came waves of harmony
> Lulling the ear with sweetness infinite.[3]

[3] This serenade is referred to again in II, iii.

There are two places in Molière where the impact of the music on the listener is mentioned. In *The Princess of Elis* (III, ii), Euryalus recalls,

> The sweetness of her voice made itself evident in that perfectly delightful song she deigned to sing, her wonderful tones penetrated to the depths of my soul, and held all my senses so enraptured that they could not recover their self-possession.

And in *The Magnificent Lovers* (I, ii), Timocles remarks "I have had my love sung by the most touching voices."

Finally, we should mention that in a performance of *The Magnificent Lovers*, Molière himself, playing the character, Clitidas, sang a song in Act Two, Scene Three.

There are two specific references in this repertoire to the use of music for dance. In Molière's *The Affected Ladies* (scene xiii) musicians are engaged for a dance and they first play for Mascarille, who sings as he dances a solo dance. Then, as he dances with Madelon, he criticizes the musicians.

> MASCARILLE. The liberty of my heart will dance a couranto as well as my feet. Play in time, musicians. Oh! what ignorant fellows! There is no possibility of dancing with them. Devil take you, can't you play in time? Steady, you village scrapers.
> JODELET. (dancing in his turn) Gently, don't play so fast, I have only just recovered from an illness.

Marivaux's *The Test* concludes with Dorian announcing, "Send for the village fiddlers, and let's end the day with a dance."

We find a nice satire on the life of the court musician in Molière's *The Impromptu of Versailles* (scene i). Here a character named Molière, "an absurd marquis," is trying to organize a rehearsal for a little play to be given before Louis XIV. He has had so little time he has written no dialogue and expects the actors to improvise it.[4] When one of them asks why he did not request more time of the king, Molière offers a sad comment on the life of the court musician,

> Ah! Mademoiselle, kings like nothing better than prompt obedience: opposition meets with little favor at their hands. Things are only acceptable at the time they are wanted; and to try to delay their entertainment is to take all the charm of it away, so far as they are concerned. They want pleasures which never keep them waiting;[5] so those that are the soonest ready are always the most agreeable to them. We should never consider ourselves when they desire anything of us: our only business is to please them; and when they command anything of us, we ought instantly to be only too glad to take advantage of the urgency of their desires. It is better to do badly what they ask of us, than not to do it soon enough; if one has the shame of unsuccessful work, there is always the renown of having instantly obeyed their commands.

Regarding the comment above, on obeying the king, we find a similar dedication in Molière's *Les Facheux* to the king.

> I had a pleasure in obeying you, which was much more useful to me than Apollo and all the Muses.

Another view of private music for the entertainment of nobles is found in Alain-Rene Lesage's *Turcaret* (II, vi), where Frontin invites a guest to dinner.

> FRONTIN. And to add to the gaiety of the occasion, you will be entertained with music and instruments.
> THE BARONNE. Music, Frontin?
> FRONTIN. Yes, Madame. The proof of it is that I am also to order a hundred bottles of [wine] for the musicians to drink.
> THE BARONNE. A hundred bottles!
> FRONTIN. It's none too much, Madame. There will be eight ensemble players, [and] four Italians from Paris, three sopranos, and two fat tenors.

[4] In fact, in the Preface to *The Impertinents*, Molière tells us he was required by the court to write this play in only fifteen days.

> In the little time that was allowed me it was impossible for me to execute so great a design, and think much upon the choice of my characters, and disposition of my subject.

[5] In one of Louis XIV's most famous remarks, made to a servant whose job was to open the door through which the king passed, Louis warned, "You almost made me wait."

M. TURCARET. Upon my word he's right. It will be none too much.

Lyrics for drinking songs are found in Molière's *Le Bourgeois Gentilhomme* (IV, i)[6] and *The Mock-Doctor* (I, vi):

> *What pleasure's so great, as the bottle can give,*
> *What music so sweet, as thy little gull, gull!*

Additional examples of entertainment music in Molière are found in *The Compulsory Marriage* (scene viii), where violins are engaged for the entertainment of the wedding guests, and in *Tartuffe* (II, iii), when Dorine refers to a ball to be held at carnival time when there will be "a good band [*la grand'bande*] with two musettes and perhaps *Fagotin*[7] and marionnettes."

Music in the Plays of Voltaire

AS WITH THE TRAGEDIES of Corneille and Racine, there is very little reference to music in Voltaire's plays, either in dialogue or in stage directions, which may be regarded in part, we believe, as an attempt to distinguish drama from the dominant influence of opera. In any case, few though these references may be, there are some worthy of mention. One offers quite a different view of the celebrated salons hosted by the upper class women of Paris. In *The Prude* (I, iv), Collette satirizes, through the nature of its associations, the performances of music in these gatherings.

> ... always at her house you will meet with good suppers, new songs, and bonmots, old wines, ice cream, liquors, new ribbons, Saxon monkeys, rich bagatelles ...

In only one play does Voltaire comment on the purpose of music, and it is the familiar purpose of offering solace to the listener. In *The Prude* (IV, v), Mme de Burlet offers to Mme Dorfise, "I have ordered him to get music, to purge your melancholy humors."

[6] In this comedy (IV, xi) a little musical play is acted out, including a song with Turkish lyrics. The music for this was composed by Lully.

[7] The musette was the specially made small bagpipes which were popular with the court, which counted among its entertainments pretending they were peasants. The meaning of "Fagotin" is unclear, but may mean small bassoons, as the musettes were sometimes played as small oboes (i.e., with the canter alone). In modern French, "fagotin" can mean a small monkey dressed in clothes or a clown. Various English translations of this passage give such diverse solutions as "the learned ape" and "an animal act."

In his *Philosophical Dictionary*, Voltaire makes a dark and curious reference to music as therapy. Here he writes a dramatic scene, from an imaginary play revolving around the cruelty of the Druids, in which Orpheus appears in the tradition of the gods who arrive at the end of plays to solve all the problems and bring about a happy ending.

> THE DRUID. I am altogether recovered. Oh, the power of good music! And who are you, divine man, who thus cures wounds, and rejoices hell itself?
>
> ORPHEUS. My friends, I am a priest like yourselves, but I never deceived anyone, nor cut the throat of either boy or girl in my life. When on earth, instead of making the gods hated, I rendered them beloved, and softened the manners of the men whom you made ferocious. I shall exert myself in the like manner in hell. I met, just now, two barbarous priests whom they were scourging beyond measure; one of them formerly hewed a king in pieces before the Lord, and the other cut the throat of his queen and sovereign at the horse gate. I have terminated their punishment, and, having played to them a tune on the violin, they have promised me that when they return into the world they will live like honest men.

The stage direction which follows this morbid dialogue ironically calls for this scene to conclude with "light and agreeable music."

The only reference in Voltaire's plays to substantial forces of instrumental or vocal music is a stage direction in *Pandora* (III, i), after Pandora laments,

> Hence, ye idle visions; cease,
> Discordant sounds,
>
> [*A Symphony is heard.*]
>
> And give me peace.

Shortly after this, another stage direction calls for the Chorus of Pleasures to "dance around her and sing." The lyrics are given for a song in which a solo voice alternates with the chorus.

The only references by Voltaire in his plays to functional music are descriptions of the military trumpet. In *Merope* (V, v), Narbas says,

> Hark! I hear on every side
> The trumpets sound, the groans of dying men ...

Similarly, in *Zaire* (I, ii), Osman mentions the "shrill trumpet heard on every side."

The sole reference to entertainment music is a curious line in *The Prude* (I, v). Here we encounter Mme Dorfise who finds no joy in the pleasures of the world. When asked even about music and dancing, she answers "they are the devil's inventions."

10 French Philosophers on Opera

As the popularity of Italian opera began to spread throughout Europe during the seventeenth century, it prompted increasing debate in France. Not only did the form itself challenge the most basic theater traditions in France, but it was a popular medium, supported commercially, whereas theater in France was a private entertainment for the aristocracy. Issues such as these, not to mention the inherent musical characteristics, fueled a wide variety of views. An early report on opera in Rome, by André Maugars, written before there was much influence felt in France itself, is full of admiration.

> There are a large number of castrati for the Dessus and the Haute-Contre, very beautiful and natural Tenors, and very few deep Basses. They are very certain of their technique and sing the most difficult music at sight. In addition, they are almost all actors by nature, and it is for this reason that they succeed so perfectly in their musical comedies. I have seen them play three or four this last winter, but I must admit that in truth they are incomparable and inimitable in music for the stage, not only for their singing but also for the expression of the words, the postures, and the gestures of the characters they play naturally and very well.
>
> As for their manner of singing, it is much more animated than ours; they have certain inflections of the voice that we do not possess. It is true that they perform their passages with more roughness, but today they are beginning to correct that.[1]

[1] André Maugars, "*Résponse faite à un curieux sur le sentiment de la musique d'Italie, écrite à Rome le premier Octobre 1639*," quoted in Carol MacClintock, *Readings in the History of Music in Performance* (Bloomington: Indiana University Press, 1979), 122.

By the end of the seventeenth century, after considerable Italian influence had come to affect the French opera, one observer, La Bruyère, found little to praise.

> The Opera is obviously the first draft of a fine spectacle; it suggests the idea of one.
> I don't know how it is that the Opera, with such perfect music and a truly regal expense, sometimes succeeds in boring me.
> There are parts of the Opera that leave one wishing for more; one finds oneself occasionally longing for the end of the whole performance: this is for lack of theatrical effects, of action and of interesting matter.
> An Opera nowadays is not poetry, but merely verse; it is not a spectacle, since machines vanished under the efficient administration of [Lully] and his tribe: it is a concert, or voices accompanied by instruments. It is an error of judgment and of taste to say, as some do, that machines are merely a childish amusement, fit only for the Marionnettes' Theater; machines enhance and embellish the imaginary action, and maintain the spectators in that delightful illusion which is the chief pleasure the theater offers, by shedding further magic over it. We need no aerial flights, no chariots, no transformation scenes, for the two *Berenices* or for *Penelope*: we need them for operas, and the characteristic of that kind of entertainment is to keep one's mind and eyes and ears beyond the same spell.
> They did it all, these busy people, they provided the stage sets, the machines, the ballets, the verse, the music, the whole entertainment, even the hall in which it was performed—including the roof and the four walls from their foundation upwards. Who can doubt but that the stag-hunt on the water, the enchanted hunting-party at the Table and the marvelous banquet in the Labyrinth were also their idea? I gather this from their activity and the self-satisfied way in which they congratulate themselves on the success of everything. If I am mistaken, if indeed they contributed nothing towards that splendid and elegant fête which went on for so long and which was planned and paid for by a single man, I wonder at two things: the calm and self-possession of the man who set everything in motion, and the fuss and self-importation of those who did nothing at all.[2]

Charles de Saint-Évremond (1613–1703), a distinguished and (rare for France) a highly educated noble, expected too

---

[2] La Bruyère, *Characters*, trans. Jean Stewart (Baltimore: Penguin Books, 1970), 220ff. Jean de La Bruyère (1645–1696) was born to a bourgeois family, studied law and in 1673 became Treasurer-General of Finance in Caen.

much from opera—he expected to have his mind stimulated. By "mind" he meant, in modern language, the left brain, that is, the rational, conceptual mind. But music does not do this, it never has and never will. Music stimulates the experiential person who is found in the right brain. Therefore, while others were debating French versus Italian opera, Saint-Évremond rejected them both.

> I shall begin by being very frank and telling you that I do not admire very much the *Comedies en Musique* as we see them at present. I admit that their magnificence pleases me, that the machines are really surprising, that the music is touching in places, that the *tout ensemble* seems marvelous; but you must admit that these marvels soon become tiresome because where the mind comes so little into play the senses necessarily languish after the first pleasure that surprise affords us ... The mind, which has given itself over in vain to outside impressions, turns to revery or is annoyed by its own weakness; finally the weakness is so great that one thinks only of leaving ...
>
> The fatigue which I ordinarily feel at the opera comes from the fact that I have never seen one which did not appear to me as despicable in the conduct of the plot and its verse. Well, it is in vain that the ear is pleased and the eyes charmed if the mind is not satisfied. My spirit agreeing with my intelligence more than with my senses secretly resists the impressions it might receive, or at least it fails to give its glad consent, without which the most voluptuous objects can give me no great pleasure. A piece of stupidity loaded with music, dance, machines and decorations is a magnificent piece of stupidity.[3]

Being by nature, as he explained, incapable of appreciating opera, he could not even understand why everything was sung!

> There is something else in the opera so unnatural that my imagination is hurt by it. That is, having the whole play sung from beginning to end as if the characters presented had ridiculously been adapted to express in music both the commonest and most important events in their lives. Can you imagine a master calling his valet or giving him a task to do by singing; that a friend sing a confidence to a friend; that one should deliberate in a council by singing; that one express his

[3] Charles de Saint-Évremond, "Lettre sur les Opera," quoted in Carol MacClintock, *Readings in the History of Music in Performance*, 251ff. Charles de Marguetel de Saint-Denis, seigneur de Saint-Évremond (1613–1703) wrote this material c. 1680, although it was not published until 1739, long after his death.

orders in song, or kill men in combat melodiously with sword strokes or spear thrusts?

He admits he does not want to ban all music from the theater, just to leave conversation to speakers and not singers. He does concede some emotions are better sung than spoken.

> Tender and tragic passions are expressed naturally by a kind of singing; the expression of a beginning love, the irresolution of a soul torn in different directions—these are matters for stanzas, and stanzas are suited to singing.

Nevertheless, in an extraordinary summary of what opera is, Saint-Évremond concludes,

> Opera is a bizarre work of verse and music where the Poet and the Musician, each hampered by the other, take a lot of trouble to create a bad work.

We might add that at the end of his letter he reveals what his real concern is.

> What annoys me the most about this infatuation with opera is that it is about to ruin tragedy, which has been the finest thing we possess, and the one most capable of forming the mind.[4]

[4] Ibid., 256.

He also provides a general outline of what he thinks an opera *should* be. Basically, his appreciation for music extended only so far as incidental music, a fine piece of spoken drama, to which one might add a prologue, intermedi and an epilogue of music—as long as it is in the spirit of the play. Thus, for him, both the mind and the senses would be satisfied.

Having observed "the little esteem the Italians have for our opera, and the great disgust we have for the Italian ones," Saint-Évremond treats the reader to a little tour of national characteristics in opera.[5]

[5] Ibid., 253ff.

> As to the manner of singing, what we call the execution in France, I think with no partiality that no nation can rival ours. The Spanish have admirable throats; but with their graces [*fredons*] and their roulades they seem in their singing to be thinking of rivaling the nightingale in the facility of their

throats. The expressiveness of the Italians is false or at least exaggerated, because they do not know exactly the nature and degree of the passions. It is bursting out laughing rather than singing when they express some joyous feeling. If they try to sigh one can hear sobs that are formed violently in the throat, not the sighs with which a loving heart gives vent to its passion in secret. Of a sad reflection they make the most powerful exclamations; tears of absence become funeral weeping; sad things become lugubrious in their mouths; they utter cries of pain instead of laments; and sometimes they express the languor due to passion as a weakness of nature. Perhaps there is some change now in their way of singing and they have profited by their contact with us to acquire a clear-cut, polished execution, just as we have profited from them to acquire the beauties of a greater and bolder composition.

I have seen comedies in England where there was much music. But to speak discreetly, I have never been able to grow accustomed to English singing. I came too late to acquire a taste so differently from any other. There is no nation which shows more courage in the men, and more beauty in the women, more wit in both sexes. But you cannot have everything. Where so many good qualities are common it is no great loss that good taste is so rare ...

There is no one slower in understanding the sense of the words and entering into the spirit of the composer than the French; there are few who understand quantity less, and who have so much trouble with the pronunciation; but when long study has enabled them to really understand what they are singing, nothing approaches their pleasantness. The same is true for instruments and especially in concerts, where nothing is sure or correct until after an infinity of rehearsals are finished. The Italians, very learned in music, bring their knowledge to our ears with no sweetness whatsoever; the French are not content to rid knowledge of its first roughness, which smacks of the hard work of composing; they find in the secrets of performing something to charm the soul, a *je ne sais quoi* very touching, which they can bring to our very hearts.

Raguenet, in 1702, provides an extensive comparison between French and Italian opera. He begins with those areas in which he finds French opera superior, beginning with the play itself, the quality of the libretto. He also finds much aesthetic virtue in the more balanced vocal forces, particularly the strong bass singers. It is true the Italian operas featured the highest voice, usually a young lady in distress. Raguenet, who took his own life in 1722, would not live long enough to see it was an idiom which would lead to the emotionally expressive music of the Classical Period.

> Our operas are written much better than the Italian; they are regular, coherent designs; and, though repeated without the music, they are as entertaining as any of our other pieces that are purely dramatic. Nothing can be more natural and lively than their dialogues; the gods are made to speak with a dignity suitable to their character, kings with all the majesty their rank requires, and the nymphs and shepherds with a softness and innocent mirth peculiar to the plains. Love, jealousy, anger, and the rest of the passions are touched with the greatest art and nicety, and there are few of our tragedies or comedies that appear more beautiful than [the librettist] Quinault's operas.
>
> On the other hand, the Italian operas are poor, incoherent rhapsodies without any connection or design; all their pieces, properly speaking, are patched up with thin, insipid scraps; their scenes consist of some trivial dialogues or soliloquy, at the end of which they foist in one of their best melodies, which concludes the scene ...
>
> Besides, our operas have a further advantage over the Italian in respect of the voice, and that is the bass, which is so frequent among us and so rarely to be met with in Italy. For every man that has an ear will witness with me that nothing can be more charming than a good bass; the simple sound of these basses, which sometimes seems to sink into a profound abyss, has something wonderfully charming in it. The air receives a stronger concussion from these deep voices than it does from those that are higher and is consequently filled with a more agreeable and extensive harmony. When the persons of gods or kings, a Jupiter, Neptune, Priam, or Agamemnon, are brought on the stage, our actors, with their deep voices, give them an air of majesty, quite different from that of the feigned bases among the Italians, which have neither depth nor strength. Besides, the interfering of the basses with the upper parts forms an agreeable contrast and makes us perceive the beauties of the one from the opposition they meet with from the other, a pleasure to which the Italians are perfect strangers, the voices of their singers, who are for the most part castrati, being perfectly like those of their women.[6]

[6] François Raguenet, "Parallèle des Italiens et des Français," (1702), quoted in Oliver Strunk, *Source Readings in Music History* (New York: Norton, 1950), 474ff.

When it came to the music, however, Raguenet could not help but admire many aspects of Italian singing.

> There is no weak part in any of the Italian operas, where no sense is preferable to the rest of its peculiar beauties; all the songs are of an equal force and are sure to be crowned with applause, whereas in our operas there are I know not how many languishing scenes and insipid melodies with which nobody can be pleased or diverted.
>
> It must be confessed that our recitative is much better than that of the Italians, which is too close and simple; it is the same throughout and cannot properly be called singing. Their recitative is little better than downright speaking, without any inflection or modulation of the voice, and yet there is this to be admired in it—the parts that accompany this psalmody are incomparable, for they have such an extraordinary genius for composition that they know how to adapt charming concords, even to a voice that does little more than speak, a thing to be met with in no other part of the world whatsoever...
>
> I observed in the beginning of this parallel how much we had the advantage over the Italians in our basses, so common with us and so rare to be found in Italy; but how small is this in comparison to the benefit their operas receive from their castrati, who abound without number among them, whereas there is not one to be found in all France. Our women's voices are indeed as soft and agreeable as are those of their castrati, but then they are far from being either so strong or lively. No man or woman in the world can boast of a voice like theirs; they are clear, they are moving, and affect the soul itself...
>
> Add to this that these soft—these charming voices acquire new charms by being in the mouth of a lover; what can be more affecting than the expressions of their sufferings in such tender passionate notes; in this the Italian lovers have a very great advantage over ours, whose hoarse masculine voices ill agree with the fine soft things they are to say to their mistresses. Besides, the Italian voices being equally strong as they are soft, we hear all they sing very distinctly, whereas half of it is lost upon our stage unless we sit close to the stage or have the spirit of divination. Our upper parts are usually performed by girls that have neither lungs nor wind, whereas the same parts in Italy are always performed by men whose firm piercing voices are to be heard clearly in the largest theaters without losing a syllable, sit where you will.

> But the greatest advantage the Italians receive from these castrati is that their voices hold good for thirty or forty years together, whereas our women begin to lose the beauty of theirs at ten or twelve years end.[7]

[7] Ibid., 482ff.

......

> In all our operas we have either some insignificant actor that sings out of tune or time, or some ignorant actress that sings false and is excused, either because she is not as yet thoroughly acquainted with the stage or else she has no voice, and then she is borne with because she has some other way of pleasing the town and withal makes a handsome figure. This never happens in Italy, where there is not a voice but what may very well be liked; they have neither man or woman but what perform their parts so perfectly well that they are sure to charm an audience by their agreeable manner of singing though their voices are not extraordinary, for music is nowhere so well understood as in Italy.[8]

[8] Ibid., 484.

On the other hand, the philosopher, Bonnet-Bourdelot, was one who found almost nothing to praise in Italian opera.

> One can say that Italian music resembles an amiable coquette, although somewhat painted, full of vivacity, always rushing about seeking to sparkle everywhere without reason, and not knowing why; like a scatter brain who shows her passions in everything she does; when it is a question of tender affection she makes it dance the gavotte or gigue. Would not one say that serious matters become comical in her hands, and that she is more suited to *ariettes* and *chansonettes* than to deal with noble subjects? In that, is she not like to those comedians who having talent only for the comic, succeed very badly, turning tragedy to ridicule when they wish to have a hand in it? One must admit that the majesty of French music treats heroic subjects with greater nobility and is more appropriate to the cothurnus and the theater; whereas in Italian music all the passions appear alike: joy, anger, sorrow, happy love, the lover who fears or hopes—all seem to be painted with the same features and the same character; it is a continual gigue, always sparkling or leaping.[9]

[9] Jacques Bonnet-Bourdelot, *Histoire de la musique, et de ses effets, depuis son origine, jusqu'à présent* (Paris, 1715), quoted in MacClintock, *Readings in the History of Music in Performance*, 242ff. Bonnet-Bourdelot (d. 1724) was a nephew of Pierre Bourdelot, an historian who died before finishing his history of music. Jacques' brother, Pierre, took up the project, but he also died before finishing. Jacques took their work, to which he added his own observations, and finished the project.

He was particularly suspicious of anything involving technique, for its tendency to detract from the sentiment of the words in the opera.

We have difficulty to accustom ourselves to the strange intervals in the recitatives of their songs, which sometimes exceed an octave, in which even the most skillful find difficulty with just intonation. Above all, the long *tenutos* make the listener impatient because they are misplaced; these holds, which we also use and which are rarely suitable except on words of repose, they make indifferently on all the words that end with vowels. I do not say there may not be a great deal of art in having a violin and a bass frolic below one of these long fermatas, but what has liberty to do with this sound that lasts a quarter of an hour? Where is the taste and expression in all of that? It very often happens that Italian music expresses something quite different from the words. I hear a Prelude that is fast and furious: I then think that some lover, repelled by the coldness of his lady, is going to give way to spite and abuse Love; not at all: it is a tender lover who praises the price of his constancy, who calls Hope to his aid, or who makes a declaration of love to his mistress.

Bonnet-Bourdelot makes a curious and revealing observation on French opera in an apparent reference to the famous French salons.

There are, however, women who decide the merit and destiny of works in the spectacles, and whom we must seek to please, above all in that art which seems to be made for them.[10]

[10] Ibid., 249ff.

Another unusually interesting passage regarding opera involves a quotation from St. Augustine which we do not find in the extant works of that Church father.

But to arrive at perfection in such a fine spectacle, it is necessary to have persons of talent who understand perfectly the principles on which St. Augustine placed the perfection of harmony, arranged in nine degrees: the first in the mind, the second in good judgment, the third in the imagination, the fourth in the emotions, the fifth in the word, the sixth in the melody, the seventh in the sound, the eighth in desire, and the ninth in the composition.

These principles embody also the perfection of the nine Muses, whom the Ancients considered divinities. Thus, to compose a perfect opera it takes at least a poet, a musician, a mathematician, a ballet master, a painter—all of whom excel in their art—and a superintendent of great perception to oversee the construction and execution of the work. Also a great prince, or a republic as powerful as that of Venice, should pay the expenses *a discretion*, for it is necessary that everything be suitable to such a great subject, which is ordinarily drawn from a fable or history or is allegorical.[11]

[11] Ibid., 249.

The reference to "a great prince" refers to the fact that opera in France at this time was sponsored by the nobility, whereas in Italy it was a private, commercial concern. Bonnet-Bourdelot returns to the French tradition when he observes,

One must admit that all these representations are at least as indebted for their perfections to the magnificence and generosity of sovereigns who have paid for them as to those who composed them; otherwise music would still be limited to the chant of the church, and bounded by private concerts, as may be seen in states where spectacles are not yet enjoyed.[12]

[12] Ibid.

In summary, he finds,

One can say also without ostentation that the French operas outdo those of Italy by the size and beauty of the choruses, by the *agrements* of the recitative, as well as by the authority of execution by the instruments of the orchestra, whose symphony is inimitable, as well as by the magnificence of the ballet *entrées* and the *danses élevées, danses bases*, or *danses figures* ... executed by dancers who know the art of characterizing the passions through movements of the dance with grace and a nobility worthy of admiration that is not found in Italy.[13]

[13] Ibid.

Charles de Brosses gives us a lengthy and very interesting account of Italian opera at the end of the Baroque. He begins his discussion of French and Italian opera by acknowledging that Italy has larger and more beautiful opera houses than France, mentioning in particular one in Rome built by a French gentleman in the service of Queen Christina. He makes the curious observation that in Italy the audience never sits on the stage. This is done only in France, where "a thousand people go to the comedy more for the spectators than for the spectacle."[14] His following remarks reflect the fact that Italian opera was much more public than that in France.

[14] Charles de Brosses, *Lettres familières écrites d'Italie en 1739 et 1740* (Paris, 1885), quoted in MacClintock, *Readings in the History of Music in Performance*, 271ff. De Brosses (1707–1777), a magistrate and president of the Parliament of Dijon, was a highly educated man in the fields of art, literature, music and the study of antiquities.

> The parterre is filled with benches, like a church, where people sit. It is no less noisy for that reason; it is a clam shell of cabals in favor of the artists, of applause when the favorite of one faction is singing ... in a word, a racket so disturbing, so indecent, that the first row of loges becomes uninhabitable. It is turned over to the disreputable women because it is too close to the parterre ...
>
> Respectable people rent the second, third, and even, if the hall is crowded, the fourth row of loges; the highest ones are for the common people ...
>
> [The loges being rented by the season], I come there as I would to my own house. You use your lorgnette to see who of your acquaintance is there, and you visit each other if you want to. The taste that those people have for spectacles and music is shown more by their presence than by the attention they pay. When the first performances are over, when the silence is rather modest, even on the parterre, it is not good manners to listen except in the interesting passages ...
>
> I took it into my head to play chess one time when I was almost alone in the La Valle theater with Rochement, at the charming *Dangerous Liberty* ... which amuses me more than their great tragedies. Chess is wonderfully suited to fill in the emptiness of those long recitations, and the music to interrupt one's too great attention to chess.

Opera being a public, commercial enterprise in Italy, De Brosses explains that one who wishes to produce an opera must rent a theater, contract singers, instrumentalists, workmen and decorators, and "often winds up going bankrupt."

In one interesting observation, De Brosses comments on the Italian tendency for several composers to use the same libretto.

> A lyric poem once set to music is common property; composer musicians are not rare; whenever one of them wants to work he seizes upon a poem already published, already set to music by several others; for this he makes new music to the same words. They especially take the operas of Metastasio; there are scarcely any of them that the famous masters have not worked on by turns. This method is useful and easy; one should use the same method in France, where operas often fail through the fault of the poet, it being impossible to compose good music to bad words.[15]

[15] Ibid., 273. De Brosses adds here that he had several times encouraged Rameau to compose operas in a different style than Lully and reports Rameau answering that he was afraid of being accused of vanity and of trying to surpass the old masters.

Tartini, according to De Brosses, complained of instrumental composers in Italy attempting to write for the voice, instead of remaining with their field of expertise.

> I have been begged to write for the theaters of Venice, and I have never been willing, knowing full well that a throat is not the fingerboard of a violin. Vivaldi, who tried to compose in both genres, was always hissed in one, while he succeeded in the other.[16]

[16] Ibid., 277.

Turning now to comparing the style of opera in France and Italy, De Brosses points out that the French prefer strange and fanciful plots, sacrificing Truth and realism in order to bring together,

> a great number of diverse amusements and the perpetual amusement of the senses. For that we have done well to choose fables, enchantments, magic which leans toward the marvelous, machines, the intrusion of divinities, varieties of festivals, dances and spectacles.[17]

The Italians, on the other hand, seem to regard opera as a means of adding music to make tragedy more effective than if it were simply recited. This, of course, was exactly the thinking which resulted in the creation of opera in the first place.

[17] Ibid., 283. De Brosses mentions with regret that Pergolesi had just died at age twenty-three [actually, twenty-six]. Had he lived, says De Brosses, he might have become as famous as his teacher, Vinci, whom he says was regarded as the Lully of Italy.

> This idea would be good if it were correct; but it has only a first appearance of truth. Indeed, in the violent movements of the soul, song, which is a kind of exaggerated voice, becomes quite natural, and it is very true that a strongly passionate sentiment will move the hearers more strongly when it is joined to music than it does with simple declamation; but except for these great movements, song becomes ridiculous in a tragedy.

This leads De Brosses to make a personal objection to the handling of the emotions in French opera and finally to state his preference for tragedy over opera, for the reason of mind above the senses.

> Another and greater fault of our best musical tragedies is that, at the moment when the action has moved you the most,

> you are diverted from your emotion because your eyes are occupied by a dance and your ears by a song, each of which forms an amusement of another kind and lets the sentiment grow cold, which the action must reheat when it returns to the stage. The opera, because it tries to present too many pleasures at one time, decreases the enjoyment: also, with many agreeable moments, there are moments of boredom, which the good French [spoken] tragedies do not have, where the interest produces its effect without diversion; it grows by degrees, and from act to act finds the heart stirred by the preceding act.
>
> The partisans of opera will say that one does not go to the opera for the subject, but for the accessories of the music, the spectacle, and the dance; that is true: it is also what makes me prefer comedy and tragedy, because the pleasures of the mind are more lively than those of the eyes or ears.[18]

[18] Raguenet, "Parallèle des Italiens et des Français," 484.

In general, however, De Brosses had genuine appreciation for the music of Italian opera.

> The Italians like to have all kinds of songs, which create the many different pictures of which music is capable. They have some very noisy ones, full of music and harmony, for brilliant voices; others have agreeable singing with delicate turns of phrase for fine and flexible voices; others are passionate, tender, touching, true in their expression of feelings, which are of a nature suitable for theatrical expression and for enhancing the play of the actor ... This music is so beautiful, so astonishing, it paints objects with such art and such truth, that one is quite willing to pardon still greater faults, like that of making a character stay on the stage to sing a very long aria at a time when danger urges him to flee.

De Brosses found recitative in general boring, claiming one day he asked an Englishman if he found the French recitative "as flat and ridiculous" as that of the Italians. "Just as ridiculous," said the Englishman, "I assure you that both are equally boring and insupportable in the highest degree."

He was particularly pleased with the new form which we recognize as opera buffa.

> These little farces have only two or three comic characters; the music is simple, gay, natural, comic in its expression, lively, and laughable in the highest degree ... Add to that

the air of truth with which it is presented by the musicians and the actors, and the strange precision of the execution. These *bouffons* weep, laugh loudly, work hard, do all kinds of pantomime, without missing the tempo by an eighth of a second. I admit that these kinds of plays, when they are like the *Maitre de Music* by Scarlatti, the *Serva padrona, Livietta e Tracollo* by my charming Pergolesi, give me more pleasure than any of the others. The intellectuals who esteem only their serious plays laugh at me for my infatuation for these farces. But I stick to my opinion that the less serious the music is, the better Italian music succeeds.[19]

[19] Charles de Brosses, *Lettres familières*, 286ff.

By 1746, the element of the drama is all but swept aside. Although Batteux offers an almost Wagnerian plea for the unity of the arts, he confesses that in opera "if music is to be preeminent, it alone has the right to display all its wares. The stage is hers to command. Poetry and dance take the second and third places."

11 Voltaire on Opera

> The opera is a public meeting place where people assemble themselves on certain days, without knowing why.[1]
> *Voltaire, 1732*

VOLTAIRE COMMENTS FREQUENTLY ON OPERA, in part no doubt due to the fact that it was generally a much discussed topic in France. We suspect he was not an avid fan of the music itself, for his commentary deals mostly with various aspects of the literary content of opera. Nevertheless, in one essay, he correctly points out that the purpose of the music in opera is not conceptual ideas, but the expression of emotions.

> All those glittering thoughts to which men have given the appellation of wit, ought never to have been admitted into great works, composed for the instruction of the public, or calculated to move the passions. I would not even hesitate to say they ought to be banished from our operas. Music expresses the passions, the sentiments, and the images: but what accents are able to express an epigram? Quinault has formerly been sometimes neglected, yet he was always natural.[2]

While today we think of Europe as having a single musical culture, whereas it's languages, food and customs vary distinctly, it is interesting that Voltaire could remark, "In no art are national characteristics more marked than in that of music."[3] In making this statement, however, it is evident he was thinking primarily of opera and the French language.

> French music, especially the vocal, is disliked by all other nations. It cannot be otherwise, because the French prosody

[1] Letter to Pierre Robert le Cornier de Cideville, quoted in Julie Sadie, "Paris and Versailles," in *The Late Baroque Era* (Englewood Cliffs: Prentice Hall, 1994), 168.

[2] "Wit," in *The Works of Voltaire* (New York: St. Hubert Guild, 1901), XXXVII, 62ff. Quinault was the librettist associated with Lully.

[3] "The Age of Louis XIV," xxxii, in Ibid., XXIII, 300.

or versification differs from that of every other country of Europe. We make the pauses always upon the last syllable, whereas all others make it upon the penult, or antepenult, as the Italians. Our language is the only one that has words terminating in *e* mute, and those *e*'s that are not pronounced in ordinary discourse ... Hence it comes, that most of our songs and recitative are insupportable to those who have not been accustomed to them. The climate denies us that flexibility of voice which it gives the Italians, and it is not custom among us, as at Rome and other Italian courts, to make eunuchs of men, in order to render their voices finer than those of women. All these things, joined to the slowness of our singing, which, by the bye, forms a strange contrast with our native vivacity, will always make the French music disagreeable to any but Frenchmen ...

Jean Baptiste Lully, who was born at Florence in 1633, and came to France at the age of fourteen, when he could perform on no instrument but the violin, was the parent of French music. He knew how to suit his art to the genius of the language, which was the only sure way to succeed: but at that time the Italian music had not begun to deviate from that gravity and noble simplicity which we still admire in Lully's recitative.

Voltaire disagrees with the criticism by the great French critic, Boileau, that the lyrics which Quinault furnished Lully were unmusical.

Those hackneyed thoughts, so wanton yet so tame,
That Lully strove to warm at music's flame.

Voltaire maintains here that it was in fact Quinault's diction which "animated the music still more than Lully's art did the words."

This last comment is given more extended discussion in a long letter of 1767 to Chabanon. Since by 1767 Lully had long past become old-fashioned, it is not particularly surprising that Voltaire here seems critical of the actual melodies of Lully and finds his strength in his understanding of the French language. The composer Voltaire praises here was Jean Benjamin de La Borde (1734–1794), a now forgotten composer of more than thirty operas. He was guillotined during the French Revolution.

I am not too much of an expert in C G C and F C F. I am hard of hearing, a bit deaf. However, I confess to you that there are tunes in *Pandora* that have given me considerable pleasure. In spite of myself, I remember for example:

Ah! You have grandeur and glory for yourself.

Other tunes have made a great impression on me and still leave a confused noise in my eardrum ...

I agree that most of Lully's ariettas are trivial tunes and Venetian barcaroles. Therefore, they are not remembered as being good but as being facile. But if one only has taste, one can fix all of poetic art and all four acts of *Armide* in one's memory. Lully's declamation is so perfect a recitative that I recite it entirely by following his notes and by only softening its intentions. [It has] a very great effect on the audience, and no one remains unmoved. Lully's declamation then is in nature. It is adapted to language; it is the expression of feeling.

If this admirable recitative no longer produces the same effect today as in the beautiful age of Louis xiv, it is because we no longer have any actors. They are in short supply in every genre, and besides Lully's ariettas have done his recitative harm and people penalize his recitative for the weakness of his symphonies. One must admit that there is considerable arbitrariness in music. All I know is that there are things in M. de La Borde's *Pandora* that have given me extreme pleasure.[4]

In one of his poems, Voltaire offers some additional insights into his personal preferences in artists associated with the opera.

> Each noble art inflamed my breast;
> Painting delights me; oft I've been,
> At the king's or duke's palace, seen
> Gazing on works with raptured eye,
> Where art with nature seems to vie;
> Paul Veronese's noble fire
> And skill divine I much admire;
> Poussin and Raphael, my sight
> Ravish with exquisite delight.
> From those rooms to the opera, I
> Upon the winds of pleasure fly;
> What there gives pleasure, from me draws
> The tribute of deserved applause.

[4] Letter to Michel-Paul Gui de Chabanon (December, 1767), in *The Selected Letters of Voltaire*, trans., Richard Brooks (New York: New York University Press, 1973), 267ff.

> In music, Mauret's sprightly strain,
> Destouche's grace, my praise obtain,
> Pelissier's art, Le More's fine voice,
> Pleasing by turns, suspend my choice.[5]

[5] "Answer to a Lady, or a Person who wrote to Voltaire as such," in Ibid., XXXVI, 180ff.

In his article on singing, in the *Philosophical Dictionary*, Voltaire, focusing again more on language than singing, suggests that others were critical of Lully. We must point out here that the reader must keep in mind that Voltaire was suffering under a both a mistranslation and a misunderstanding of Aristotle's comments about music in Tragedy. The fact is we do not know today exactly what the role of music was in Greek theater, but judging by Aristotle it was a role much more important than just having the "Chorus" recite a kind of recitative.

> It is very probable that the *melopée*, or modulation, regarded by Aristotle in his poetic art as an essential part of tragedy, was an even, simple chant, like that which we call the preface to mass, which in my opinion is the Gregorian chant, and not the Ambrosian, and which is a true *melopée*.
> When the Italians revived tragedy in the sixteenth century the recitative was a *melopée* which could not be written; for who could write inflections of the voice which are octaves and sixths of tone? They were learned by heart. This custom was received in France when the French began to form a theater, more than a century after the Italians. The *Sophonisba* of Mairet was sung like that of Trissin, but more grossly; for throats as well as minds were then rather coarser at Paris. All the parts of the actors, but particularly of the actresses, were noted from memory by tradition. Mademoiselle Buaval, an actress of the time of Corneille, Racine, and Molière, recited to me, about sixty years ago or more, the commencement of the part of Emilia in *Cinna*, as it had been played in the first representations by La Beaupré. This modulation resembled the declamation of the present day much less than our modern recitative resembles the manner of reading the newspaper.
> I cannot better compare this kind of singing, this modulation, than to the admirable recitative of Lully, criticized by adorers of double crochets, who have no knowledge of the genius of our language, and who are ignorant what help this melody furnishes to an ingenious and sensible actor.[6]

[6] *Philosophical Dictionary*, "Singing," in *The Works of Voltaire*, XIII, 209ff.

In as much as opera was a constant subject of discussion in Baroque France, it is no surprise to find references to it in Voltaire's poetry. It is also no surprise to find him employing his love of satire on this subject in his poem "The Temple of Taste." His principal targets here are the cultural pretense of aristocrats and the encroachment of Italian opera on the French language.

> This was a concert given by a gentleman of the long robe, infatuated with music, which he never learned, and chiefly with the Italian music, which he had no knowledge of, but from some indifferent airs which were never heard at Rome, and which are very badly sung in France by some girls belonging to the opera.
>
> They then caused a long French recitative, set to music by an Italian, who did not understand our language, to be performed. It was to no purpose to remonstrate to him, that as this sort of music is nothing more than notated declamation, it is of consequence, subjected to the genius of the language; and that nothing can be as ridiculous as French scenes sung in the Italian taste, except Italian ones sung in the French taste.
>
>> Nature ingenious, fertile, wise,
>> Earth with gifts various beautifies;
>> She speaks to all in language fit,
>> They differ both in tongue and wit;
>> Their tone, their voices suit; each note
>> Is by the hand of nature wrote;
>> And every difference must appear
>> To a refined, judicious ear.
>> Music to charm in France, the tone
>> Of France must imitate alone.
>> Lully could to our taste descend,
>> Not strive to alter but amend.
>
> No sooner were these judicious remarks made, but the pretended connoisseur, shaking his head, cried, "Come, come, you shall soon see something new." We could not refuse to enter, and immediately after, the concert began.
>
>> The rivals then of Lully's fame,
>> Their taste and skill in art the same,
>> French verse most dissonantly played
>> With the Italian music's aid:
>> A lady, with distorted eyes,

Acted a thousand ecstasies.
A coxcomb, of his dress quite vain.
Quavered and thrilled a frantic strain,
And beat time false, which made them soon
All equally play out of tune.[7]

In this same poem there is also a brief exchange between the most famous critic of poetry, Boileau, and the librettist of Lully's operas, Quinault.

Boileau, at the express command of the God of Taste, was reconciled to Quinault, who may be considered as a poet, formed by the graces, as Boileau was by reason.

But Boileau, satirist severe,
Whilst he embraced could scarce forbear.
The lyric poet to revile,
Yet Quinault pardoned with a smile.

"I'll never be reconciled to you," said Boileau, "except you acknowledge that there are many insipid lines in those agreeable operas." "That's very possible," answered Quinault, "but you must at the same time acknowledge that you were never capable of writing *Atys* or *Armida*."[8]

And once again, Voltaire incorrectly suggests that it is Quinault, and not Lully, whom history will remember.

Quinault was much superior in his way to Lully. The former will always be read, whereas the latter, setting aside his recitative, cannot even be sung: yet in his own time [Quinault] was supposed to be indebted to Lully for his reputation: but time judges all things.[9]

In his poem, "The Worldling," Voltaire mentions his one high hope for the future of French opera, Rameau.

To the opera house he must repair,
Dance, song and music charm him there.
The painter's art to strike the sight,
Does there with that blest art unite;
The yet more soft, persuasive skill,
Which can the soul with pleasure thrill.
He may to damn an opera go,
And yet perforce admire Rameau.[10]

[7] "The Temple of Taste," in Ibid., XXXVI, 45ff.

[8] "The Temple of Taste," in Ibid., XXXVI, 67.

[9] "Notes on Some of the Writers who Lived in the Age of Louis XIV," in Ibid., XXXVIII, 207.

[10] "The Worldling," in Ibid., XXXVI, 87.

But in his poem, "Envy," there is the suggestion that Rameau fared little better with the critics than Voltaire.

> Orpheus alone should dare to hiss Rameau;
> Venus to criticize is Psyche's right;
> But why should we in censure thus delight?
> No beauty she acquires who blames a face ...[11]

[11] "Envy," in Ibid., XXXVI, 185.

Interestingly enough, Voltaire himself served as the librettist for several operas by Rameau. The only one of these which he discusses at any length in his correspondence is *Samson* (1733), which was never produced. Rameau later used some of this music in *Zorocastre* in 1749, using a new librettist.

> I committed a great blunder by writing an opera, but the desire to work for a man like M. Rameau carried me away. I thought only of his genius and did not understand that mine is not at all suited for the lyric genre. Therefore I informed him some time ago that I would rather have written an epic poem than fill in someone else's outlines. I certainly do not scorn that sort of work. None of it is despicable, but this is a talent which I believe I lack entirely. Perhaps with tranquility of mind, care, and the advice of my friends, I may succeed in achieving something less unworthy of the talents of our Orpheus. But I predict that the production of this opera will have to be postponed until next winter. It will only be improved and be more sought after by the public. Our great musician, who doubtless has enemies in proportion to his merit, must not feel sorry that his rivals are getting ahead of him. The point is not to be performed soon, but to be successful. It is better to be applauded late than to be hissed early.[12]

[12] Letter to M. Berger (c. February, 1734), in *The Selected Letters of Voltaire*, 32.

Another letter on the same subject, two years later, includes the following.

> I would hope that the indulgence with which this work has just been received might encourage our great composer Rameau to place renewed confidence in me and complete his opera on Samson along the lines I have always had in mind. My work was solely for him, I departed from the ordinary road in the poem only because he does the same in music. I thought it time to open opera to a new career. Since the

beauties of Quinault and Lully have become commonplace on the tragic stage, few persons will be bold enough to advise M. Rameau to create music for an opera in which love is absent from the first two acts. But he must have the courage to set himself above prejudice ... Let his self-interest and pride give him courage; let him promise to act entirely in concert with me; let him especially not wear his music out by having it played from house to house; let him adorn the pieces I have written for him with new beauties. I will send him the play when he wishes; M. de Fontenelle will be the examiner. I feel sure that the Prince de Carignan will be its patron and that, in the end, of all the works by this great musician it will unquestionably bring him the greatest honor.[13]

[13] Letter to M. Berger (February, 1736), in Ibid., 52ff.

Voltaire also writes extensively on the subject of national styles in opera. His most extensive discussion of this aspect of opera is contained in an essay on ancient and modern tragedy, addressed to an Italian bishop.[14] He begins with the interesting contention that music, specifically opera, has contributed to the decline of Italian tragedy.

[14] Contained in a letter to cardinal Quirini, bishop of Brescia, quoted in *The Works of Voltaire*, XXXVII, 116ff.

If your nation has not always equaled the ancients in tragedy, it is not to be attributed to your language, which is copious, flexible, and harmonious, adapted to all subjects: but it is in my opinion, extremely probable that the great progress you have made in music has in some measure put a stop to your improvement in tragedy: one perfection has destroyed another ...

One of your most celebrated authors tells us, that since the golden age in Athens, Tragedy, deserted and forsaken, wanders about from country to country in search of some kind friend that will assist and restore her to her former honors, but has as yet found none; if he means by this that no nation among the moderns has theaters where choruses are almost always on stage, singing strophes, antistrophes, and epodes, accompanied with serious dances; that we do not set our actors on stilts, or cover their faces with masks that express joy on one side and grief on the other: if he means that the declamation of your tragedies is not notated and accompanied with instruments, he is certainly in the right, and I don't know whether all this is not rather in our favor; perhaps our manner, by approaching more nearly to nature, is fully as eligible as that of the Greeks, which had much more splendor and magnificence.

But if he only designed to insinuate that this noble art is not in general so much considered since the restoration of letters as it was formerly; that there are nations in Europe who have treated with ingratitude the successors of Sophocles and Euripides; that our theaters are not like those superb edifices which the Athenians were so proud of; and that we do not take the same pains as they did in representations, which have become so necessary in large and opulent cities; we cannot but entirely agree with him.

Where shall we find any public spectacle at present that can give us any idea of the Greek stage? Perhaps in your tragedies, or operas. What say the critics, an Italian opera like the theater of Athens? Yes, the Italian recitative is exactly the *mélopée* of the ancients, a declamation in notes, and accompanied with instruments of music: this *mélopée*, which is tiresome and disagreeable in your bad tragic operas, is admirable in those few which are good. The choruses which you have added in late years approach still nearer to the ancient chorus, as the music in them is different from that of the recitative; in the same manner as the strophe, antistrophe, and epode, among the Greeks were set to music, though they differed from the *mélopée* of the dialogue ...

I am sufficiently aware that these tragedies, which are so agreeable from the music and magnificence of the spectacle, have indeed one fault which the Greeks always avoided; a fault which has often turned pieces finely written, and in all other respects extremely regular, into monstrous and unnatural productions; I mean, the fault of bringing into every scene little songs and catches that interrupt the action, merely to show off the quavers of an effeminate voice that exerts itself to the utter destruction of probability and good sense. [Metastasio] has taken several of his tragedies from French writers, and has, by the force of his genius in some measure remedied this absurdity, which has become, as it were, necessary. The words of his songs or sonnets embellish the subject; they are full of pathos and passion ...

But what are the greatest beauties when out of their proper place? What would an Athenian audience have said, if Oedipus and Orestes, just in the very minute of discovery, the most interesting part of the drama, had entertained them with quavering out a fine song ...? We must therefore, after all, acknowledge that the opera, so bewitching to an Italian ear by its musical attractions, though on the one hand it may be said to have revived, has notwithstanding on the other, in effect, destroyed the true Greek tragedy.

Our French opera deviates still more from the right point: as our *mélopée* differs more than yours from natural declamation, and is withal more languid. It will not allow our scenes their proper length, but requires short dialogues and little sententious remarks, every one of which makes a kind of sonnet.

Let those who are thoroughly acquainted with the state of literature in other nations, and whose knowledge is not confined to the songs of our own ballets, recollect that admirable scene in *La Clerienza di Tito*, between Titus and his favorite, who had conspired against him ... Or let them read the soliloquy that follows ...

These two scenes, comparable to the finest which Greece ever produced, if not superior to them; these two scenes, worthy of Corneille when he is no declaimer, or of Racine when he is not flimsy; these two scenes, which are not founded on opera love, but on the noblest sentiments of the human heart, are at least three times as long as the longest scenes in our musical tragedies: but these would not be allowed in our Lyric theater, which is only supported by maxims of gallantry, and ill-painted passions, except the *Armida*, and some fine scenes in *Iphigenia*, works more admired than imitated among us.

Among the many faults of our operas, we have, like you, a number of little detached songs, even in the most tragical parts, and which are more inexcusable than yours, because they have less affinity to the subject; the words are generally submitted entirely to the composers, who not being able to express themselves in the manly and vigorous terms of our language, require soft, vague, and effeminate words, foreign to the action, and adapted as well as they can to little ballads, like those which at Venice are called "Barcarole." Where, for instance, is the connection between Theseus, just discovered by his father on the point of being poisoned by him, and this ridiculous speech:

The wisest men often fall in love,
And engage themselves they know not how.

But with all these faults I am still of the opinion, that our good tragic operas, such as *Atys*, *Armida* and *Theseus*, may give us some idea of the Greek theater, because they are sung like the ancient tragedies, and because the chorus, even defective as it now is, consisting of tedious panegyrics on the morality of love, does notwithstanding, in some measure, resemble the Grecian chorus, by continuing on the stage almost throughout the piece ...

Several learned men, who are well acquainted with the works of antiquity, seem to think with me, that they are at once the copy and the destruction of the Athenian stage; a copy of it, as they admit of the *mélopée*, the choruses, machines, and deities, and at the same time the destruction of it; as they have taught our young men to be fonder of sound than sense; to prefer the tickling of their ears to the improvement of their minds; the non-sense of sing-song to sublimity of sentiment; and have besides contributed to the success of many insipid and ill-written performances, which have been supported by a few pleasing songs: and yet, in spite of all these faults, that enchantment which arises from a happy mixture of fine scenes, choruses, dances, symphony, and a variety of decorations, bears all before it, and silences even criticism itself; insomuch that the best comedy or tragedy we have is never seen so often by the same people with half the pleasure that a middling opera is. Beauties which are regular, noble, and severe are seldom much sought after by vulgar minds.

In another place, Voltaire also suggests that the tradition of the long romantic poems, such as those by Ariosto and Tasso, may have also lost favor because of opera.

What has chiefly contributed to their fall is the great perfection the stage has arrived at. In a good tragedy, or a good opera, we meet with a much greater number of sentiments than are to be found in all these enormous volumes: these sentiments are at the same time much better expressed, and there appears a much clearer knowledge of the human heart.[15]

Given the above discussion, it is surprising to find, in a discourse addressed to the French people, he acknowledges the debt of French opera to Italy.

You will allege that you are extremely successful in comic operas: but can you deny that you are indebted to Italy for your comic as well as your serious operas?[16]

But, in a letter to Chabanon, he longs for a new savior of French opera.

[15] "Notes on Some of the Writers who Lived in the Age of Louis XIV," in Ibid., XXXVIII, 277.

[16] "A Discourse to the Welsh," in Ibid., XXXVII, 94.

> I am willing to believe that Orpheus was a great musician, but if he were to return among us to create an opera, I would advise him to attend the school of Rameau.
>
> I certainly realize that today the [Parisians] only have their comic opera, but I am persuaded that geniuses like you can bring the age of Louis XIV back to them. You are the one to rekindle the remains of the sacred fire that has not yet been completely extinguished.[17]

Another general observation, in his essay, "The Ignorant Philosopher," speaks of the censorship of literature and the changing of taste.

> Most philosophical works are like La Fontaine's "Tales," which were at first burned, but were in the end brought upon the stage at the Comic Opera.[18]

Voltaire is at his outspoken best when he surveys the general decline of opera, which he dates from the preferences of the court of Louis XIV. Thinking of Duché, a *valet de chambre* of Louis XIV, Voltaire notes,

> His opera of *Iphigenia at Tauris* is his best piece. It is written in the sublime taste; and, though it is but an opera, it affords a strong idea of the best things in the Greek tragedies. This taste did not last long, and soon after we were reduced to simple ballets, consisting of detached acts, made solely for the sake of introducing the dances; thus, even the opera began to degenerate, at the same time that almost every other theatrical production was on the decline.[19]

It is apparent that Voltaire had little appreciation for the inevitable dance in opera, as we can see in a sarcastic remark in a letter to Catherine the Great.

> For some time now there has been an excellent dancer at the Paris opera. She is said to have very lovely arms. The last comic opera was not very successful, but another is to be put on which will be the wonder of the world.[20]

Returning to Voltaire's views on the decay of opera, we find another somewhat sarcastic comment, which follows a brief summary of the evolutionary climb of mankind.

---

[17] Letter to Michel-Paul Gui de Chabanon (September, 1764), in *The Selected Letters of Voltaire*, 253.

[18] "The Ignorant Philosopher," in *The Works of Voltaire*, XXXV, 298.

[19] "Notes on Some of the Writers who Lived in the Age of Louis XIV," in Ibid., XXXVIII, 283.

[20] Letter to Catherine of Russia (August, 1771), in *Voltaire and Catherine the Great*, trans. A. Lentin (Cambridge: Oriental Research Partners, 1974), 113.

Finally, after other ages, things got to the point at which we see them. Here we represent a tragedy in music; there we kill one another on the high seas of another hemisphere, with a thousand pieces of cannon. The opera and a ship of war of the first rank always astonish my imagination. I doubt whether they can be carried much farther in any of the globes with which the heavens are studded.[21]

[21] *Philosophical Dictionary*, "Man," in *The Works of Voltaire*, XI, 186.

He seemed particularly disturbed that librettists and composers relied on such things as the ancient myths, rather than legitimate plot, to attract the audience.

An Asiatic, who should travel to Europe, might well consider us as pagans; our week days bear the names of Mars, Mercury, Jupiter, and Venus; and the nuptials of Cupid and Psyche are painted in the pope's palace; but, particularly, were this Asiatic to attend our opera, he would not hesitate in concluding it to be a festival in honor of the pagan deities.[22]

[22] *Philosophical Dictionary*, "Contradictions," in Ibid., VII, 264.

......

At the opera, and in more serious productions, the gods are introduced descending in the midst of tempests, clouds, and thunder; that is, God is brought forward in the midst of the vapors of our petty globe. These notions are so suitable to our weak minds, that they appear to us grand and sublime.[23]

[23] *Philosophical Dictionary*, "Heaven of the Ancients," in Ibid., X, 17.

Some of the most curious remarks on opera by Voltaire are on the subject of manners. Voltaire never thought well of the dance and indeed in his poem, "The Maid of Orleans," the opera dancer is classed together with "the lover of a brothel's wanton joy."[24] He thought it particularly odd that members of the audience, in Paris, were allowed to climb upon the stage and dance with the actors, as he mentions in a letter to the English ambassador to Constantinople:

[24] "The Maid of Orleans," in Ibid., XL, Canto II.

We ought certainly to reflect, that everything in this world depends upon custom and opinion: the court of France have danced on the stage with the actors of the opera, and we thought there was nothing strange in it, but that the fashion of this kind of entertainment should be discontinued.[25]

[25] Letter to Mr. Falkener, in Ibid., XIX, 15.

In a letter of August 1765, to Mme Clairon, Voltaire mentions this again relative to the king himself.

Louis XIV, at the peak of his greatness, danced with dancers from the opera house within view of all Paris when he returned from the celebrated campaign of 1672.[26]

Some of Voltaire's reflections on contemporary manners were clearly intended to be humorous. In an essay, we find a fictional observer is worried that the theater is taking away the audience of the church. An "Italian" answers,

> The case is not the same at Rome, and in the other states of Europe. When a fine mass has been sung at St. John of Lateran, or St. Peter's church, with grand choruses in four parts, and when twenty castrati have sung a hymn with quavering voices, all is ours; those who composed the congregation go in the evening to drink chocolate at the opera of St. Ambrose, and nobody takes umbrage at this. Churchmen take care not to excommunicate [the famous singers] la Signora Cuzzoni, la Signora Faustina, la Signora Barbarini, and above all Signor Farinelli, knight of Calatrava, and actor of the opera, who is possessed of diamonds as big as my thumb.[27]

Finally, Voltaire had a long and close relationship with Frederick the Great in Potsdam. We find it most interesting, in a poem written for Frederick the Great, that Voltaire mentions a projected opera which apparently Frederick had planned to compose.

> Great Frederick to Berlin with speed shall repair,
> And the joy of his triumphs his true subjects shall share;
> And by a new opera, of his own writing,
> Himself shall exhibit his achievements in fighting.[28]

[26] Quoted in *The Selected Letters of Voltaire*, 257.

[27] "Dialogue between the Intendant des Menus and the abbé Brizel," in *The Works of Voltaire*, XXXVII, 252ff.

[28] "To the King of Prussia," in Ibid., XXXVI, 198.

12 Music in French Fiction

THE DEBATE OVER THE QUESTION of the ideals of ancient Greece versus contemporary virtues which permeated all facets of French intellectual society is also mentioned in the works of fiction. In Fénelon's *Telemachus*, we find the ancient Greek's use of "harmony" as a metaphor for good government, with the head of state being analogous to the conductor.

> The government of a kingdom demands a certain harmony, like Music, and just proportions, like that of architecture. If you will allow me, I will again make use of the comparison of these arts, and make you conceive what ordinary understandings those men have who govern by the detail. He who in a consort of music sings only some certain parts, although he sings them perfectly well, he is no more than a singer; he alone is the master of music who governs the whole consort, and at once regulates all the parts of it.[1]

In this same book, Fénelon makes the important point that one learns about music from performance, not from books.

> Who is it that taught you to know good and bad poets? It was frequent reading and reflection with such persons as had a true taste that way. Who is it that procured you that judgment in music? It was the same application of mind in observing musicians.[2]

Cyrano de Bergerac's *Other Worlds* [*L'Autre Monde*] of 1650 is a reflection of society's interest in the possibility of life on the other planets at a time when, even though astronomy

---

[1] Fénelon, *The Adventures of Telemachus, Son of Ulysses*, Book XII, (London: Garland Publishing, 1979, facsimile of the 1720 edition), II, 235. He continues with a similar distinction between the mason and the architect. François de Salignac de La Mothe-Fénelon (1651–1715) was a courtier, bishop of Cambrai and royal tutor to a grandson of the Louis XIV, the Duke of Burgundy.

It was as tutor for the duke of Burgundy that Fénelon wrote the most widely read French book of its time, and the following century, the *Continuation of Homer's Odyssey*. However, this book, known today as *The Adventures of Telemachus*, angered Louis XIV in its description of a tyrant. Fénelon and his friends were banished from the court, the printer was arrested and the police attempted to confiscate all copies.

[2] Ibid., Book XXIV, II, 270.

had fostered this interest, telescopes were not yet sufficient to reject the possibility that even the Moon might be inhabited. It is indeed to the Moon that the central figure of this novel first travels and a citizen of that body explains both the nature of hearing and provides a curious explanation for how music communicates emotions to the listener.

> The operation of hearing is not more difficult to conceive and for the sake of brevity let us simply consider the case of the notes of a lute touched by the hands of a virtuoso. You will ask me how I can possibly perceive something so far away from me and which I cannot see at all. Does a sponge come out of my ears and soak up this music in order to bring it to me? Or does the musician beget another little musician inside my head with a little lute and instructions to sing the same tunes to me like an echo? No; the miracle is due to the fact that the plucked string strikes the air which is composed of little bodies and drives it into my brain, gently piercing it with these little bodily nothings. If the string is taut the note is high, because it drives the atoms more vigorously and once the organ is thus penetrated it furnishes my imagination with sufficient of them from which to make its picture. If it is not so taut, it happens that when our memory has not yet completed its image, we are obliged to repeat the same sound to it; so that, for example, from the materials furnished by the measures of a saraband, it takes enough to complete the portrait of this saraband.
>
> But this operation is by no means as wonderful as those by which we are moved now to joy, now to anger with the aid of the same organ. This occurs when in the course of their movement the little bodies meet others inside us which are moving in the same manner, or whose own shape makes them susceptible to the same type of vibration. The new arrivals excite their hosts to imitate their motion and in this way when a violent tune encounters the fire of our blood, it makes it take up the same dance and excites it to thrust itself outwards, and that is what we call "the ardor of courage." If the sound is sweeter and has only the strength to raise a lesser, more quavering flame, by causing this to travel along the nerves and membranes and through the apertures in our flesh, it excites that tickling sensation which we call "joy." The other passions are aroused in the same way, according to the greater or lesser violence with which these little bodies are hurled at

us, according to the motion resulting from their contact with other impulses and according to the mobility they find in us.3

[3] Cyrano de Bergerac, *Other Worlds*, trans. Geoffrey Strachan (London: Oxford University Press, 1965), 84ff.

The characteristic, with regard to the perception of music, which most interested both the ancient philosophers and those of the Middle Ages, was that music is the only art which you cannot see. It is from this perspective that we find in Fénelon's *Telemachus* King Inachus's description of Music as an "odor," as if you can *smell* music, if you cannot see it.

> He holds in his hand a golden harp, and with eternal raptures sings the wonderful works of the gods: from his heart and his mouth an exquisite odor takes its being; the melody of his lyre and the voice were enough to ravish the gods as well as men.4

[4] Fénelon, *The Adventures of Telemachus, Son of Ulysses*, Book XIX, II, 158ff.

Only in Fénelon's *Telemachus*, among the fictional works, do we find insights into the purpose of music, and here they are all related to the communication of emotions.

> This said, Termosiris gave me a flute, of such sweetness, that the echoes of the hills, which carried the sound of every side, soon drew each neighboring shepherd round about me. My voice was endued with a Divine harmony: I found myself transported and moved, as by a superior power, to sing the graces which Nature has conferred upon the country. We passed the days and part of the nights in singing together.5

[5] Ibid., Book II, I, 36.

> ......
>
> The hollow valleys shall ring again with the consorts of shepherds, who along the crystal brooks shall sing to their pipes both of their amorous pains and pleasures.6

[6] Ibid., Book XII, I, 286.

In one place Fénelon casts this more in the example of the "ethos" of the ancient Greeks, the ability of music to change the character of the listener.

> Apollo [came to] teach the shepherds what are the charms of harmony; soften their savage hearts, show them the amiableness of virtue, and make them feel how sweet it is to enjoy, in this retirement, the innocent delights that nothing can deprive a shepherd of.7

[7] Ibid., Book I, I, 36.

Fénelon's *Telemachus* is also rich in descriptions of art music set in pastoral scenes, reminiscent of the ancient lyric poets.

Every day was a festival; nothing was heard but the warbling of the birds, or the soft whispering of the zephyrs, sporting amidst the trembling boughs, or the murmur of a transparent stream descending from some rock, or songs which the Muses inspired into the shepherds who followed Apollo.[8]

[8] Ibid., Book II, I, 35.

And,

There was at Tyre a young Lydian called Malachon, of marvelous beauty, but voluptuous, effeminate, and swallowed up in pleasure; his own study was how to preserve the delicacy of his complexion, to comb his flaxen locks, which waved upon his shoulders, to perfume himself, to adjust his robe in the nicest manner, to sing amorous songs to the music of his lute.[9]

[9] Ibid., Book III, I, 65

He paints a rather romantic picture of Egypt, with meadows full of grazing cattle, workers bending under the weight of fruit they are harvesting, and,

Shepherds that made the Echoes on every side repeat the melodious sound of their warbling flutes and pipes.[10]

[10] Ibid., Book II, I, 22.

In another place, he credits the Egyptians with the invention of "instruments of music to ravish the soul."[11]

[11] Ibid., Book VIII, I, 184.

We might also mention that in this same book, Fénelon writes a line which reminds us of the minstrel schools of the late Middle Ages.

And now the shepherd comes home again with his flute, and sings to the assembled family such new songs as he learnt in the adjacent hamlets.[12]

[12] Ibid., Book XII, I, 284.

Other references to art music are found in Marivaux's *La vie de Marianne*, where there is a brief mention of a specially composed song honoring newlyweds, "a very fine epithalamium sung to soft music"[13] and in Cyrano de Bergerac's *Other Worlds*, where a visitor from the Earth visits the Sun and finds there, among other implausible curiosities, people who have turned themselves into birds. These birds and the visitor engage in a musical dialogue, the description of which suggests that the author himself had heard art songs which were emotionally quite sensitive.

[13] Marivaux, *The Virtuous Orphan*, trans. Mary Collyer (Carbondale: Southern Illinois University Press, 1965), 506. Pierre de Marivaux (1688–1763), born Pierre Carlet, was a minor playwright and novelist. An epithalamium is a wedding song.

We serenaded one another by turns with the musical stories of our mutual loves. In my airs I sang that I was not only comforted but that I even rejoiced at my disaster since it had won me the honor of being lamented in such beautiful songs ...

I replied in my turn with all the raptures, all the tenderness, and all the subtleties of a passion so moving that two or three times I saw it on the branch ready to die of love. In truth, I mixed so much skill with the sweetness of my voice and surprised its ear with touches so cunning and ways so little frequented by its own species, that I had its fair soul at the mercy of all the passions to which I wished to subject it.[14]

[14] Cyrano de Bergerac, *Other Worlds*, 161.

Curiously, opera is not as frequently mentioned in fiction as it is in all other forms of literature. It is no doubt an accurate reflection of the times that in Crébillon, fils' *Letters from the Marchioness de M****, opera is described as a place to meet one's lover.

If it must be so, my Lord, I permit you to be at the opera, and am infinitely obliged to you for your industry, to be informed what box I shall appear in; and since you so much desire it, I shall take care to have you accommodated with a place: But, as tender as the music may be, all opera nights are not alike; and whatever soft things you may tell me, with relation to Armida and Rinaldo, I shall remember too well that I have been the one, ever to allow you to be the other.[15]

[15] Claude Prosper Jolyot de Crébillon, fils, *Letters from the Marchiness de M*** to the Count de R****, ed. Josephine Grieder (New York: Garland, 1972), 259.

Alain René Lesage, in his *Le Diable Boiteux*, presents two descriptions, remarkable in their detail, of serenades. While the novel is set in Madrid, we may assume his familiarity with serenades was gained in Paris. The first passages gives us much information about the musicians, and their literature of the latest songs sung in a "sweet" style. First we are told of the arrangements.

You may assure your cousin that I will in all things follow her advice; and that tomorrow, without fail, in the middle of the night, the street shall resound with one of the most gallant concerts that was ever heard in Madrid. And away went the intendant to secure the assistance of a celebrated musician, to whom he communicated his project, and whom he charged with the care of its execution.[16]

[16] Alain René Lesage, *Asmodeus, or The Devil on Two Sticks* [1707] (The Bibliophilist Society, 1932), 99ff. Lesage (1668–1747) was educated by the Jesuits at Vannes and traveled to Paris to study law. After serving as a tax collector, he became disgusted and turned to writing.

The lady herself is alerted that Don Como, governor of the pages, will "gratify you with the sound of music and sweet voices, in an evening serenade."

> The night came, and with it appeared, before the balcony of the lady, two carriages, from which descended the gallant Como and his confidant, accompanied by six musicians, vocal and instrumental, who commended a very decent concert, which lasted for a considerable time. They performed many of the newest songs, and sang all the songs in vogue whose verses told the power of love in uniting hearts despite the obstacles of fortune, and the inequality of rank; while at every couplet, which the general's daughter perceived to be directed to herself, her merriment knew no bounds.
> When the serenade was over, and the performers had departed in the carriages which brought them, the crowd which the music had attracted dispersed, and our lover remained in the street with Domingo alone.

Later we are told that this concert, "including the carriages and the enormous quantity of wine which its bibulous performers had consumed, cost Don Como upwards of a hundred ducats."

The second serenade which Lesage describes is unique for its high drama. Here Asmodeus, Zambullo and Don Cleophas are out walking when they hear instruments tuning at the end of the street, preparing for a serenade.

> I am a great admirer of this sort of concert, replied Zambullo; let us by all means get near them; there may chance to be some decent voices among the lot ...
> The serenade was commenced by the instruments alone, which played some new Italian songs; and then two of the voices sang alternately the following couplets:
>
> *List, while the thousand charms I sing,*
> *Which round thee such enchantment fling,*
> *that even Love has plumed his wing*
> *To seek thy bower.*
> *Thy neck, that shames the mountain snow,*
> *Thy lip, that mocks the peach's glow,*
> *Bit Cupid's self a captive bow*
> *Beneath thy power ...*

> The couplets are gallant and delicate, cried the Student. They seem so to you, replied the Devil, because you are a Spaniard: if they were translated into French, for instance, they would not be greatly admired. The readers of that nation would think the expressions too figurative; and would discover an extravagance of imagination in the conceptions, which would be to them absolutely laughable. Every nation has its own standard of taste and genius, and will admit no other: but enough of these couplets, continued he, you will hear music of another kind.
>
> Follow with your eyes those four men who have suddenly appeared in the street. See! they pounce upon the serenaders: the latter raise their instruments to defend their heads, but their frail [instruments] yield to the blows which fall on them, and are shattered into a thousand pieces.

Two cavaliers come to the rescue, one of whom paid for the serenade and is killed by the attackers.[17]

In the end, it is the evidence of the contemplative listener which confirms the presence of art music. In Fénelon's *Telemachus* we find,

> He played on his flute, and all the other shepherds resorted to the shady elms and limpid streams, to listen to his songs.[18]

In another place he makes this point much more vivid.

> Mentor took up a harp, and played on it in so masterly a manner, that Architoas let his drop from him in very spite: his eyes struck fire; his troubled face turned pale; everybody took notice of his disorder and confusion: but at the same moment Mentor's harp entirely transported the souls of all the bystanders; none of them hardly durst breathe, for fear of breaking in upon the profound silence, and so losing something of the divine music, still fearing least it would be too soon over. Mentor's voice was by no means effeminate, but tuneable, strong, and expressive of every passion he turned it to.[19]

The subjects of his songs included the praises of Jupiter, the wisdom of Minerva, the misfortunes of young Narcissus and of the death of Adonis.

> All that heard him broke into resistless tears, and felt a secret pleasure in weeping. When he gave over singing, the

[17] Ibid., 161ff.

[18] Fénelon, *The Adventures of Telemachus, Son of Ulysses*, Book II, I, 34.

[19] Ibid., Book VIII, I, 179ff.

Phoenicians looked at one another with amazement: one said, this is Orpheus, for thus with his harp he used to soften the wild beasts.

One who wished to congratulate the singer was so overcome with emotion he could not speak,

> Arichitoas ... did now begin to bestow on Mentor some commendations, but he blushed at the same time and could not proceed.

Montesquieu, in his *Persian Letters*, which describe an imaginary visit to Paris by a Turk, and his subsequent comments on the manners of society he found there, makes fun of the serious attention given to the ancient philosophers. In this work we find music for dancing where Montesquieu describes a pastoral festival in the kingdom of the Troglodytes,

> They instituted festivals in honor of the gods. Maidens, adorned with flowers, and young men celebrated them with dancing and rustic minstrelsy; then followed banquets ... It was at these gatherings that artless nature spoke.[20]

And Brantôme mentions a tradition in villages of the use of the tabor and flute to accompany the young girl to the church on her wedding day.[21]

There is also a brief reference to military music in Fénelon's *Telemachus*, which speaks of "trumpets that filled the air with martial clangors."[22]

Regarding instances of entertainment music, there are two references to banquet music in Fénelon's *Telemachus*:

> Adoam caused a magnificent repast to be brought in ... the rowers seats were all filled with musicians playing upon the flute: Architoas now and then made them pause, to introduce the sweet harmony of his voice and lyre, fit to be heard at the table of the gods, and to ravish the ears of Apollo himself.[23]

......

> At other times Ulysses appeared to him of a sudden in those feasts where joy shines forth amidst delights, and where you might hear the soft harmony of a voice, with a harp more melodious than the harp of Apollo, or the voice of all the Muses.[24]

---

[20] Montesquieu, *The Persian Letters* (London: Athenaeum, 1901), 27. The Troglodytes are mentioned in both Aristotle and Herodotus as bestial tribes living in Africa. Later, in Ibid., 262, he describes a gentleman in Paris who is so enchanted by ancient Rome that he not only collects artifacts, but travels on the old Roman roads, even though it requires him to travel miles out of his way. Charles-Louis de Secondat, Baron de Montesquieu (1689–1755), was born to a family of sufficient wealth that he was able to spend much of his time in study. Although his *L'Esprit des lois* (1748) is better known today, the *Persian Letters* became very popular and inspired Voltaire's *Lettres sur les Anglais*, 27.

[21] Brantôme, *Lives of Fair and Gallant Ladies*, trans. A. R. Allinson (New York: Liveright, 1933), 367.

[22] Fénelon, *The Adventures of Telemachus, Son of Ulysses*, Book X, I, 230.

[23] Ibid., Book VIII, I, 177ff.

[24] Ibid., Book XVIII, II, 123.

Finally, Alain Rene Lesage, in his *Le Diable boiteux*, briefly refers to a trio sung in a tavern by "a lusty Flemish captain, a chorister of the French opera, and an officer of the German guard." They have been drinking since eight in the morning and, for honor of country, each is determined to be the last standing.[25]

[25] Alain René Lesage, *Asmodeus*, 25.

Music in Fiction by Voltaire

ALL OF VOLTAIRE'S fictional romances are to some degree disguised philosophy, and the most interesting of these today are those which seem to comment on contemporary events. For example, his most famous romance, *Candide*, was written as a direct response to the earthquake in Lisbon, in November 1755, in which 30,000 were killed. The quake hit on All Saints' Day, a very significant church festival day in Europe, and thus it was the fact that so many of the faithful were among the dead that so shook Voltaire's faith. The response by some, such as Rousseau (who said man himself was to blame for being in church) and the followers of Leibniz's philosophy of optimism, astonished Voltaire. In *Candide*, Candide and Professor Pangloss (representing Leibniz) journey to Lisbon in time for the earthquake. Pangloss explains, of the tragedy,

> All this was indispensable for private misfortune makes the general good, so that the more private misfortunes there are, the greater is the general good.

Curiously, as he sometimes did, Voltaire pretended this was not his work.

> What is this brochure entitled *Candide* which people say is being scandalously circulated and is said to come from Lyons? ... It is claimed that there are people impertinent enough to impute this work, which I have never seen, to me![26]

[26] Letter to Gabriel Cramer (February, 1759), in *The Selected Letters of Voltaire*, trans. Richard Brooks (New York: New York University Press, 1973), 198.

Perhaps such statements were made in self-defense, to protect himself against the repetition of earlier unpleasant experiences with the critics. This seems all the more evident in the fact that *Candide* also includes several satirical views of the critics. Later one of these critics speaks of the "official rules" of writing drama.

> Whoever neglects any one of these rules, though he may write two or three tragedies with tolerable success, will never be reckoned in the number of good authors.[27]

[27] *Candide*, in *The Works of Voltaire* (New York: St. Hubert Guild, 1901), I, 160.

In his fictional romances, Voltaire offers humorous references to several aspects of contemporary discussion on music and society. "André Des Touches in Siam," begins with a concise reflection of Voltaire's opinion of contemporary French music and includes a reference to his favorite composer.

> André Des Touches was a very agreeable musician in the brilliant reign of Louis XIV, before the science of music was perfected by Rameau, and before it was corrupted by those who prefer the art of surmounting difficulties to nature and the real graces of composition.[28]

[28] "André Des Touches in Siam," in *The Works of Voltaire*, IV, 5.

This same romance includes a passage which reflects the ongoing discussion in France on the relative virtues of ancient and contemporary art. In the course of this story, Des Touches interviews an official from Siam named Croutef. Des Touches wants to discuss the music of Siam, which sounds discordant to him, but Croutef only wants to speak of the "harmony" of society, in the Platonic sense.

> DES TOUCHES. Tell me, I beseech you, sir, if in Siam you divide the tone major into two commas, or into two semi-commas, and if the progress of the fundamental sounds are made by one, three, and nine?
> CROUTEF. By Sammonocodom, you are laughing at me. You observe no bounds. You have interrogated me on the form of our government, and you speak to me of music!
> DES TOUCHES. Music is everything. It was at the foundation of all the politics of the Greeks. But I beg your pardon; you have not a good ear, and we will return to our subject. You said that in order to produce a perfect harmony—
> CROUTEF. I was telling you that formerly the tonsured Tartar pretended to dispose of all the kingdoms of Asia, which occasioned something very different from perfect harmony ...

However, all things go on; people divert themselves, they dance, they play, they dine, they sup, they make love; this makes every man shudder who entertains good intentions.
DES TOUCHES. And what would you have more? You only lack good music. If you had good music you might call your nation the happiest in the world.[29]

Another reference to the ancient-modern debates is found in "A Dialogue between Marcus Aurelius and a Recollet Friar." In the passage in question, the friar is bringing the famous emperor and philosopher up to date on changes in Rome since his death hundreds of years before. Among these, the friar observes,

> Peace and the fine arts flourish here eternally. The ancient masters of the world are now become music-masters. Instead of sending colonies into England, we now send them eunuchs and fiddlers.[30]

Another reference to castrati is found in *Candide*.

> I was born in Naples, he said, where they make eunuchs of thousands of children every year; some die of the operation; some acquire voices far beyond the most tuneful of your ladies; and others are sent to govern states and empires [in the East]. I underwent this operation very successfully, and was one of the singers in the princess of Palestrina's chapel.[31]

In the romance, *Jeannot and Colin*, music is included in a humorous discussion of the limited value of education for a person of high birth. There is a complaint that "the genius of young persons is smothered under a heap of useless knowledge."

> A man of quality, like the young marquis, should not rack his brains with useless sciences ... Did anybody ever so much as think of talking of geometry in good company?[32]

It is decided that it would be a virtue if the young marquis would learn to dance, especially as he seemed to have a natural talent for music.

> Nature, which does all, had given him a talent that quickly displayed itself surprisingly; it was that of singing ballads

[29] Ibid., 11ff.

[30] "A Dialogue between Marcus Aurelius and a Recollet Friar," in Ibid., IV, 68.

[31] *Candide*, in Ibid., I, 101.

[32] "Jeannot and Colin," in Ibid., III, 10ff.

agreeably. The graces of youth, joined to this superior gift, caused him to be looked upon as a young man of the brightest hopes. He was admired by the women; and having his head full of songs he composed some for his mistress. He stole from the song, "Bacchus and Love," in one ballad; from that of "Night and Day" in another; from that of "Charms and Alarms," in a third. But as there were always in his verses some superfluous feet, or not enough, he had them corrected for twenty Louis d'or a song.[33]

[33] Ibid., 12.

Finally, in "The Blind as Judges of Color," Voltaire presents a brief story of the blind in a hospital who pretend to be authorities on color. We take this as a satire on self-proclaimed experts on topics of which they know nothing, as well, perhaps, a reflection of the Scholastic views of the University of Paris, which held that one can only "know" music in its conceptual form ("speculative music") rather than by the ear. This story concludes with the observation by a deaf man that the "deaf were the only proper judges of music."[34]

[34] "The Blind as Judges of Color," in Ibid., IV, 13ff.

Is this outrageous? Did the universities really believe this? One recalls that Petrarch, in his "Remedies for Fortune Fair and Foul" (II, xcvii), wrote this curious contention:

> A deaf person can know the tones and numbers characterizing the intervals of fifth and octave, as well as the other proportions of the musical scale with which musicians work. Although one does not hear the sounds of the human voice, of strings or the organ, he nevertheless may understand in his mind their fundamental canon and, doubtless, will prefer the intellectual pleasure to a mere titillation of the ear.

We find art music in "The Princess of Babylon," where Voltaire employs a pastoral scene, so often used in Renaissance and Baroque literature, as the setting for the singing of love songs. Here there is an ensemble of birds singing the soprano and alto parts, with shepherds singing the tenor and bass. One listener, with tears flowing from her eyes, calls the resulting music "consolatory and voluptuous."[35]

[35] "The Princess of Babylon," in Ibid., III, 206.

Voltaire included two satiric views of opera in his romances. He was no lover of Italian opera, as is clear in this passage from *Candide*.

While dinner was being prepared Pococurante ordered a concert. Candide praised the music to the skies. "This noise," said the noble Venetian, "may amuse one for a little time, but if it were to last more than a half-hour, it would grow tiresome to everybody, though perhaps no one would care to admit it. Music has become the art of executing what is difficult; now, whatever is difficult cannot be long pleasing.

I believe I might take more pleasure in an opera, if they had not made such a monster of that species of dramatic entertainment as perfectly shocks me; and I am amazed how people can bear to see wretched tragedies set to music; where the scenes are contrived for no other purpose than to lug in, as it were by the ears, three or four ridiculous songs, to give a favorite actress an opportunity of exhibiting her vocal-pipes. Let who will die away in raptures at the trills of a eunuch quavering the majestic part of Caesar or Cato, and strutting in a foolish manner upon the stage, but for my part I have long ago renounced these paltry entertainments, which constitute the glory of modern Italy, and are so dearly purchased by crowned heads."[36]

[36] *Candide*, in Ibid., I, 178ff.

In "The Princess of Babylon," Voltaire satirizes the Church's objections to opera, various excesses of opera itself and the apparent tradition of nobles dating the ladies of the opera after the show, all set in the period of ancient Babylon.

After dinner he was conducted to a place of public entertainment which was enchanting, but condemned, however, by the Druids, because it deprived them of their auditors, which, therefore, excited their jealousy. The representation here consisted of agreeable verses, delightful songs, dances which expressed the movements of the soul, and perspectives that charmed the eye in deceiving it. This kind of pastime, which included so many kinds, was known only under a foreign name. It was called "an Opera," which formerly signified in the language of the Seven Mountains, work, care, occupation, industry, enterprise, business. This exhibition enchanted him. A female singer, in particular, charmed him by her melodious voice and the graces that accompanied her. This child of genius, after the performance, was introduced to him by his new friends. He presented her with a handful of diamonds, for which she was so grateful that she could not leave him all the rest of the day. He supped with her and her companions, and during the delightful repast he forgot his sobriety and became heated and oblivious with wine ... What an instance of human frailty![37]

[37] "The Princess of Babylon," in Ibid., III, 247ff.

In "The Princess of Babylon," Voltaire presents several views of functional court music, including a master of ceremonies preceded by twenty trumpets and "a great number" of musicians seated near the buffet table.[38] That this is purely functional dinner music is made clear by the following:

[38] Ibid., 169, 182ff.

> The music, which continued during the repast, furnished every prince with an opportunity of conversing with his female neighbor.

Voltaire makes several references to Church music. "The White Bull," set in the Old Testament time of Nebuchadnezzar, includes the description of a religious procession with 100 girls playing "the sacred sistrums" and priests singing in chorus "with a harmony which ravished the soul, and which melted it."

> And at every pause was heard the sound of the sistrums, of cymbals, of tabors, of psalteries, of bagpipes, harps, and sackbuts.[39]

[39] "The White Bull," in Ibid., II, 238ff.

A character in "The Study of Nature" voices an opinion which was probably near to Voltaire's own.

> If God cannot change any of the affairs of the world, what is the use of teasing him with prayers, or of singing hymns to his praise.[40]

[40] "The Study of Nature," in *The Complete Romances of Voltaire*, 312.

A final reference which should be mentioned is found in *Candide*, a work which reflects the deep impression made on Voltaire by the great earthquake in Lisbon. In a typical example of his biting satire, Voltaire writes that the Church arranged for an *auto-da-fe*, a burning of the unfaithful, as "an infallible preventive of earthquakes."[41] In his description of this execution he portrays a scene which included the singing of an anthem (which he later identifies as a *Miserere*) accompanied by bagpipes. As odd as this seems, it is a fact that the execution of the Huguenots in Paris was accompanied by lively music.

[41] *Candide*, in *The Works of Voltaire*, I, 80ff, 89.

13 Music in French Non-Fiction

OUR PURPOSE IN THIS CHAPTER is to present a sampling of first-hand observations of manners relative to the practice of music, taken from letters and memoirs of the aristocracy. We begin with a comment on the general cultural environment, as expressed in a letter from Charles de Saint-Évremond to the playwright, Corneille, in 1668.

> I believe the influence of ill taste is upon the decline; and that the first piece you shall give the public will show, by the return of their former applause, both the recovery of good sense and the restoration of reason.[1]

The "ill taste," among the aristocracy, of which Saint-Évremond speaks, is described in much more vivid terms in a letter by the Duchesse d'Orléans.

> All the young people are dreadfully debauched and given to every vice, nor are they above lying and cheating and they think that it would be a disgrace to take pride in being honorable people; all they can do is guzzle, debauch others, and use filthy language, and whoever among them is the most unmannerly is admired and esteemed the most.[2]

In a letter of 1698 she begins to complain that her own son is falling into this pattern of life, observing,

> He has changed so much that one does not recognize either his face or his temperament, and since he leads this life he no longer takes pleasure in anything; his pleasure in music, which used to be a passion, is gone too.[3]

[1] Saint-Évremond, Letter to d'Hervart, February, 1675, quoted in *The Letters of Saint-Évremond*, ed. John Hayward (Freeport, NY: Books for Libraries Press, 1971), 76. Charles de Marguetel de Saint-Denis, sieur de Saint-Évremond (1610–1703) was trained in law, but spent much of his career in the military. A letter critical of the Treaty of the Pyrenees forced him to leave France and live his remaining years in London.

[2] Letter to the Duchess Sophie, May 18, 1685, quoted in *A Woman's Life in the Court of the Sun King*, trans. Elborg Forster (Baltimore: Johns Hopkins University Press, 1984), 53. In a letter of 1700 [Ibid., 123], she mentions that the Duke d'Estrées was placed in the Bastille after a wild drinking spree in which several houses were set on fire. Elisabeth Charlotte, Duchesse d'Orléans (1652–1722), born Liselotte von der Pfalz, was a sister-in-law to Louis XIV. After the king's death, her son became Regent.

[3] Ibid., 106.

While the Duchesse praises her son's "pleasure in music," above, she placed quite a different value on actual musicians. In a letter of 1699, regarding the character of the Monsieur, she observes that he "prefers the company of lowly people, of painters and musicians, to that of people of rank."[4] This attitude reflects an attitude which had become increasingly prominent since the latter part of the sixteenth century, that a gentleman should not engage in music because he should never spend his time on any activity which requires extraordinary effort. We can see this clearly in a letter of 1647 by Saint-Évremond, when he observes,

[4] Letter to the Electress Sophie, July 26, 1699, Ibid., 114.

> Study has something cloudy and melancholy in it, which spoils that natural cheerfulness, and deprives a man of that readiness of wit, and freedom of fancy, which are required for polite conversation.[5]

[5] Quoted in Hayward, *The Letters of Saint-Évremond*, 1.

Fifteen years later, we find the gentleman's viewpoint has not changed.

> I never was much addicted to reading; and if I employ any hours that way, they are the most idle, without design, without order, when I cannot enjoy the conversation of ingenious Gentlemen, and find myself debarred from pleasurable entertainments. Do not therefore expect that I should speak to you profoundly of those things, which I have but cursorily examined, and upon which I have but slight reflections...
>
> Mathematics have, indeed, much more certainty: but when I consider the profound meditation they require, and that they draw us from the actions and pleasures, to employ us entirely in speculation, its demonstrations seem to me to be very dearly bought; and a man must be very fond of Truth to pursue it at that price.[6]

[6] Ibid., 32ff.

When contemplating a visit to London, Saint-Évremond at least expressed a preference for music over science, as he explains to d'Hervart,

> I cannot understand how I can have made you think that I was going to apply myself to [scientific experimentation], for of all things in the world, it is least to my taste... Should I visit England... I should prefer the duke of Buckingham's violin to his laboratory, however curious it might be.[7]

[7] Ibid., 94ff.

There was, in this regard, an exception made for aristocratic ladies, music being an acceptable means of spending a life of insignificant employment. No doubt many of them became proficient musicians as we can see in the instance when the Duchesse d'Orléans regrets that a talented young lady, Louise-Adelaide, is going to become a nun.

> It is a pity for this girl; she has many good traits, is most pleasing in appearance, tall, well-built, with a pretty and pleasant face, a beautiful mouth, and teeth like pearls; she dances well, has a lovely voice and is a fine musician who can sing from sight anything she likes, without grimacing and very prettily.[8]

[8] Letter to the Raugrafin Luise, March 31, 1718, quoted in Ibid., 212.

The Duchesse d'Orléans, who often complains of court manners, finds the nobles superficial even in the emotions they feel for their departed friends. She relates that after the funeral of the Dauphine, the court immediately resumed its card playing, "hunting in the afternoon, music at night."

> If this were a matter of strength of character one might perhaps appreciate it and admire them for it, but that is not the reason, for as long as they see the sad spectacle they cry, but as soon as they leave the room they laugh again and forget all about it.[9]

[9] Letter to the Duchess Sophie, June 12, 1690, quoted in Ibid., 69.

This attitude is confirmed by the Duke of Saint-Simon who observes that even the death of Louis XIV, after having reigned seventy years, was little regretted and that few persons felt a sense of loss, apart from his personal servants.[10]

[10] *The Memoirs of the Duke of Saint-Simon*, trans. Bayle St. John (London: George Allen, 1926), III, 28.

There are a number of references by the aristocratic ladies which suggest they were active performers, listeners, collectors and even composers of songs. Several times in her correspondence, Mme de Sevigne mentions singing in private. For example, in a letter of 1695,

> I have received your two letters from Chaulnes, my dear cousin; we found some verses in them that delighted us; we have sung them with extreme pleasure, and more than one person will tell you so.[11]

[11] *Letters of Madame de Sévigné*, ed. Richard Aldington (London: Routledge, 1937), II, 195. In a letter of 1680 [Ibid., II, 76], she uses the figure of speech, "We are in good tune when we are together."

In an earlier letter to the Count de Grignan, she apologizes,

I should likewise have sent you the music you desired, but have not yet been able to procure it.[12]

[12] Ibid., I, 21.

The Duchesse d'Orléans provides very interesting information about the nature of some of these songs privately sung by the ladies.

> I also have a very big book of songs. It was given to me by the good Grande Mademoiselle [the niece of Louis XIII] before she died, and it amuses me very much. At the late Monsieur's court there were many clever people who made up the funniest songs. There are people in Paris who have ten or twelve big volumes of these old songs and take very good care of them. In France one can find out about every period from songs, because songs are written about everything. They are a much better way to learn about the court than the history books; for these are full of flattery, but in the songs they sing what is really going on.[13]

[13] Letter to the Electress Sophie, January 24, 1700, quoted in *A Woman's Life in the Court of the Sun King*, 121.

Even Saint-Évremond, who often claimed he was not particularly fond of formal concerts and opera, nevertheless could quote the lyrics of popular songs in his correspondence, as for example in a letter to the Comte de Lionne in 1668.

> *Pains of Love are sweeter far*
> *Than all the other pleasures are.*[14]

[14] Quoted in *The Letters of Saint-Évremond*, 63.

In a letter to the same the following year, we find,

> Now you are perfectly cured, relish the pleasure of it, and let me make melancholy reflections on the song you have taught me:
>
> > *But oh! when Age benumbs our veins,*
> > *No longer sprightly Joy remains!*
>
> If there be any songs as agreeable as this in the music of [*Les Plaisirs de l'Isle enchantée*], I desire you to send them to me [arranged with accompaniment].[15]

[15] Ibid., 79.

As the correspondence and memoirs by these French aristocrats rarely mention general philosophical problems in aesthetics, we are not surprised to find the same is true with regard to music. We should like to mention, however, two comments relative to the purpose of music. First, in a letter to the Earl of St. Albans in 1677, Saint-Évremond writes of the familiar purpose of music to soothe the listener. He recommends, in this case, preparing for approaching death in the manner of Monsieur des Yveteaux of Paris.

> He died at eighty years of age, causing a saraband to be played to him, a little before he expired, that his soul, as he expressed himself, might slide away the easier.[16]

Mme de Sevigne mentions, if indirectly, the purpose of music to communicate feeling in a letter to Mme de Grignan. She recalls that after a performance of Molière's *Tartuffe*, the minuet and gigues played at a ball "nearly reduced me to tears, for they brought you so fresh to my remembrance."[17]

Saint-Évremond, in a letter to d'Hervart on the subject of opera, is particularly interesting for its contention that music communicates feelings, but spoken words communicate action.

> I do not deny but that the music may be very beautiful in some places, and the dances marvelous, but that opera, seeing how it is composed, should be perfect in every part, is an impossibility ... There is nothing so ridiculous as having an action sung, whether it be the deliberation of a Council, the giving of orders in battle, or anything else. Where the Gods are concerned there may be singing: every Nation has worshiped them in song, and chanted their praises. We can sing what we feel and suffer, for grief and affection are naturally expressed by a kind of tender and melancholy song. But our actions require no other expression but the spoken word. Moreover, operas are so contrived that all the spirit of the production is lost in our enjoyment of the music, which is not worth it, however enchanting it may be. For where the mind has too little to do, it is impossible, in the long run, that our senses, which we are most eager to please, should not begin to languish. The best poet is obliged to degrade himself in favor of the musician, since his lines must be arranged, less for the meaning he would have them represent, than for the convenience of the musician and the smoothness of his songs.[18]

To another correspondent, however, he is quick to note that he himself is not moved by the emotions of opera!

[16] Ibid., 189. In Vigneul Marville, *Mélanges d'histoire et de litterature* (Paris, 1725), I, 177, this same Frenchman is described.

> He ended his days in a world of his own, dressed as a shepherd, the birds hopping on to his flute piped to an imaginary flock ...

[17] Letter of 1671, in *Letters of Madame de Sévigné*, I, 68.

[18] Letter to d'Hervart, February, 1675, quoted in *The Letters of Saint-Évremond*, 161ff.

> The passionate songs at the opera make no impression upon me of themselves; they have no manner of influence over me.[19]

In the correspondence of several persons we are given the information that the opera, like the theater, was under attack by the Church. A letter of 1680 by Mme de Sévigné mentions in passing the censorship of opera.

> The opera (*Proserpine*) is superior to every other. The Chevalier tells me he has sent you several of the songs, and that he saw a gentleman who said he had sent you the words; I dare say you will like it. There is a scene in it, between Mercury and Ceres, which requires no interpreter to be understood; it must have been approved, since it has been performed; but you will judge for yourself.[20]

The Duchesse d'Orléans, as well, cannot understand why the Church is opposed to opera and plays, as she mentions in a letter to the Electress Sophie in December 1694.

> If the rumors that are flying are true, the boredom here will soon get worse, for they say that all operas and plays are to be done away with and that the Sorbonne has orders to work on this. I am certain that this will be no more to Your Grace's taste than it is to mine, and what seems most peculiar is that they go after such innocent things and forbid them, even though the most dreadful vices are in vogue now, such as murder by poison, assassination, and abominable sodomy; but nobody objects to these and the preachers only preach against the poor plays, which do not hurt anyone and in which one sees vice punished and virtue rewarded.[21]

In a letter of 1701, she mentions that the king no longer attends the opera[22] and in 1709 she reveals,

> My confessor does not forbid me to go to the opera or to the theater, except on the day before confession; he would be pleased if I did not go at all, but since I know what I do there is not sinful I have no scruples whatsoever about it.[23]

There are a few interesting comments relative to the practice of opera performance in the Court at this time. Saint-Simon recalls the celebration of the marriage of the Duke

---

[19] Letter to Duchesse Mazarin, 1676, quoted in Ibid., 168.

[20] *Letters of Madame de Sévigné*, II, 57ff.

[21] Letter to the Electress Sophie, December 16, 1694, quoted in *A Woman's Life in the Court of the Sun King*, 85.

[22] Ibid., 140. In a letter of 1716, however, she mentions the king was fond of music.

[23] Ibid., 176.

de Burgundy lasted several days and suggests that such festivities often concluded with an opera.

> The king took them into the theater, where Destouches's opera of *Issé* was very well performed. The opera being finished, everybody went his way, and thus these marriage-fêtes were brought to an end.[24]

Regarding this same duke, who became the Regent following the death of Louis XIV, Saint-Simon tells us that he regularly attended the opera at five o'clock and sometimes returned with an "opera girl" as one of his mistresses.[25] In another place he observes that the opera in question was in the Palais Royal, that it was well-guarded on the days of a performance and that a machine had been built to cover the pit when the opera was used for balls.[26] Of another noble, he mentions that "Paris loved Monseigneur, perhaps because he often went to the opera."[27]

One of Saint-Simon's most interesting comments is relative to the vanity of Louis XIV.

> Without voice or musical knowledge, he used to sing, in private, the passages of the opera prologues that were fullest of his praises! He was drowned in vanity; and so deeply, that at his public suppers—all the Court present, musicians also—he would hum these self-same praises between his teeth, when the music they were set to was played![28]

Among the correspondence and memoirs of the French aristocrats we also find some interesting descriptions of, and information regarding, actual performances which they heard. A letter of 1676 by Mme de Sévigné seems to imply there was rather frequent music at court.

> There is always music, to which [the king] occasionally listens, and which has an admirable effect; in the meantime, he chats with the ladies, who are accustomed to have that honor.[29]

The Duke of Saint-Simon agrees that Louis XIV regularly listened to music in "Madame de Maintenon's rooms," and on one occasion describes this as "a grand concert."[30]

Among the participants, Saint-Évremond mentions "Mademoiselle Sivert, who sings Italian songs better than any I have

---

[24] *The Memoirs of the Duke of Saint-Simon*, I, 109.

[25] Ibid., III, 59.

[26] Ibid., III, 61. The duke also observes [Ibid., III, 125],

> The Regent, without having the horrible vice or the favorites of Henry III, had even more than that monarch become notorious for his daily debauches, his indecency, and his impiety.

In another place [Ibid., III, 410], the duke mentions that the Regent had said he would like to die suddenly. After the latter's death, Saint-Simon reflected,

> I shudder to my very marrow, with the horrible suspicion that God, in His anger, granted his desire.

[27] Ibid., I, 206.
[28] Ibid., II, 359.

[29] Quoted in *Letters of Madame de Sévigné*, I, 238.

[30] *The Memoirs of the Duke of Saint-Simon*, II, 348.

heard in my life,"[31] and the Duke of Saint-Simon recalls one noble lady, Madame la Duchesse, who "had the art of writing witty songs."[32] Regarding "witty" songs, the Duchesse d'Orléans mentions in several of her letters popular songs written in satire of the king. In one letter she suggests that these feelings were not deeply felt.

> I know the French; they may be angry at their king, but their anger goes no further than the singing of songs against his Majesty, and for all that, every one of them would rather starve to death than leave their king without money.[33]

Nevertheless, in another letter she mentions,

> I am sending Your Grace a song … expressing discontent with the king and the Prince de Conti, which I could not send through the mail.[34]

Functional music can become art music under circumstances that included a contemplative listener. We have such a case, regarding more serious vocal music, when Mme de Sévigné, writes of the funeral service for Chancellor Peter Seguier in 1672.

> As the for the music, it was fine beyond all description. Lully exerted himself to the utmost and was assisted by all the king's musicians. There was an addition made to that fine *Miserere*, and there was a *Libera* which filled the eyes of the whole assembly with tears. I do not think the music in heaven could exceed it.[35]

Regarding instrumental music at court, Saint-Évremond mentions several harpsichordists in his correspondence, beginning with a performance by Jacques Chambonnières, the great keyboard player employed by Louis XI.

> Monsieur de Chambonnière's Corantos, which you sent me, are pretty, but they are not his best; the Sarabande is very agreeable, and in his true manner. I once heard him play a Suite of Corantos in a concert at the Duc de Joyeuse's, with which I was enraptured. I have asked you to send me his *Springtime*, for which Monsieur Servien wrote the words; it begins with a Coranto, continues with a Sarabande, and ends

[31] Letter to d'Hervart, July, 1669, quoted in *The Letters of Saint-Évremond*, 96.

[32] *The Memoirs of the Duke of Saint-Simon*, I, 83.

[33] Letter to the Electress Sophie, December 22, 1702, quoted in *A Woman's Life in the Court of the Sun King*, 149.

[34] Ibid., 150.

[35] *Letters of Madame de Sévigné*, I, 110.

with a Chaconne. I shall be obliged if you can send them all, as well as *Young Zephyrs* and the *Suite of Corantos*. All this is a burden, but as they are old pieces, they will not be difficult to obtain, and you could certainly have them copied by some scholar who is familiar with Monsieur de Chambonnière's style.[36]

In other places he mentions "Baillon, who is an excellent performer on the harpsichord,"[37] and an English artist.

It would be agreeable to visit Mrs. Bond. You are certain there of winning a little, and of hearing the harpsichord played better than anyone you can hear in England.[38]

Nevertheless, in a letter of 1671, he comments,

The elegant harmony of concerts, engages me not so much.[39]

The Duchesse d'Orléans, in a letter during one of the coldest winters in recent memory, describes a failed concert.

Last night we had a concert, but it was not very good because half of the musicians could not make their way up the hill in their hackney coach, for all the streets are icy.[40]

As might be expected for a court environment, this literature contains references to a wide variety of functional music. One of the more curious of these is in a letter of 1680 by Mme de Sévigné which mentions the execution of a noble lady, Catherine Monvoisin, who enjoyed a local reputation in Paris as a provider of poison to needy nobles. Among the latter was Racine, of whom it was rumored that he murdered his mistress, Therese du Parc.[41] Mme de Sévigné described "La Voisin" singing psalms in mockery in her cell in the days before her execution.

There are numerous references to more traditional Church music. Saint-Évremond makes his most fervent comments about music when it is that of the Church, as we can see in a letter to Monsieur Justel in 1681.

Nor is your austerity less wild in the silencing our music, than in condemning our images. You ought to remember that David recommended nothing so earnestly to the Jews, as the

[36] Letter to d'Hervart [1669], quoted in *The Letters of Saint-Évremond*, 93ff.

[37] Letter to Duchesse Mazarin, 1691, quoted in Ibid., 294.

[38] Letter to Mme de la Perrine (c. 1700–1703), quoted in Ibid., 370.

[39] Letter to Mareschal de Crequi, [1671], quoted in Ibid., 115.

[40] Letter to the Electress Sophie, February 7, 1709, quoted in *A Woman's Life in the Court of the Sun King*, 171.

[41] To protect Racine, the king had the court records suppressed, hence the details are lost to history.

celebrating of the praises of the Almighty with all sorts of instruments. Music in churches exalts the soul, purifies the mind, moves the heart, inspires and raises devotion.[42]

[42] Quoted in *The Letters of Saint-Évremond*, 234.

The Duchesse d'Orléans, Elisabeth Charlotte, being German-born, was usually bored when hearing the music of the Church sung in Latin and French. On one occasion when a cough kept her from sleeping for three days,

> I remembered that I always sleep in church as soon as I hear preaching and nuns singing. Therefore I drove to a convent where there was to be a sermon. The nuns had barely begun to sing when I went to sleep, and I slept throughout the three-hour service; that made me feel much better.[43]

[43] Letter to the Duchess Sophie, March 19, 1693, quoted in *A Woman's Life in the Court of the Sun King*, 81.

She mentions this again a few years later.

> If your Grace were Catholic and had to go to mass, she would find it even more boring, for not only is it always exactly the same, but one never hears anything but the singing of vowels, like "aaaa eeee oooo iiii"; it is enough to make one burst out of one's skin with sheer impatience.[44]

The Duke of Saint-Simon mentions that the musicians of Louis XIV always sang an anthem when he went to mass.[45]

The Duchesse d'Orléans also writes of the music of the Lutherian church.

[44] Letter to the Electress Sophie, January 15, 1696, quoted in Ibid., 89. In a letter of 1719, she mentions that Louis XIV never used trumpets and timpani in church.
[45] *The Memoirs of the Duke of Saint-Simon*, III, 22.

> What has become of the hymns that used to be sung in Hanover during Advent? In my day, no Advent passed without the hymn "Now Comes the Heathens' Savior . . ." It seems to me that the Lutherans rarely have musical instruments in their churches; in my day we did not have any and everyone sang together, just as Your Grace does in her church. It seems to me that singing alone is much more entertaining than the finest instrumental music. If the angels in heaven can assume human shape and human voices, they must sing beautifully, but I doubt that Our Lord is all that amused by instruments.[46]

In another letter she mentions the Lutheran hymn, "O Man Repent Your Grievous Sins."

[46] Letter to the Electress Sophie, December 16, 1699, quoted in *A Woman's Life in the Court of the Sun King*, 118.

> I still know the melody and at least six stanzas of this very long hymn. It is really much more agreeable when one can

sing along instead of having to listen to some bawling in a language that one does not even understand.47

And in yet another letter she mentions the music for New Year's.

"In dulci jubilo-ho-ho, sing, Christians, and rejoy-hoy-hoyce, our hearts' deli-hi-hight lies in praesepio-ho-ho, and sparkles like the su-hu-hun, matris in gremio-ho-ho, alpha es et o-ho-ho, alpha es et o." If Your Grace has not sung this herself today, I am certain at least that the timpani and trumpets have played it for her, since today is New Year's Day for Your Grace.48

We have a glimpse of ceremonial music heard by the public, when the Duchesse d'Orléans describes a ceremony to lay a cornerstone.

Today I rose a good hour later than usual because I had gone to bed an hour late yesterday. I did not return from Paris until ten o'clock at night; I had driven there at half past ten in the morning in order to perform a most tiresome and long-winded ceremony in a monastery called l'Abbeye au Bois, namely, the laying of a cornerstone for a new church. I was quite embarrassed, for I was received to the sound of timpani, trumpets, shawms, pipes, tambors and gun salutes. I had to walk through an alley along the foundation with all that noise ahead of me ... You can imagine how this attracted the populace. Before this fine procession I had already heard mass with beautiful music at the monastery. At the place of the foundation stone the priests sang three psalms in Latin and also recited some prayers of which I did not understand a word.49

We find descriptions of rather unusual civic music when the Duke of Saint-Simon relates the drums began to march through Paris at five o'clock in the morning when the king requested the Parliament to meet at the Tuileries50 and an instance in 1717 when "guards with drums at each end of the street" were used to control traffic.51

Regarding music for dance, Mme de Sévigné, referring to the son of one of her noble lady friends mentions, "he took a hautboy with him, and they danced till midnight."52 The Duchesse d'Orléans, on the other hand, complains,

[47] Ibid., 158. In a letter to Sophie of May 24, 1705, she mentions an interesting anecdote regarding the death of the Emperor Leopold.

> When the emperor, having received the sacraments, asked the doctors whether they knew of anything else that might help him. When they answered this question with "No," he called for all his musicians, sang hymns to their accompaniment, and thus died singing.

[48] Letter to the Electress Sophie, March 8, 1699, quoted in Ibid., 111.

[49] Letter to the Raugrafin Luise, June 9, 1718, quoted in Ibid., 213ff.

[50] *The Memoirs of the Duke of Saint-Simon*, III, 138ff.

[51] Ibid., III, 223.

[52] *Letters of Madame de Sévigné*, II, 138.

I spent the first days of carnival being sick and the last days being bored by watching poorly danced minuets.[53]

The Duke of Saint-Simon mentions the capture of military timpani—an important symbol of victory in the field.

We took all their cannon ... a quantity of flags, and some pairs of timpani. The victory was complete.[54]

Several correspondents refer to the elaborate entertainment music provided at Versailles. A letter of Mme de Sévigné, of 1676, mentions "they went afterwards in gondolas upon the canal, where there was music."[55] The Duchesse d'Orléans, describes the entertainments given on Monday, Wednesday and Fridays by the king in a new gallery built to connect his apartments with those of the queen. These evenings, called, "*jours d'appartement*," began with the men and women assembling separately,

> Thereupon everyone goes to the salon of which I spoke, and from there to a large room where there is music for those who want to dance. From there one goes to a room where the king's throne stands. There one finds various kinds of music, concerts and singing. From there one goes into the bedchamber, where three tables for playing cards are set up, one of the king, one for the queen and one for Monsieur. From there one goes to a room that could be called a hall, where more than twenty tables, covered with green velvet cloth with a gold fringe, have been put up for all kinds of games. From there one goes to a large antechamber containing the king's billiard table, and then to another room with four large tables for the collation, all kinds of things like fruit cakes and preserves ... After one is done with the collation, which is taken standing up, one goes back to the room with the many tables; now everyone sits down to a different game, and it is unbelievable how many varieties of games are being played: lansquenet, trictrac, picquet, l'hombre, chess, ... every conceivable game. When the king and the queen come into the room, no one gets up from the game. Those who do not play, like myself and a great many others, just stroll from room to room, now to the music and now to the game room, for one is allowed to go wherever one wishes; this lasts from six until ten, when one goes to supper.[56]

[53] Letter to the Electress Sophie, February 10, 1701, quoted in *A Woman's Life in the Court of the Sun King*, 129.

[54] *The Memoirs of the Duke of Saint-Simon*, I, 33.

[55] *Letters of Madame de Sévigné*, I, 239.

[56] Letter to the Electress Wilhemine-Ernestine, December 6, 1682, quoted in *A Woman's Life in the Court of the Sun King*, 38ff.

In a letter of 1695, she reveals her own preference, "if there is *appartement* I listen to the music."[57]

[57] Ibid., 86.

We also find some description of the musical performances hosted by lesser nobles. A letter of Mme de Sévigné of 1677 describes the music at a party in a garden of the Hotel de Conde.

> There were water-works, bowers, terraces, six hautboys in one corner, six violins in another, the most melodious flutes; a supper which seemed to be prepared by enchantment, an admirable bass-viol, and a resplendent moon, which witnessed all our pleasures.[58]

[58] Quoted in *Letters of Madame de Sévigné*, I, 262.

She also writes of her visit to the Marquis de Termes in 1677.

> They brought one of the musicians belonging to the opera with them; he plays better than Lully, and amuses us highly. There is, besides, a little impertinent hump-backed fellow, who is always singing, and who imagines himself an admirable performer; he is a perpetual source of laughter to us.[59]

[59] Ibid., II, 1.

The Duke of Saint-Simon mentions entertainment music provided for banquets by the king's famous ensemble, the "twenty-four violins." He relates that on the annual fête of St. Louis (August 25) the order of the day was that,

> The drums and oboes, assembled beneath the king's windows, should play their accustomed music as soon as he awoke, and that the twenty-four violins should play in the ante-chamber during his dinner.[60]

[60] *The Memoirs of the Duke of Saint-Simon*, II, 351.

He describes the celebration of the Peace of Utrecht, in April 1713, as including a *Te Deum* sung at Notre Dame, a fireworks display and a great banquet at the Hotel de Ville for the leading officials of Paris with music performed by the king's "twenty-four violins."[61]

[61] Ibid., II, 248.

We should mention another instance of entertainment music recalled by the Duke of Saint-Simon, although it was probably not appreciated by the guest of honor. He tells of a palace joke by which the Swiss guards with drums were sent in to awaken a lady in the morning "by their horrid din."[62]

[62] Ibid., I, 258.

Finally, Mme de Sévigné gives us a brief glimpse of the local peasant music near her country estate.

> I am vexed that you cannot see the *bourrées* of this country; it is the most surprising sight imaginable; the peasantry dance in as true time as you do, and with such an activity, a sprightliness that, in short, I am quite in raptures with them. I have a little band of music every evening, which costs me a mere trifle.[63]

[63] Letter of 1676, quoted in *Letters of Madame de Sévigné*, I, 226.

14 On French Military Music of the Baroque

DURING THE FIRST PART of the seventeenth century, military music in France centered on the trumpet, of which most companies had two but those with more than two hundred soldiers being assigned a third.[1] Each regiment also maintained a Trumpet-major, who was necessary to train new trumpeters in a repertoire which was not yet notated. During parades the trumpets rode before the commander in front of the troops. In battle, however, both the trumpets and the commander were placed safely in the rear.[2] Mersenne commented on the psychological value of the trumpet.

> But its principal usage is destined for war ... It is easy to conclude ... how they would prepare the heart and mind of the soldier for going to war, for attacking, and engaging in combat.[3]

Mersenne describes a number of specific trumpet signals and concludes with some interesting details,

> The first is called the "cavalcade," used when the army or one of its regiments approaches towns, through which it passes going to a siege or places of combat, to warn the inhabitants and make them participants in the cheerfulness and expectation of winning the victory. The second is named "to the saddle," used for breaking up camp, and then follows the "call to saddle." In the third place is sounded "on horseback"; and then "to the standard," and "the charge." Further is sounded the "watch"; but all these ways of sounding are most often distinct only through the interval of meter ... Thus two or more trumpets are easily heard a quarter league away and

[1] Paris, National Archives (MS 01/715, vol. 171, 173, 179, 181ff).

[2] Georges Kastner, *Manuel général de musique militaire* (Paris, 1838), 107ff.

[3] Marin Mersenne, *Harmonie universelle* (Paris, 1636), 331.

make many discourses which can take the place of speech. Still there is nothing particular in that, except that they can be heard from further away than the other instruments, which can be similarly used to hold some desired discourse.[4]

Several sources mention a trumpet signal called *la sourdine*, which Kastner says was used to march "with little noise."[5] A treatise of 1631 adds,

> the mute is used when there is a risk of being discovered by the enemy or when it is wished to surprise them, as also when it is desired to decamp or secretly withdraw.[6]

The importance of these signals in the field necessitated some care in the selection of the man assigned this responsibility. One French treatise commented on the character needed in the trumpeter as follows:

> The trumpet must be a man of patience and vigilance, to be ready at all hours to execute the orders of the calls ... The trumpet must be a discreet man, primarily when he is used in the negotiations, where he must never use other terms than those he is instructed with, never interfere by giving counsel, in order that in conferences and treaties there will be no ambiguity or statements contrary to those proposed.[7]

Another contemporary treatise adds an interesting comment on the relationship of the trumpeter and his horse.

> The trumpets are the instruments best to use of horse dancing because they [the horses] can learn to breathe when the trumpets breathe. There is no instrument more agreeable to the horse, because it is martial, and the horse which is naturally generous, likes to be animated by its sound.[8]

In spite of such testimonials to the importance of the cavalry trumpeter, a contemporary officer testifies that he often had the experience of finding, in an army of 12,000 or 15,000 men, ten trumpets who did not know their signals.[9]

The timpani appears for the first time in the French cavalry at the time of Louis XIV, although the first instruments were those captured from German troops and only those French units which had achieved such an acquisition were permitted

---

[4] Ibid., 332.

[5] Kastner, *Manuel général*, 107.

[6] Pierre Trichet, *Traité des instruments de musique* (Bourdelois, 1631). A copy can be found in F-Psy [MS.1070].

[7] Alain Mallet, *Les travaux de Mars, ou l'Art de la guerre* (Paris, 1691), III, 96.

[8] Claude Ménestrier, *Des Ballets anciens et modernes selon les règles du théâtre* (Paris, 1682), 238.

[9] Lieutenant-Colonel Lecoq Madeleine, quoted in Kastner, *Manuel général*, 117.

to use them. Thus the timpani became prized emblems of a regiment's honor and when abroad the timpanist was preceded by four Cavaliers for protection. In the end, however, it was the responsibility of the player to prevent the capture of his instruments.

> The timpanist must be a man of heart, preferring to perish in combat rather than surrendering his timpani. He must have good arm movement and an accurate ear, and be able to divert his master with agreeable tunes. There is no other instrument which gives a more martial sound than the timpani, especially when it is accompanied by trumpets.[10]

One observer maintained that the timpani also had a positive effect on the character of the horse.

> The beating of the timpani, which controls the stamping and the marching of the horses, also insures that these animals march with the most noble pride.[11]

The timpanist rode (the instruments carried in front of the saddle) in front of the commander during parades and to the rear of the action in war time. According to Titcomb, the timpanist usually performed as part of an ensemble with two or three trumpets, improvising with their signals, but at the same time forming the harmonic bass to their parts.

> The "Charge" for the kettledrum is nothing but a very great noise produced by animated rolls, which go from the right timpani to the left and from the left to the right, with some detached strokes; as this noise constitutes exactly the underlying bass for the trumpets, it suffices that the kettledrummer must have a good ear to fulfill this air.[12]

The technique of the timpanist even included certain special effects, such as simulated echoes.[13]

The tambour performed the same role for the foot soldiers, the infantry and dragoons, that the trumpet performed for the mounted cavalry. The tambour was made of oak, but sometimes brass or a different wood. Iconography shows the instrument played in a near vertical position by the left leg.[14]

When on parade, the tambours—rather like sheep dogs—were placed before and after the troops in an effort to keep

---

[10] Mallet, *Les travaux de Mars*, III, 98. The comment on the need of a good ear refers to the role of the timpani in supplying the bass of the trumpet choir.

[11] Claude Ménestrier, *Des Représentations en musique anciennes et modernes* (Paris, 1681), 124.

[12] Caldwell Titcomb, "Baroque Court and Military Trumpets and Kettledrums," *Galpin Society Journal* (June, 1956), 61ff. One of the most interesting manuscripts in F-Pn is a huge volume, *Airs Propres pour le Timpanon*, consisting of nothing but pages of exercises, "airs," and signals for the timpanist.

[13] Ibid., 71, 75–76.

[14] Mersenne (1636), quoted in Michel Brenet, "French Military Music in the Reign of Louis XIV," in *Musical Quarterly* (July, 1917), 344.

them together.[15] This was probably also necessary in order for each soldier to be able to hear clearly the beat. Apparently by the seventeenth century the soldiers generally did march to a beat. A late seventeenth century French chronicle gives an interesting and detailed explanation for the coordination of feet and drums.

> A company of soldiers marches to the beating of the drums and give seven beats; some are given by the drums and others are rests. They pick up one foot on one, suspend it on two; on three they put that foot down and begin to lift the other. On four the suspend it, on five they put it down and on six they affirm it. The seventh is a rest, after which they begin again.[16]

This same writer discusses the manner of marching to tambours in various countries. The Swiss, for example,

> who are much more weighty in their marching, the French being more agile, will move the first on four *breves* and push on a *longue*, afterwards they have two pauses, which the *Pata pata pan* ... expresses. The *longues* are the *Pan*, the *breves* [*les brefs*] are *Pata* and the very brief are *Frrr*.[17]

The basic seventeenth century tambour signals for battle are given by a contemporary writer, Mallet, in 1671.

> In each company, it is mandatory to have two, or at the very least one Tambour player. The duty of the player is to beat the *Marche* for entering a campaign, the *Allarme* for running to take arms, the *Chamade* for calling the Soldiers, and the *Blanc* for warning them. In each Regiment there is a Tambour player who commands all the others of the same Corps, and this Drummer is called the Tambour Major.[18]

Some confusion among the troops when hearing the signal, *l'assemblée*, led to an official clarification in 1670 and a new signal, *la générale*, created by the king himself.

> His Majesty—wishing to see to it that no confusion arises among his infantry troops because of different drum beats, and that when one regiment is to begin fighting, everyone knows if the entire army or the whole infantry corps should march or only the regiment which is to fight—His Majesty has ordained and ordains, wishes and means that, when in

[15] Kastner, *Manuel général*, 111.

[16] Claude Ménestrier, *Des Représentations en musique anciennes et modernes* (Paris, 1681), 124.

[17] Early percussion notation is often expressed in syntax.

[18] Quoted in Susay Sandman, "Wind Band Music Under Louis XIV" (Unpublished dissertation, Stanford, 1974) who also reproduces signals from the Philidor Collection of 1705 in F-Pn [Res.F.671].

the army there is an order for the entire infantry to march, the first begins to fight because of the beat newly ordained by His Majesty, which is called *la générale*; for the second the usual *l'assemblée* and then in the time that the soldiers are coming out of their tents the beat that was ordained for the entrance and the exit from the camp; and when it is only one regiment and not the whole infantry corps which has orders to march, then the drums beat, for the first, *aux champs*; for the second, the former *l'assemblée*, then the exit and then *en marche*.[19]

Some years later, in 1725, this new signal, together with some additional new ones, was discussed by Guignard:

> *La Générale* which is played when the entire infantry corps is to take up arms; *l'assemblée* to give notice to assemble and get ready to take up arms; *le Drapeau* to get the flags and get ready for battle, and to lay down arms in a pile in the *Corps de Garde* or in quarters; *aux champs* to march, or to show the first group to march when the entire infantry is not to take up arms; *la Retraite* to retreat into camp or into quarters or to cease combat; *la Fassine* or *Breloque* to give notice to the workers to go to work, and the hour at which they stop working to eat or leave—this drum beat serves also to give notice that mass is going to begin; *appeller* to assemble the officers and soldiers and to instruct them to gather in an assigned place; *le Ban* to introduce and receive an officer, and to read the prohibitions or publications of rules from the King or General; and *la Diane* for reveille.[20]

As in the case of the trumpet, these signals not only gave directions for movement, but provided last-minute inspiration for the soldiers, as a contemporary observed:

> The tambour is not only a great help in the armies for the marching of the infantry, serving as a sign for moving on, marching, retiring, for assembly and the other orders which would otherwise be difficult to carry about at the same time, and to make as many people hear, but they also animate the soldiers and give them heart when they must crush the enemy in combat. The trumpets, timpani and oboes have nearly the same effect. The beating of the timpani, which controls the stamping and the marching of the horses, also insures that these animals march with the most noble pride.[21]

In addition to the use of tambours for military movement, and the field related uses mentioned above, they were also

[19] Kastner, *Manuel général,* 393ff, translation by Sandman, "Wind Band Music Under Louis XIV," 79.

[20] Claude Guignard, *L'Ecole de Mars* (Paris, 1725), 695.

[21] Ménestrier, *Des Représentations.*

used as a means of giving peaceful salutes from one troop to another.[22] They could also perform diplomatic roles, carrying on a dialog with the drummer of the enemy. An eye-witness to the surrender of Luxembourg, in 1684, mentions the use of the tambour in this regard.

[22] Marcelle Benoit, *Versailles et les Musiciens du Roi* (Paris, 1971), 238.

> ... as he was coming back at dawn, the drummer of the besieged beat a *petite Diane* and an *Appelle*. As soon as he was finished an officer appeared on the bastion and cried that he was sent from the Prince de Chimay and that he wished to send envoy—officers to speak with the General to arrange the surrender and that he would send hostages ... None of this was of any use, the drummers dispersed, our fire continued for a while and then diminished a little ... The drummers came and cried, after having played, that they had come to call for capitulation.[23]

[23] Charles Sevin, Marquis de Quincy, *Histoire militaire du règne de Louis le Grand* (Paris, 1726), II, 81, 83.

Finally, there are a few contemporary accounts which offer insights into the actual technique of the drummers, apart from the descriptions of the nature of the signals. First, a rather early seventeenth century account (1626) implies variation in touch and even muting.

> The French *batterie* is the finest of all, and the *Marche* sounds better, and the Tambour gives a clearer cadence than in the practice of any other nation; because the drum gives distinct mark to the fundamental step of the soldier. For the *allarmes*, the Tambour Colonel himself should give a more compact batterie with a light touch and rather tight play. When it is necessary to dislodge secretly, the Tambour must be covered with a small cloth in order to deafen its sound. After sounding the *allarem*, the Tambour player should raise his hand, for it is a mistake to say that the sound continues to live, even though it ceases to be commanded. Therefore, the player should stop promptly and cut short without refrain, omitting the customary ramble [*ballade*], which drags on for a long time.[24]

[24] René François, *Essay des merveilles de nature, et des plus nobles artifices* (Rouen, 1626), 140ff.

In another early seventeenth century account, Mersenne mentions the stick technique:

> If I had some musical characters at my command, I should have placed here all the ways of beating of the French drum ... and I should have explained what the *baton rond*, the *baton*

rompu, and the *baton mesle* are; I can only say that the beat of the *baton rond* is made when the two sticks strike each blow one after the other; that of the *baton rompu*, when each hand strikes twice in succession; and the beat of the *baton mesle* when each beats sometimes once with each hand and sometimes twice. As to retreat, the two sticks beat all together.[25]

Kaster adds that the Mousquetaires used drums which were much smaller than those of the infantry, and that they beat "in a very different way, which was much more gay." Unfortunately he provided no further details.[26]

Militarily and musically, the most important development in military movement was the reintroduction of coordinated marching, a practice which had been lost since the ancient Romans. In France this seems to have begun with attempts to march to drums[27] during the sixteenth century, as suggested by Arbeau.

> Were it not for these, the men would march confusedly and without order, which would cause them to be in danger of being overthrown and defeated.[28]

One French military leader who argued strongly for coordinated marching was the general, Maurice de Saxe (1696–1750).[29] He was also one who reminded his colleagues of the forgotten tradition of the ancient armies.

> I begin with the *marche*; the necessity to discuss this may seem extravagant to the ignorant.
> No one knows what the ancients understood by the word *Tactique*; many soldiers use it and believe it to mean (only) the movement of troops in battle. The whole world beats a march without knowing its tradition and everyone thinks this noise is nothing but an ornament of the military.
> We should have a better opinion of the ancients and the Romans, who should be our teachers. It is absurd to believe that this war noise served no more unique purpose than to deafen their ears!

The general pictures the army without the beat of the drum: "Every soldier walks according to his own ease, some slow and some fast." If one is marching and orders the front to quicken the pace, the rear unavoidably loses ground before

[25] Mersenne, *Harmonie universelle*, 556.

[26] Kastner, *Manuel général*, 111.

[27] The French drum signals of the seventeenth century are discussed in detail by René François, *Essay des merveilles de nature, et des plus nobles artifices* (Rouen, 1626), 140ff and by Mersenne, *Harmonie universelle*, 556.

[28] Thoinot Arbeau, *Orchésographie* (1588), trans. Peter Warlock (New York, 1925), 26.

[29] Maurice, Comte de Saxe, *Les Rêveries ou mémoires sur l'art de guerre* (Hague, 1756), I, vi, 23ff.

they perceive the order. Then, the rear runs to catch up, whereupon the front also begins to run, throwing everything into disorder.

In addition to solving these problems, the use of a beat helps prevent the troops from getting tired. The general offers his readers what he calls "extraordinary" proof of this fact.

> There isn't anyone who has not seen people dance all night with continuous energy. But if you have someone dance even two hours *without* music, he will protest! This proves that music [*les tons*] have a secret power over us which disposes us to exercise our bodies and makes it easy at the same time.

It was this secret, the general suggests, that enabled the Roman armies to cover such great areas of Europe. He contends that they could march twenty-four miles in five hours, by marching to a cadence! Just try that with your own troops, he says, and see if you can do as well (without music).

> What would one say if I prove that it is impossible to vigorously charge the enemy without this cadence, or without it one always arrives with the ranks out of order? What a monstrous mistake! I believe that for the previous three or four centuries no one has paid any attention to this.

The real progress came in the seventeenth century with the establishment of standing armies, in place of the long European tradition of calling up troops only as the need presented itself. The presence of standing armies made feasible the creation of standing musical groups and so the appearance of the Hautboisten band (oboes and bassoons) marks the beginning of true coordinated marching to music as it had been known to the ancient Greeks and Romans. The most knowledgeable authority suggests that the Hautboisten band were added to companies of the Mousquetaires in the year 1665.[30] According to Grove, these four "oboes" were two trebles, a tenor [*taille des hautbois*] and a bassoon.[31]

It appears that the additional advantages which a commander could enjoy with an oboe band, as opposed to mere drums or trumpets, caused them to become widely popular.

[30] Marcelle Benoit, *Versailles et les musiciens du roi* (Paris, 1971), 236.
[31] XII, 311.

This additional cost became a concern to the king and in 1633 he issued the following edict,

> His Majesty, knowing that inmost of his infantry companies there are several tambours, and even *fifres* and hautbois in some whose service is not only useless, but also causes an expense for the captains to maintain them, and His Majesty, wishing, therefore, to limit the number of said tambours, that he henceforth wants to be maintained in his French infantry troops, and to eliminate completely the hautbois, His Majesty has ordained and ordains, wishes and means that henceforth, in each French infantry company, there can be only a single tambour and in a regiment of a single *fifre* which will be attached to the colonel's company, with no hautbois, and without the number of tambours being permitted to be increased for whatever reason or for any pretext whatsoever.[32]

[32] Quoted in Kastner, *Manuel général*, 394–395.

The military Hautboisten bands accompanied the troops to battle, but, judging by an account from the Battle of Mons in 1691, they also must have performed music beyond that required by marching troops.

> One day, during the siege of Mons, after the tragic spectacle which had offered murderous hostilities, the artillery became silent suddenly around 11 a.m. and the frightful sound of bombs was replaced by an oboe concert which the officers of the King's regiment were giving for the women of the city. The musicians had installed themselves on the still burning remains of the city which our troops had just taken possession of. It seems that the women of the city were sensitive to this homage, because they rushed up to the ramparts to hear the concert, and returned only after it had ceased.[33]

[33] Ibid., 103, fn 1.

A French newspaper[34] preserves an account of another military concert, held in a tent during the Siege of Namur in 1692.

[34] *Mercure Galant* for May, 1692.

> The king having invited the ladies to dinner the next day treated them to a war-like concert, composed of 120 tambours of the Gardes, 40 tambours of the Swiss Guards, with trumpets and timpani of the Gardes du Corps, the Light-Guard, to the number of 36, and all the oboes of the Mousquetaires and the Regiment of the king. Altogether they played a French march, and then the Swiss march. The trumpets and timpani

gave separately the pleasure of a march on horseback. Mr. Philidor, whom the king had put in charge of the concert, had arranged a great finale for the entire ensemble. The oboes played airs from *La Grotte de Versailles* and Mr. Philidor played with them. The trumpets and timpani then gave a divertimento of the old *airs de guerre*, which they did in two choirs, interspersed with menuets played by the oboes. All the tambours, timpani and trumpets then played "la charge" at the same time and the king had them repeat it three times. After that one heard the three last arias from *Psiche* ... All of these airs were well played, nicely orchestrated, and played by all of these excellent men, each outstanding in his profession.

There were also some forms of military music, at least trumpets, on the ships of the French navy during the Baroque.

One of the strangest moments in the annals of military music of the Baroque, however, must have been the reappearance, after ages beyond number, of the conch in 1689. For some reason these were instituted especially for the campaign against the bandits of Catalan, who were fighting for the Spanish. According to Guignard, in each company there was a man who played this "instrument," which was used in place of the tambour. He describes it as a "great snail-shell from the sea played by a hundred men." The sound was described as "surprisingly rustic and at the same time martial."[35]

[35] Guignard, *L'Ecole de Mars*, I, 722.

Bibliography

1 On Some Views of French Baroque Musicians

Bacilly, Bénigne de. *L'Art de bien chanter*. Paris (1668).
Barzun, Jacques. *Rameau's Nephew and Other Works*. Garden City: Doubleday, 1956.
Brossard. Sebastien de. "Largo." In *Dictionaire de Musique*. Paris (1703).
Buelow, George J. "Music and Society in the Late Baroque Era." In *The Late Baroque Era*. Englewood Cliffs: Prentice Hall, 1994.
Couperin, François. *L'Art de toucher*. Paris, 1717, reprinted Wiesbaden: Breitkopf & Härtel, 1933.
Donnington, Robert. *The Interpretation of Early Music*. New York, 1964.
Harris, Ellen. "Voices." In *Performance Practice: Music after 1600*. New York: Norton, 1989.
Kuyper, Jon. "Marc-Antoine Charpentier's *Règles de Composition*." Iowa City: University of Iowa, unpublished dissertation, 1971.
MacClintock, Carol. *Readings in the History of Music in Performance*. Bloomington: Indiana University Press, 1979.
Maland, David. *Culture and Society in Seventeenth-Century France*. New York: Scribner's, 1970.
Masson, Charles. *Nouveau Traité*. Paris, 1699.
Mermet, Louis Bollioud de. *De la corruption*. Lyon, 1746.
Morgenstern, Sam. *Composers on Music*. New York: Pantheon, 1956.

Norman, Gertrude and Miriam Shrifte. *Letters of Composers.* New York: Knopf, 1946.

Rameau, Jean Philippe. *Observations sur notre instinct pour la musique, et sur son principe* [1734].

———. *Treatise on Harmony.* Translated by Philip Gossett. New York: Dover, 1971.

———. *Le Nouveau système de musique théorique* [1726].

Rousseau, Jean. *Traité de la viole.* Paris, 1687.

Sadie, Julie Anne. "Paris and Versailles." In *The Late Baroque Era.* Englewood Cliffs: Prentice Hall, 1994.

Saint-Lambert, Michel de. *Principes du clavecin.* Paris, 1702.

Schmitz, Hans-Peter. *Die Kunst der Verzierung im 18. Jahrhundert.* Kassel: Bärenreiter, 1955.

Walls, Peter. "Strings." In *Performance Practice: Music after 1600.* New York: Norton, 1989.

2 *Mersenne on the Nature of Music*

Duncan, David. "Persuading the Affections: Rhetorical Theory and Mersenne's Advice to Harmonic Orators." In *French Musical Thought, 1600-1800.* Ann Arbor: UMI Research Press, 1989.

Mersenne, Marin. *Harmonie universelle*, II, ii. Translated by John Egan. Bloomington: Indiana University, unpublished dissertation, 1962.

———. *Fourth Treatise of the Harmonie universelle.* Edited by Robert Williams. Rochester: Eastman School of Music, unpublished dissertation, 1972.

———. *Treatise Three*, Book One, *Traitez de la voix, et des chants.* Translated by Edmund LeRoy. New York: Julliard School, unpublished dissertation, 1978.

———. *Treatise Three, Book Two ("Second Book of Songs") of the Traitez de la voix, et des chants ...* Translated by Wilbur F. Russell. Princeton: Westminster Choir College, unpublished dissertation, 1952.

———. *Treatise Five, Traite des instruments.* Translated by Roger Chapman. The Hague: Nijhoff, 1957.

3 Voltaire on Music

Voltaire. *Select Letters of Voltaire*. Translated by Theodore Besterman. London: Nelson, 1963.
———. *The Works of Voltaire*. New York: St. Hubert Guild, 1901.

4 Mersenne on Performance

Doni, Giovanni Battasta. *Compendio del trattato de' generi e de' modi*. Rome, 1635.
Donnington, Robert. *The Interpretation of Early Music*. New York, 1964.
Lippman, Edward. *Musical Aesthetics: A Historical Reader*. New York: Pendragon Press, 1986.
Mersenne, Marin. *Fourth Treatise of the Harmonie universelle*. Edited by Robert Williams. Rochester: Eastman School of Music, unpublished dissertation, 1972.
———. *Harmonie universelle*, II, ii. Translated by John Egan. Bloomington: Indiana University, unpublished dissertation, 1962.
———. *Treatise Three, Book Two ("Second Book of Songs") of the Traitez de la voix, et des chants ...* Translated by Wilbur F. Russell. Princeton: Westminster Choir College, unpublished dissertation, 1952.
———. *Treatise Five, Traité des instruments*. Translated by Roger Chapman. The Hague: Nijhoff, 1957.

5 French Philosophers on Music

André, Yves Marie. *L'Essai sur le beau* [1741].
Batteux, Charles. *Les beaux arts réduits à un même principe*. Paris, 1746.
Bonnet-Bourdelot, Jacques. "Histoire de la musique, et de ses effets, depuis son origine jusqu'à présent." Paris, 1715. Quoted in Carol MacClintock. *Readings in the History of Music in Performance*. Bloomington: Indiana University Press, 1979.
Du Bos, Jean-Baptiste. *Réflexions critiques sur la poésie et sur la peinture*. Paris, 1719.

Brossard, Sebastien de. *Dictionnaire de Musique*. Paris, 1703.

La Bruyère, Juan de. *Characters*. Translated by Jean Stewart. Baltimore: Penguin Books, 1970.

Le Cerf de la Viéville. "Traite du bon gout en musique." In Oliver Strunk, *Source Readings in Music History*. New York: Norton, 1950.

Fénelon, François de Salignac de La Mothe-. *Fénelon's Dialogues on Eloquence*. Translated by Wilbur Howell. Princeton: Princeton University Press, 1951.

———. *Fénelon's Letter to the French Academy* [1716]. Translated by Barbara Warnick. New York: University Press of America, 1984.

Hays, William, ed. *Twentieth-Century Views of Music History*. New York: Scribner's, 1972.

Huray, Peter le and James Day. *Music and Aesthetics in the Eighteenth and Early-Nineteenth Centuries*. Cambridge: Cambridge University Press, 1981.

Lang, Paul Henry. "Musical Thought of the Baroque: The Doctrine of Temperaments and Affections." In William Hays, ed. *Twentieth-Century Views of Music History*. New York: Scribner's, 1972.

MacClintock, Carol. *Readings in the History of Music in Performance*. Bloomington: Indiana University Press, 1979.

Maugars, André. "Response faite à un curieux sur le sentiment de la musique ... " In Carol MacClintock. *Readings in the History of Music in Performance*. Bloomington: Indiana University Press, 1979.

Montesquieu, Charles de Secondat, Baron de. *The Spirit of Laws* [1748]. Translated by Thomas Nugent in *Great Books*, XXXVIII. Chicago: Encyclopedia Britannica, 1952.

Raguenet, François. "Parallèle des Italiens et des Français." [1702]. Quoted in Oliver Strunk. *Source Readings in Music History*. New York: Norton, 1950.

Strunk, Oliver. *Source Readings in Music History*. New York: Norton, 1950.

Yates, Frances. *The French Academies of the Sixteenth Century*. Nendeln: Kraus, 1968.

6 French Philosophers on the Character of French Musicians

Bonnet-Bourdelot, Jacques. "Histoire de la musique, et de ses effets, depuis son origine jusqu'à présent." Paris, 1715. In Carol MacClintock. *Readings in the History of Music in Performance*. Bloomington: Indiana University Press, 1979.

Brosses, Charles de. "Lettres familières écrites d'Italie en 1739 et 1740." Paris, 1885. Quoted in Carol MacClintock. *Readings in the History of Music in Performance*. Bloomington: Indiana University Press, 1979.

Le Cerf de La Viéville. *Histoire de la musique*. Amsterdam, 1725.

Donnington, Robert. *The Interpretation of Early Music*. New York, 1964.

Maugars, André. "Response faite à un curieux sur le sentiment de la musique d'Italie, écrite a Rome le premier Octobre 1639." Quoted in Carol MacClintock. *Readings in the History of Music in Performance*. Bloomington: Indiana University Press, 1979.

Raguenet, François. "Parallèle des Italiens et des Français." [1702]. Quoted in Oliver Strunk. *Source Readings in Music History*. New York: Norton, 1950.

7 Descartes on Music

Bianconi, Lorenzo. *Music in the Seventeenth Century*. Cambridge: Cambridge University Press, 1989.

Blom, John. *Descartes*. New York: New York University Press, 1978.

Descartes, René. *Compendium of Music*. Translated by Walter Robert. American Institute of Musicology, 1961.

———. *Philosophical Letters*. Translated by Anthony Kenny. Oxford: Clarendon Press, 1970.

———. *The Philosophical Writings of Descartes*. Translated by John Cottingham, Robert Stoothoff and Dugald Murdoch. Cambridge: Cambridge University Press, 1985.

8 On Court Music in the French Baroque

Benoit, Marcelle. *Versailles et les musiciens du roi*. Paris, 1971.
———. "Paris, 1661–87: the Age of Lully." In *The Early Baroque Era*. Englewood Cliffs: Prentice Hall, 1994.
———. *Musiques de cour*. Paris, 1971.
Bianconi, Lorenzo. *Music in the Seventeenth Century*. Translated by David Bryant. Cambridge: Cambridge University Press, 1989.
Couperin, François. *Concerts royaux*. Paris, 1722.
Ecorchville, Jules. "Quelques documents sur la musique de la Grand-Écurie du Roi." In *Sammelbande des Internationalen Musikgesellschaft*. 1903.
———. *Vignt suites d'orchestre*. Paris, 1906.
Furetière, Antonine. *Dictionnaire universel*. The Hague, 1690.
Isherwood, Robert. *Music in the Service of the King*. Cornell University Press.
Massip, Catherine. "Paris, 1600–61" In *The Early Baroque Era*. Englewood Cliffs: Prentice Hall, 1994.
National Archives, Paris. MS.Bundle 01/2830, Nr. 86, 88; MS. Bundle 01/878, Nr. 401.
Recherches sur la musique française classique. Paris, 1968.
Rousseau, Jean-Jacques. "Copiste." In *Dictionnaire de Musique*. Paris, 1767.
La Ruelle. *Obsequies of Charles III*. Nancy, 1608.
Saint-Simon, Louis de Rouvroy. *Memoirs of Louis XIV and the Regency*. London, 1901.
Trichet, Pierre. *Traité des instruments de musique*. Bordeaux, c. 1640.
Walther. *Musikalisches Lexikon*. Leipzig, 1732.
The Works of Mr. de Moliere. New York: Benjamin Blom, 1967.

9 Music in the French Dramatic Theater

Corneille, Pierre. *The Liar*.
Lesage, Alain-René. *Turcaret*.
Marivaux, Pierre de. *Double Infidelity*.
———. *Money Makes the World Go Round*.
———. *The Test*.

Molière [Jean-Baptiste Poquelin]. *The Affected Ladies.*
———. *Le Bourgeois Gentilhomme.*
———. *The Compulsory Marriage.*
———. *Les Facheux.*
———. *The Hypochondriac.*
———. *The Impromptu of Versailles.*
———. *Love the Best Physician.*
———. *The Magnificent Lovers.*
———. *The Mock-Doctor.*
———. *Monsieur de Pourceaugnac.*
———. *The Princess of Elis.*
———. *The School for Wives Criticized.*
———. *Tartuffe.*
Racine, Jean-Baptiste. *Athaliah.*
Voltaire. *Merope.*
———. *Pandora.*
———. *The Prude.*
———. *Zaire.*

10 French Philosophers on Opera

Bonnet-Bourdelot, Jacques. "Histoire de la musique, et de ses effets, depuis son origine jusqu'à présent." Paris, 1715. Quoted in Carol MacClintock. *Readings in the History of Music in Performance.* Bloomington: Indiana University Press, 1979.

Brosses, Charles de. "Lettres familières écrites d'Italie en 1739 et 1740." Paris, 1885. Quoted in Carol MacClintock. *Readings in the History of Music in Performance.* Bloomington: Indiana University Press, 1979.

La Bruyère, Jean de. *Characters.* Translated by Jean Stewart. Baltimore: Penguin Books, 1970.

Maugars, André. "Response faite à un curieux sur le sentiment de la musique d'Italie, écrite a Rome le premier Octobre 1639." Quoted in Carol MacClintock. *Readings in the History of Music in Performance.* Bloomington: Indiana University Press, 1979.

Raguenet, François. "Parallèle des Italiens et des Français." [1702]. Quoted in Oliver Strunk. *Source Readings in Music History*. New York: Norton, 1950.

Saint-Évremond, Charles de. "Lettre sur les Opéra." Quoted in Carol MacClintock. *Readings in the History of Music in Performance*. Bloomington: Indiana University Press, 1979.

11 *Voltaire on Opera*

Sadie, Julie. "Paris and Versailles." In *The Late Baroque Era*. Englewood Cliffs: Prentice Hall, 1994.

Voltaire. *The Selected Letters of Voltaire*. Translated by Richard Brooks. New York: New York University Press, 1973.

———. *Voltaire and Catherine the Great*. Translated by A. Lentin. Cambridge: Oriental Research Partners, 1974.

———. *The Works of Voltaire*. New York: St. Hubert Guild, 1901.

12 *Music in French Fiction*

Bergerac, Cyrano de. *Other Worlds*. Translated by Geoffrey Strachan. London: Oxford University Press, 1965.

Brantôme, Pierre de Bourdeille, seigneur. *Lives of Fair and Gallant Ladies*. Translated by A. R. Allinson. New York: Liveright, 1933.

Crébillon, fils, Claude Prosper Jolyot de. *Letters from the Marchiness de M*** to the Count de R****. Edited by Josephine Grieder. New York: Garland, 1972.

Fénelon, François de Salignac de La Mothe-. *The Adventures of Telemachus, Son of Ulysses*. London: Garland Publishing, 1979 (facsimile of the 1720 edition).

Lesage, Alain René. *Asmodeus, or The Devil on Two Sticks* [1707]. The Bibliophilist Society, 1932.

Marivaux, Pierre de. *The Virtuous Orphan*. Translated by Mary Collyer. Carbondale: Southern Illinois University Press, 1965.

Montesquieu, Charles-Louis de Secondat, Baron de. *The Persian Letters*. London: Athenaeum, 1901.

Voltaire. *The Selected Letters of Voltaire*. Translated by Richard Brooks. New York: New York University Press, 1973.
———. *The Works of Voltaire*. New York: St. Hubert Guild, 1901.

13 Music in French Non-Fiction

Letters of Madame de Sévigné. Edited by Richzard Aldington. London: Routledge, 1937.
The Letters of Saint-Évremond. Edited by John Hayward. Freeport, NY: Books for Libraries Press, 1971.
Marville, Vigneul. *Mélanges d'histoire et de litterature*. Paris, 1725.
The Memoirs of the Duke of Saint-Simon. Translated by Bayle St. John. London: George Allen, 1926.
A Woman's Life in the Court of the Sun King. Translated by Elborg Forster. Baltimore: Johns Hopkins University Press, 1984.

14 On French Military Music of the Baroque

Arbeau, Thoinot. *Orchésographie* [1588]. Translated by Peter Warlock. New York, 1925.
Benoit, Marcelle. *Versailles et les musiciens du roi*. Paris, 1971.
Brenet, Michel. "French Military Music in the Reign of Louis XIV." *Musical Quarterly* (July, 1917).
François, René. *Essay des merveilles de nature, et des plus nobles artifices*. Rouen, 1626.
Kastner, Georges. *Manuel général de musique militaire*. Paris, 1838.
Mallet, Alain. *Les travaux de Mars, ou l'Art de la guerre*. Paris, 1691.
Ménestrier, Claude. *Des Ballets anciens et modernes selon les règles du théâtre*. Paris, 1682.
———. *Des representations en musique, anciennes et modernes*. Paris, 1681.
Mersenne, Marin. *Harmonie universelle*. Paris (1636).
Sandman, Susay. "Wind Band Music Under Louis XIV" Unpublished dissertation, Stanford, 1974.

Saxe, Maurice, Comte de. *Les Rêveries ou mémoires sur l'art de guerre*. Hague, 1756.

Sevin, Charles, Marquis de Quincy. *Histoire militaire du règne de Louis le Grand*. Paris, 1726.

Titcomb, Caldwell. "Baroque Court and Military Trumpets and Kettledrums." *Galpin Society Journal* (June, 1956).

Trichet, Pierre. *Traité des instruments de musique*. Bourdelois, 1631. A copy can be found in F-Psy [MS.1070].

About the Author

Dr. David Whitwell is a graduate ("with distinction") of the University of Michigan and the Catholic University of America, Washington DC (PhD, Musicology, Distinguished Alumni Award, 2000) and has studied conducting with Eugene Ormandy and at the Akademie für Musik, Vienna. Prior to coming to Northridge, Dr. Whitwell participated in concerts throughout the United States and Asia as Associate First Horn in the USAF Band and Orchestra in Washington DC, and in recitals throughout South America in cooperation with the United States State Department.

At the California State University, Northridge, which is in Los Angeles, Dr. Whitwell developed the CSUN Wind Ensemble into an ensemble of international reputation, with international tours to Europe in 1981 and 1989 and to Japan in 1984. The CSUN Wind Ensemble has made professional studio recordings for BBC (London), the Köln Westdeutscher Rundfunk (Germany), NOS National Radio (The Netherlands), Zürich Radio (Switzerland), the Television Broadcasting System (Japan) as well as for the United States State Department for broadcast on its "Voice of America" program. The CSUN Wind Ensemble's recording with the Mirecourt Trio in 1982 was named the "Record of the Year" by *The Village Voice*. Composers who have guest conducted Whitwell's ensembles include Aaron Copland, Ernest Krenek, Alan Hovhaness, Morton Gould, Karel Husa, Frank Erickson and Vaclav Nelhybel.

Dr. Whitwell has been a guest professor in 100 different universities and conservatories throughout the United States and in 23 foreign countries (most recently in China, in an elite school housed in the Forbidden City). Guest conducting experiences have included the Philadelphia Orchestra, Seattle Symphony Orchestra, the Czech Radio Orchestras of Brno and Bratislava, The National Youth Orchestra of Israel, as well as resident wind ensembles in Russia, Israel, Austria, Switzerland, Germany, England, Wales, The Netherlands, Portugal, Peru, Korea, Japan, Taiwan, Canada and the United States.

He is a past president of the College Band Directors National Association, a member of the Prasidium of the International Society for the Promotion of Band Music, and was a member of the founding board of directors of the World Association for Symphonic Bands and Ensembles (WASBE). In 1964 he was made an honorary life member of Kappa Kappa Psi, a national professional music fraternity. In September, 2001, he was a delegate to the UNESCO Conference on Global Music in Tokyo. He has been knighted by sovereign organizations in France, Portugal and Scotland and has been awarded the gold medal of Kerkrade, The Netherlands, and the silver medal of Wangen, Germany, the highest honor given wind conductors in the United States, the medal of the Academy of Wind and Percussion Arts (National Band Association) and the highest honor given wind conductors in Austria, the gold medal of the Austrian Band Association. He is a member of the Hall of Fame of the California Music Educators Association.

Dr. Whitwell's publications include more than 127 articles on wind literature including publications in *Music and Letters* (London), the *London Musical Times*, the *Mozart-Jahrbuch* (Salzburg), and 50 books, among which is his 13-volume *History and Literature of the Wind Band and Wind Ensemble* and an 8-volume series on *Aesthetics in Music*. In addition to numerous modern editions of early wind band music his original compositions include five symphonies.

David Whitwell was named as one of six men who have determined the course of American bands during the second half of the twentieth century, in the definitive history, *The Twentieth Century American Wind Band* (Meredith Music). A doctoral dissertation by German Gonzales (2007, Arizona State University) is dedicated to the life and conducting career of David Whitwell through the year 1977. David Whitwell is one of nine men described by Paula A. Crider in *The Conductor's Legacy* (Chicago: GIA, 2010) as "the legendary conductors" of the twentieth century.

> "I can't imagine the 2nd half of the 20th century—without David Whitwell and what he has given to all of the rest of us."
> Frederick Fennell (1993)

About the Editor

CRAIG DABELSTEIN began studying the piano at age seven and took up the saxophone at age twelve. Mr Dabelstein has Bachelor of Arts (Music) and Bachelor of Music degrees from the Queensland Conservatorium of Music and a Graduate Diploma of Learning and Teaching and a Graduate Certificate in Editing and Publishing from the University of Southern Queensland. He has held the principal saxophone chairs in the Australian Wind Orchestra and has been an augmenting member of the Queensland Philharmonic and Symphony Orchestras. He was a member of the Queensland Saxophone Quartet and has previously been a saxophone teacher at the Queensland Conservatorium of Music. He is a regular conductor of the Queensland Wind Orchestra and has been a research associate for the *Teaching Music Through Performance in Band* series of books. He is the editor of more than forty books by Dr. David Whitwell including *A Concise History of the Wind Band, Foundations of Music Education, Music Education of the Future, The Sousa Oral History Project, Wagner on Bands, Berlioz on Bands, The Art of Musical Conducting, Aesthetics of Music* (8 volumes) and *The History and Literature of the Wind Band and Wind Ensemble* (13 volumes). He currently teaches saxophone and clarinet, and conducts bands at St Joseph's College, Gregory Terrace.

Books by David Whitwell

- The Sousa Oral History Project
- The Art of Musical Conducting
- The Longy Club: 1900–1917
- La Téléphonie and the Universal Musical Language
- Extraordinary Women
- A Concise History of the Wind Band
- Essays on the Modern Wind Band
- Essays on Performance Practice
- A New History of Wind Music
- The College and University Band
- The Early Symphonies of Mozart
- Band Music of the French Revolution
- A Conductor's Diary

On Philosophy and Performance Practice

- Essays on Music of the German Baroque: Philosophy and Performance Practice
- Essays on Music of the French Baroque: Philosophy and Performance Practice
- Essays on Italian and Spanish Music of the Baroque: Philosophy and Performance Practice
- Philosophy and Performance Practice of Music during Jacobean England
- Philosophy and Performance Practice of Music during Restoration England

On Composers

- Wagner on Bands
- Berlioz on Bands
- Chopin: A Self-Portrait
- Liszt: A Self-Portrait
- Schumann: A Self-Portrait in His Own Words
- Mendelssohn: A Self-Portrait in His Own Words

On Education

- Philosophic Foundations of Education
- Foundations of Music Education
- Music Education of the Future

Aesthetics of Music

- Aesthetics of Music in Ancient Civilizations
- Aesthetics of Music in the Middle Ages
- Aesthetics of Music in the Early Renaissance
- Aesthetics of Music in Sixteenth-Century Italy, France and Spain
- Aesthetics of Music in Sixteenth-Century Germany, the Low Countries and England
- Aesthetics of Baroque Music in Italy, Spain, the German-Speaking Countries and the Low Countries
- Aesthetics of Baroque Music in France
- Aesthetics of Baroque Music in England

The History and Literature of the Wind Band and Wind Ensemble Series

- Volume 1 The Wind Band and Wind Ensemble Before 1500
- Volume 2 The Renaissance Wind Band and Wind Ensemble
- Volume 3 The Baroque Wind Band and Wind Ensemble
- Volume 4 The Wind Band and Wind Ensemble of the Classical Period (1750–1800)
- Volume 5 The Nineteenth-Century Wind Band and Wind Ensemble
- Volume 6 A Catalog of Multi-Part Repertoire for Wind Instruments or for Undesignated Instrumentation before 1600
- Volume 7 Baroque Wind Band and Wind Ensemble Repertoire
- Volume 8 Classical Period Wind Band and Wind Ensemble Repertoire
- Volume 9 Nineteenth-Century Wind Band and Wind Ensemble Repertoire
- Volume 10 A Supplementary Catalog of Wind Band and Wind Ensemble Repertoire
- Volume 11 A Catalog of Wind Repertoire before the Twentieth Century for One to Five Players
- Volume 12 A Second Supplementary Catalog of Early Wind Band and Wind Ensemble Repertoire
- Volume 13 Name Index, Volumes 1–12, The History and Literature of the Wind Band and Wind Ensemble

Ancient Voices

- Ancient Views on Music and Religion
- Ancient Views on the Natural World
- Ancient Views on What Is Music
- Contemporary Descriptions of Early Musicians
- Early Views of Music and Ethics
- Early Thoughts on Performance Practice
- Music Performance in Ancient Societies

Renaissance Voices

- Essays on Renaissance Philosophies of Music
- Renaissance Men on Music

www.whitwellbooks.com